Microsoft Enterprise Mobility Suite: Planning and Implementation

Peter Daalmans
Kent Agerlund

PUBLISHED BY
Deployment Artist
http://deploymentartist.com

Warning and Disclaimer

Every effort has been made to make this book as complete and as accurate as possible, but no
warranty or fitness is implied. The information provided is on an "as is" basis. The authors and the
publisher shall have neither liability nor responsibility to any person or entity with respect to any
loss or damages arising from the information contained in this book.

Feedback Information

We'd like to hear from you! If you have any comments about how we could improve the quality
of this book, please don't hesitate to contact us by visiting http://deploymentartist.com, sending an
email to feedback@deploymentartist.com, or visiting our Facebook site
http://facebook.com/DeploymentArtist.

Foreword

The world is a fast-moving, complicated place, and in the world of IT, you're constantly faced with a barrage of business requirements and user demands. In my opinion, there is no more exciting technology to work with than those that enable your users, without sacrificing the protection you need to deliver for your business. Two or three years ago, this book would have suggested that you "might want to think about, maybe, enabling people to be productive on the go."

Today, mobile productivity is business imperative. It's your imperative.

People the world over now take productivity with them in their pocket, using Microsoft Office, Salesforce, Dynamics, or whatever app it takes. That's a given. This book is about using the best tools available to you, in the shape of Microsoft Enterprise Mobility Suite, to provide your businesses with the best solution to the problem of protected mobile productivity.

You're going to learn how to harness Azure AD, a hyper-scale identity platform in the cloud that handles 1.3 billion daily authentications. You're going to learn how Multi-Factor Authentication and advanced security reports will catapult your organization to the forefront of adaptive risk mitigation practices. Not only that, but you'll understand how to do it without your users having to learn yet another password that they just write down, or even changing their behavior much.

This book is written by two guys (Kent and Peter) who love Microsoft Intune's ability to deliver the promise of hybrid management but more importantly have thousands of hours of real time, hands-on experience, partnering with their customers. They show you how to leverage groundbreaking features in EMS, like Conditional Access, a risk mitigation feature that deeply integrates Azure AD, Office 365, devices, and your network in a way no other solution can.

Azure AD Rights Management gives you the power to protect your data in any cloud and on any device. Each time a user needs access, they must prove who they are. This book explains how this amazing technology fits into your world.

If you're looking to make the next move in your career, or get in on the next big thing: Congratulations! You just found it! Enterprise Mobility Suite is taking the world by storm. It's probably the fastest growing enterprise mobility management product out there today. The time you invest in this book, the skills you learn in this book, the knowledge you gain from this book, will pay off handsomely. I know because I've been on this journey for the past couple of years, and I've never been more excited about a technology than I am about EMS.

Let's get started.

Simon May

Principal Program Manager, Enterprise Mobility, Microsoft

Acknowledgments

This book would not exist without the support from our families, Julie, Nanna, Susanne, Samantha, and Stef. Thank you for your patience and understanding. Love you all.

Thank you, Johan Arwidmark, Chris Nelson, Brian Mason, Kenny Buntinx, Marius Skovli, Eddie Hönig, Ami Casto, and Tim De Keukelaere for your support with reviewing this book, raising the right questions and not taking simple answers as real answers.

- Peter Daalmans and Kent Agerlund

As always, a special thanks to my colleagues at Coretech, with whom I'm proud to be associated. These guys are by far the best and most creative team I have ever worked with. Guys, you'll Never Work Alone.

- Kent Agerlund

About the Authors

Peter Daalmans

Peter Daalmans is a Senior Technical Consultant working for IT-Concern in the Netherlands. Peter has a primary focus on System Center Configuration Manager, Microsoft Exchange, and Enterprise Mobility. Peter has been awarded the Microsoft Most Valuable Professional (MVP) in Enterprise Mobility every year since 2012.

Peter shares his knowledge on his blog ConfigMgrBlog.com. Peter is also one of the founders and leads of the Windows Management User Group Netherlands.

Peter speaks at local and international group meetings and conferences like TechEd (Australia / New Zealand), IT/Dev Connections, Midwest Management Summit (MMS), BriForum (UK and USA), TechDays Netherlands, and ExpertsLive Netherlands.

You can connect with Peter on Twitter @pdaalmans and on LinkedIn at http://www.linkedin.com/in/pdaalmans.

Kent Agerlund

Kent Agerlund is Chief Technical Architect and System Center specialist working as a certified trainer, consultant, and event speaker. Kent started his computer endeavors back in the late 80s working with databases like dBase, Paradox, and FoxPro. From almost the beginning of his professional computer career, Kent has worked as a certified trainer and consultant. Today Kent works for Coretech, a Danish System Center house, where he also contributes by writing articles and sharing tips and tricks on http://blog.coretech.dk.

In recent years, Kent has travelled the globe delivering his Mastering Configuration Manager and Mastering Enterprise Mobility classes and speaking at various conferences like Ignite, MMS, and IT/Dev Connections. Through the years, Kent has attained various certifications and achievements, such as Windows 2012 R2 Enterprise Administrator, MCSE+A, and MCT, and been awarded Microsoft Most Valuable Professional (MVP) in Enterprise Mobility.

You can connect with Kent on Twitter @Agerlund and on LinkedIn at http://www.linkedin.com/in/kentagerlund

Contents

Introduction

Today's challenges in the IT industry remind us about the era in the 80s during which a PC went from being something only a select few were using to something that quickly became an industry factor. Back then, the lack of true systems management systems left most IT pros with overwhelming challenges in terms of supporting users, devices that they might not even have understood fully, and a lack of company policies. They knew little back then about managing users, applications, or outside security threats. They had almost no control over users, and floppy disks with confidential data were all over the place.

At ViaMonstra, we are fortunate to have an IT manager who was around back then and is capable of seeing the parallels between the "old days" and the challenges of today. Today it's not floppy disks but smartphones, tablets, and users who are constantly online that pose the biggest challenges. For many, the challenges seem overwhelming, and often IT pros do not know where to begin.

Our best advice is to take a deep breath and focus on the one thing that is the real asset of any organization: *data*. Thus, our main concern is not lost or stolen devices, or application management. *Our primary concern is data—access to data, protecting data, and sharing data*. For ViaMonstra, it is important that the business control the tools and not the other way around. IT management, with support from the CEO, has defined a new set of strategic IT policies that set clear employee expectations:

- Company data must be accessible from any supported device at any given time.

- Access to company data must be controlled, and confidential data must never be shared between internal or external resources without written approval and a signed NDA.

- Employees must be provided with better self-service options to lower the overall IT operational costs while enhancing productivity.

ViaMonstra also is struggling with its mobile device inventory. Today the inventory list is in Excel and often not updated with latest information.

Sales people often have to wait to follow up with customers until they are at the office or have a reliable VPN connection, which causes lost orders. Most sales people are on the road for days at the time, and these delays continue to cost the company profits. ViaMonstra will develop a managed application that will be installed as a required application on all company-owned devices.

ViaMonstra will allow company-owned devices access to internal resources like company Wi-Fi, email, and VPN. Personally owned devices will be allowed access only to the guest Wi-Fi network and corporate mail *if the device is compliant with the security policies*.

With that in mind, ViaMonstra has chosen to implement the Microsoft Enterprise Mobility Suite, also known as Microsoft EMS. It is important to understand from the beginning that EMS is not a single product, but rather a set of services to which ViaMonstra subscribes. Microsoft EMS provides ViaMonstra with the agility needed to run the business and the security required to protect data. It's our firm believe that this book demonstrates how Microsoft Azure Active Directory, Azure Rights Management, Microsoft Intune, Microsoft System Center Configuration Manager, and Advanced Threat Analytics can be combined into a real enterprise mobility solution that suits the challenges in your organization.

Real World Note: We still see many mobile device projects that do not succeed. According to our experience, the keys to success lie in getting a project sponsor from the management level. Define nontechnical business goals and technical goals. It is very important that you do not mix the business goals with the technical goals.

Say Hello (Possibly Again) to ViaMonstra Inc.

In this book, you implement a mobility service platform for the fictional ViaMonstra Inc. ViaMonstra is a midsized company with a single location and 6000 employees. Its site is located in New York, and the company uses the Enterprise Mobility Suite (EMS) and System Center for its system management solution.

BTW, the name ViaMonstra comes from *Viam Monstra*, Latin, meaning "Show me the way."

How to Use This Book

This book is packed with step-by-step guides, which means you can build your solution as you read along. This book is different from other books published by Deployment Artist, as we are describing two environments. This also means that you will need two different environments if you want to follow all the scenarios. In addition to the main chapters in the book, you also find detailed test scenarios in Appendix C.

In numbered steps, we have the all names and paths in bold typeface. We also used a standard naming convention throughout the book when explaining what to do in each step. The steps normally are something like this:

1. On the **Advanced Properties** page, select the **Confirm** check box, and then click **Next**.

Sample scripts are formatted like the following example, on a grey background.

```
DoNotCreateExtraPartition=YES
MachineObjectOU=ou=Workstations,dc=corp,dc=viamonstra,dc=com
```

Code and commands that you type in the guides are displayed like this:

1. Install MDT 2013 by running the following command in an elevated PowerShell prompt:

```
& msiexec.exe /i 'C:\Setup\MDT 2013\
MicrosoftDeploymentToolkit2013_x64.msi' /quiet
```

The step-by-step guides in this book assume that you have configured the environment according to the information in Chapter 2, "ViaMonstra Inc. and the Proof-of-Concept Environment," and in Appendix A.

Sample Files

You can download all the sample files used in this book from http://deploymentfundamentals.com.

Additional Resources

In addition to all tips and tricks provided in this book, you can find extra resources like articles and video recordings on our blogs, blog.coretech.dk/kea and ConfigMgrBlog.com.

Standalone vs. Hybrid

As an Enterprise Mobility administrator, you will immediately face a major choice for your mobile device management (MDM) authority:

- Run Microsoft Intune standalone

- Integrate Microsoft Intune with Microsoft System Center Configuration Manager (also known as *hybrid*)

In this book, we describe how you can work with both mobile device authorities. To be able to do that, we have two completely different environments whereas you likely have only one.

Topics Not Covered

This book is not intended to be an identity management cookbook. We cover some but far from all aspects of Active Directory Federated Services also known as AD FS. Likewise, we also cover aspects of Azure RemoteApp, Web Application Proxy, and Office 365, though not in-depth.

Chapter 1

Getting Started with EMS

The Microsoft Enterprise Mobility Suite you are using at ViaMonstra is not one product that you can take off the shelf. It is a suite of products that fit together and allow you to control your mobile devices and the data and applications stored on those devices. In this chapter, you get a crash course in the various services and other things used in this book, which should help you to plan your proof-of-concept (PoC) environment.

Enterprise Mobility Suite Components

First, look at the components in Microsoft Enterprise Mobility Suite (EMS) and see how they fit together. With EMS, you are able to manage not only the mobile devices, but also their applications, the data that are stored or created on the devices, and the identities of the users who are accessing the devices and data.

Looking at the four following layers, you can translate those to the products in the suite:

- **Identity.** Microsoft Azure Active Directory Premium

- **Data.** Microsoft Azure Rights Management service

- **Applications.** Microsoft Intune (Mobile Application Management)

- **Device.** Microsoft Intune (Mobile Device Management)

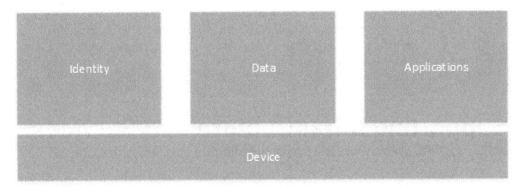

Layers of protection in Microsoft EMS.

Before you set up your ViaMonstra PoC environment, you need to create your project plan: how to approach this PoC, what you want to achieve, and how you want to measure whether the PoC is successful.

Next, you identify what you need to use EMS and where to get it: http://ref.ms/ems.

Microsoft Intune

Microsoft Intune is a purely cloud-based service and management platform in which users enroll their devices, such as Windows computers, Android devices, Windows Phones, and Apple iPhones. You can use Microsoft Intune as the mobile device authority platform for managing devices or as a proxy management platform where System Center Configuration Manager is the mobile device management authority.

Azure Active Directory Premium

For years, IT pros have managed directories of users and other resources on premises. With the cloud services offered by Microsoft, you also need to maintain a directory in the cloud. Besides being a resource database, Azure Active Directory also provides other services like Multi-Factor Authentication, activity reports, and self-service password resets. Azure Active Directory comes in a few flavors; the one you will be working with is the Premium edition.

Azure Rights Management Service

Azure Right Management is a core feature when it comes to protecting and securing data. With Azure Right Management, ViaMonstra can control who can share data and which applications can be used to share data both on premises and on the road.

Microsoft Advanced Threat Analytics

Microsoft Advanced Threat Analytics (ATA) is an on-premises solution to help IT professionals protect their enterprises from advanced attacks by automatically analyzing, learning and identifying normal and abnormal entity (user, devices and resources) behavior. ATA uses behavioral analysis to understand normal entity behavior, reducing false positives by applying contextual insight into traffic produced by engaged entities.
A key benefit of ATA is the ability to detect advanced attacks. Real-time detection, combined with awareness of existing security risks and behavioral analysis using Machine Learning algorithms help flag and foil sophisticated attacks.
.

EMS Supporting Infrastructure and Services

In addition to the core EMS components, other supporting infrastructure and services are used with EMS.

Azure Active Directory Synchronization

Azure Active Directory Synchronization performs synchronization between your on-premises directory and your directory in the cloud. Directory Synchronization is one of the frequently updated tools. The version used in this book allows you to select the objects you want to synchronize, the object attributes like password hash, and how often you want the synchronization to occur. Always use the latest version available.

Active Directory Federation Services (AD FS)

Active Directory Federation Services (AD FS) is not a technical requirement when working with other services like Windows Intune and Azure RemoteApps. However, many organizations feel a bit more secure when their on-premises directory server provides authentication instead of Azure Active Directory. With Active Directory Proxy Services (a sub component of AD FS), you also can control who can access what services and from what devices.

If you want to try AD FS in your environment, you find detailed instructions in Appendix D.

Web Application Proxy

Web Application Proxy is a service often used to provide devices access to corporate resources. The service is most often implemented with Azure Active Federation Services. To control this, you create *claims*. A claim is an XML rule that grants access to resources based on device type, user control, user group control, and network.

Office 365

Office 365 is a subscription-based online service that provides organizations with access to Microsoft Office, Skype for Business, and Exchange Online.

System Center Configuration Manager

System Center Configuration Manager (ConfigMgr) is properly the most popular systems management tool we have worked with in the past 10–15 years. The product is superior when it comes to managing on-premises servers and desktop clients, and it can be integrated with Microsoft Intune to provide management for devices enrolled in Microsoft Intune.

PowerShell

PowerShell is a scripting language that is installed by default in every Microsoft operating system since Windows Server 2008 and Windows Vista. It has to be one of the coolest technologies ever developed by Microsoft. PowerShell, or Windows PowerShell, is Microsoft's framework for task automation. It consists of a command-line shell, with an associated scripting language built on top of it. It integrates with the .NET Framework, having access to all COM objects and direct access to WMI. PowerShell allows you to perform administrative tasks on both local and remote Windows systems. Since the release of WinPE 4.0, PowerShell also can be added to the boot images used in OSD.

It is a bit unfair to list samples of what you can do in PowerShell because there are no real limits. You can do every type of automation task you can imagine in PowerShell, but here are a couple samples:

- Configure the Azure service account password to never expire using PowerShell:

```
Set-MsolUser -UserPrincipalName
AzureAD_SVC@emsking.onmicrosoft.com -PasswordNeverExpires
$True
```

- Create a device collection in ConfigMgr:

```
New-CMDeviceCollection -Name "All Windows Phones"
-LimitingCollectionName "All Mobile Devices"
```

For editing PowerShell scripts, we recommend using the built-in ISE editor available in Windows 7 and greater. It provides you with cmdlets help and intelligence when writing PowerShell scripts.

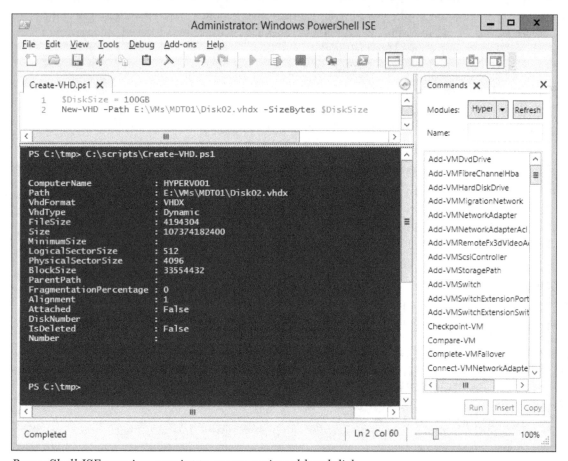

PowerShell ISE running a script to create a virtual hard disk.

Hydration

Hydration is the concept of using a deployment solution, like MDT 2013, to build a fully automated lab, proof-of-concept (PoC) environment, or production environment. We provide a hydration kit (see Appendix A) which builds the environment used in this book.

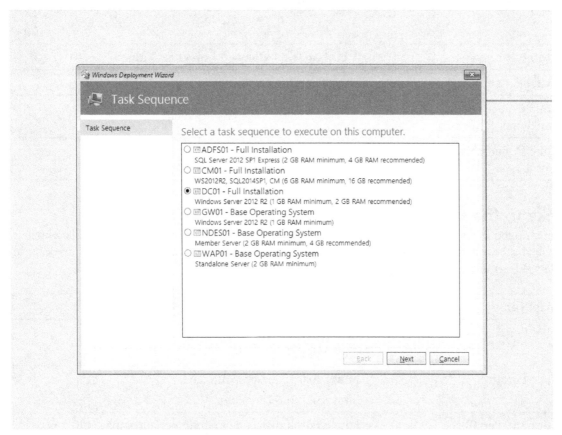

Creating the virtual machines used in this book. See Appendix A for details.

Domains

For setting up a Microsoft EMS environment, you need to have access to your internal domain and at least one external domain name. The following table lists the values for this PoC.

Public domain names are unique, and for that reason, you cannot use the examples we are using in the book. Instead, you have to register a new public domain name and use it in your PoC. For your convenience, we have added an empty column for you to add your values. You also can use the Excel spreadsheet in the book sample files to document your values together with the service accounts described in Chapter 2.

Note: As you learned in the introduction, as an Enterprise Mobility administrator, you must make an immediate major choice for your mobile device management (MDM) authority: either to use Microsoft Intune standalone, or to integrate Microsoft Intune with Microsoft System Center Configuration Manager. The following table lists the domains for both solutions, though you will use only one depending on which solution you set up.

Setting	ViaMonstra Values	Your Values
Local Domain Name	corp.viamonstra.com	
Public Domain Name EMS Standalone	emskings.com	
Public Domain Name EMS Hybrid	mdmhybrid.com	

Links to the Portals

As mentioned in the introduction, Microsoft EMS is a suite of services with many portals which you need access to during you daily management. We highly recommend that you bookmark these portals as part of your planning process.

Portal Links	Address
Azure Portal	https://manage.windowsazure.com https://portal.azure.com
Intune Portal	https://manage.microsoft.com https://portal.Azure.com
Office 365 Portal	https://portal.office.com/admin/default.aspx
Azure Self-Service	https://myapps.microsoft.com
Web Company Portal	https://portal.manage.microsoft.com
Intune Account Portal	https://portal.office.com/admin/default.aspx

Chapter 2

ViaMonstra Inc. and the Proof-of-Concept Environment

As you remember from the introduction, ViaMonstra Inc. is the fictional company we use throughout this book. In this chapter, we describe the company in more detail, as well as the proof-of-concept environment we use in our step-by-step guides. You can find detailed installation instructions on how to set up the initial environment in Appendix A.

ViaMonstra Inc.

ViaMonstra Inc. was invented for the very purpose of having a "real" company for which to build an enterprise client management solution. This solution comes from multiple real-world consulting engagements we have done.

ViaMonstra has 6000 employees with its headquarters in New York and multiple locations worldwide.

Public Domain Name

To be able to start the proof of concept, ViaMonstra needs a public domain name. Because ViaMonstra already uses viamonstra.com in the production environment, the company needs to buy a public domain name to complete the PoC and not interfere with the production environment. There are many providers offering that service. ViaMonstra has chosen to use GoDaddy to acquire the domain name.

For this book, we acquired a public domain name (emskings.com) for the EMS standalone solution described in Chapter 4, and for the EMS hybrid solution described in Chapter 5, we acquired the emshybrid.com domain instead.

Get a Domain Name for EMS Standalone

In this guide, you acquire the public domain name for the EMS standalone solution. If you plan to work with the EMS hybrid solution instead, skip to the next section, "Get a Domain Name for EMS Hybrid," instead.

> **Note:** We used the emskings.com domain for the EMS standalone solution when we created this book. Be sure to register your own domain because you cannot reuse the emskings.com domain.

1. Start your Internet browser and browse to **https://godaddy.com**. Fill in the domain name you want to buy for the EMS standalone solution and click **Search Domain**.

2. If the domain is available, click **Select** (otherwise, click **search again**) and click **Continue to Cart**.

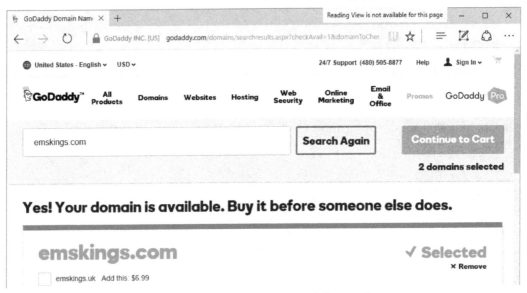

Purchasing the public domain name for the EMS standalone solution.

3. Choose the (optional) options like Make It Private or website options and click **Continue to Cart**.

4. Review the information, select the **Term** and click **Proceed to Checkout**.

5. Next, you need to proceed as a new customer and register yourself or log on as a returning customer and supply the information to place your order.

6. Select the **I agree to the following: Universal Terms of Service Agreement / Domain Name Registration Agreement** check box and click **Place Your Order**.

7. Next, finalize the payment and become the owner of the new domain name.

Real World Note: As stated, you can use your own DNS provider; the most important thing is that you are able to manage the domain name and add the DNS records as described later in this book.

Get a Domain Name for EMS Hybrid

In this guide, you acquire the public domain name for the EMS hybrid solution.

Note: We used the mdmhybrid.com domain for the EMS hybrid solution when we created this book. Be sure to register your own domain because you cannot reuse the mdmhybrid.com domain.

1. Start your Internet browser and browse to **https://godaddy.com**. Fill in the domain name you want to buy for the EMS hybrid solution and click **Search Domain**.

2. If the domain is available, click **Select** (otherwise, click **search again**) and click **Continue to Cart**.

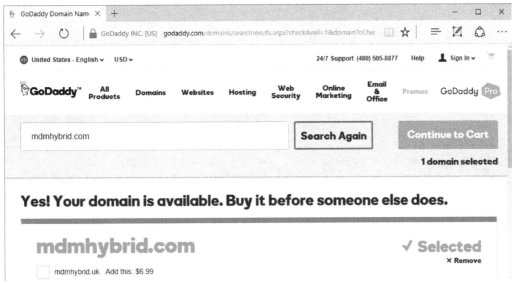

Purchasing the public domain name for the EMS hybrid solution.

3. Choose the (optional) options like Make It Private or website options and click **Continue to Cart**.

4. Review the information, select the **Term** and click **Proceed to Checkout**.

5. Next, you need to proceed as a new customer and register yourself or log on as a returning customer and supply the information to place your order.

6. Select the **I agree to the following: Universal Terms of Service Agreement / Domain Name Registration Agreement** check box and click **Place Your Order**.

7. Next, finalize the payment and become the owner of the new domain name.

> **Real World Note**: As stated, you can use your own DNS provider; the most important thing is that you are able to manage the domain name and add the DNS records as described later in this book.

Service Accounts

One of the most common mistakes we see in a cloud-enabled project is the use of private accounts. When implementing EMS, you encounter several account requirements. It is very important that those accounts are corporate accounts and well documented. In this project, ViaMonstra uses the accounts discussed in the following sections. Use the third column in the tables to document your account information. You also can use the Excel spreadsheet found in the book sample files to document your account information.

Service Accounts for EMS Standalone

This section covers the accounts used for an EMS standalone solution. If you plan to work with the EMS hybrid solution instead, skip to the "Service Accounts for EMS Hybrid" section instead.

> **Note:** We used the accounts in these sections for the EMS standalone solutions when we created this book. Be sure to register your own accounts because you cannot reuse these accounts. So replace "emskings" with your values, and you are good to go!

Account	Description	Your Account Information
AzureAD_SVC@emsking.onmicrosoft.com	Service account for Azure Active Directory synchronization	
admin@emskings.onmicrosoft.com / admin@emskings.com	Global Azure Active Directory Administrator	
admin@emskings.onmicrosoft.com / admin@emskings.com	Office 365 Administrator	
admin@emskings.onmicrosoft.com / admin@emskings.com	Microsoft Intune Administrator	
emskings@outlook.com	Apple ID	
emskings@outlook.com	Microsoft Account	
emskings@outlook.com	Google ID	

Set Up a Microsoft Account

The first account you need is a *corporate* Microsoft account. This is the account you will use when you register different services like Apple and Google IDs. Even though you might already have a *personal* Microsoft account, it is highly recommended that you create a new one for your organization and keep it protected just like you protect your on-premises Active Directory domain administrator account.

1. Go to **http://outlook.com** and click **Sign up now**.

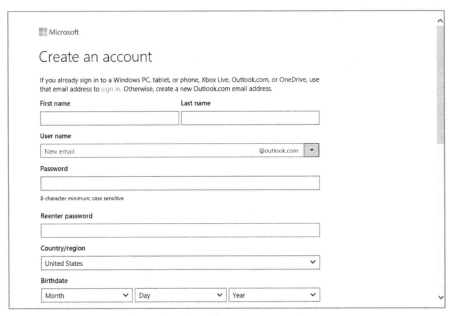

Creating the Microsoft Outlook account.

2. On the Create an account screen, supply your information like first name, last name, password, and other information before choosing a new user name for the new @outlook.com Microsoft account.

Set Up an Apple ID

To be able to manage Apple iOS devices, you need an Apple ID to request a Push Notification Certificate.

1. Go to **https://appleid.apple.com/** and click **Create an Apple ID**.

2. On the **My Apple ID** page, fill in the information needed to create an Apple ID.

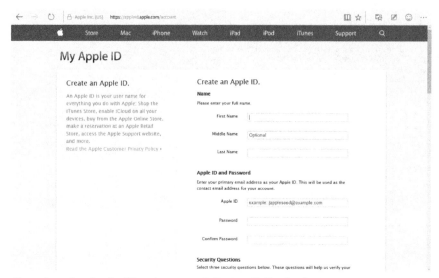

Creating the Apple ID using your Microsoft Outlook account.

3. After filling out the information, click **Create Apple ID**.

4. Next, a verification email with the subject **Verify your Apple ID** is sent to the email address you supplied. Click the **Verify Now** link in the email.

5. On the Apple website, you need to fill in your email address and password again to verify the Apple ID.

Real World Note: Users who have iOS devices must also have a personal Apple ID in order to install apps from the Apple App Store.

Set Up a Google Account

1. Go to **https://google.com/**, click **Sign in**, and then click **Create account**.

2. On the **Create your Google Account** page, fill in the information needed to create a Google ID.

3. After you fill out the information, a verification email message with the subject **Verify your Google ID** is sent to the email address you supplied. Click the **Verify Now** link in the email.

Service Accounts for EMS Hybrid

The section lists the accounts for an EMS hybrid solution with ConfigMgr.

> **Note:** We used these accounts for the EMS hybrid solution when we created this book. Be sure to register your own accounts because you cannot reuse these accounts. So replace "mdmhybrid" with your values, and you are good to go!

Account	Description	Your Account Information
AzureAD_SVC@mdmhybrid.onmicrosoft.com	Service account for Azure Active Directory synchronization	
admin@ mdmhybrid.onmicrosoft.com / admin@ mdmhybrid.com	Global Azure Active Directory Administrator	
admin@ mdmhybrid.onmicrosoft.com / admin@ mdmhybrid.com	Office 365 Administrator	
admin@ mdmhybrid.onmicrosoft.com / admin@ mdmhybrid.com	Microsoft Intune Administrator	
mdmhybrid@outlook.com	Apple ID	
mdmhybrid@outlook.com	Microsoft Account	
mdmhybrid@outlook.com	Google ID	

Set Up a Microsoft Account

The first account you need is a *corporate* Microsoft account. This is the account that you will use when you register different services like Apple and Google IDs. Even though you might already have a *personal* Microsoft account, it is highly recommended that you create a new one for your organization and keep it protected just like you protect your on-premises Active Directory domain administrator account.

1. Go to **http://outlook.com** and click **Sign up now**.

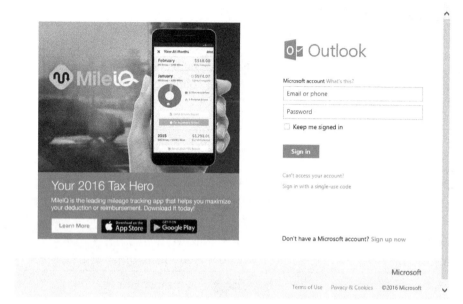

Creating the Microsoft Outlook account.

2. On the Create an account screen, supply your information like first name, last name, password, and other information before choosing a new user name for the new @outlook.com Microsoft account.

Set Up an Apple ID

To be able to manage Apple iOS devices, you need an Apple ID to request a Push Notification Certificate.

1. Go to **https://appleid.apple.com/** and click **Create an Apple ID**.

2. On the **My Apple ID** page, fill in the information needed to create an Apple ID.

Creating the Apple ID using your Microsoft Outlook account.

3. After filling out the information, click **Create Apple ID**.

4. Next, a verification email with the subject **Verify your Apple ID** is sent to the email address you supplied. Click the **Verify Now** link in the email.

5. On the Apple website, you need to fill in your email address and password again to verify the Apple ID.

Real World Note: Users who have iOS devices must also have a personal Apple ID in order to install apps from the Apple App Store.

Set Up a Google Account

1. Go to **https://google.com/**, click **Sign in**, and then click **Create account**.

2. On the **Create your Google Account** page, fill in the information needed to create a Google ID.

3. After you fill out the information, a verification email message with the subject **Verify your Google ID** is sent to the email address you supplied. Click the **Verify Now** link in the email.

Real World Note: When working with multiple accounts that all require you to sign in via internet browsers like Google Chrome or Internet Explorer, ensure that you are familiar with the private browsing feature. That way you can log in using multiple accounts without having to close the browser.

Microsoft Subscriptions

In order to follow the exercises in this book, you need to establish a 30-day Microsoft EMS trial account. Included in the Microsoft EMS license, you get a subscription to Microsoft Intune, Azure Rights Management, and Azure Active Directory Premium services. We detail the configuration of the EMA trial account in the solution chapters: Chapter 4 for the EMS standalone solution and Chapter 5 for the EMS hybrid solution.

Servers

The New York site has the following servers related to software distribution and other supporting infrastructure. All servers are running Windows Server 2012 R2. You can find detailed configuration of each server in the "Servers (Detailed Information)" section in this chapter.

Friendly Reminder: In Appendix A, you can find detailed step-by-step guidance on how to deploy the servers used in the book.

- **DC01.** Domain Controller, DNS, PKI, and DHCP
- **GW01.** Virtual Router (optional server used for Internet access)
- **ADFS01.** Member Server, and SQL Server 2012 SP1 Express
- **WAP01**. Standalone Server.
- **NDES01**. Member Server
- **CM01.** SQL Server 2014 SP1 and ConfigMgr

Note: The CM01 server is required only if you want to learn or use hybrid device management with System Center Configuration Manager.

Clients

In addition to the servers, you need to have lots of mobile devices and machines for testing. The machines and mobile devices need to comply with the following minimum versions.

- **Windows 10 Enterprise.** Any machine with Windows 10 Enterprise
- **Windows 10 Mobile.** Any Windows 10 Mobile device with build 1511 or higher
- **iPhone.** Any iPhone with iOS 7.1 or higher
- **iPad.** Any iPad with iOS 7.1 or higher
- **Android phone.** Any Android Knox-enabled phone with version 4.0 or higher
- **Windows Phone.** Any Windows phone with version 8.1 or higher
- **Mac OS X device.** Mac OS X 10.9 or later.

Internet Access

Fundamental to working with cloud services is access to the Internet. This book requires you to have Internet access on the virtual machines and mobile devices. We commonly use a virtual router, running in a virtual machine (VM), to provide Internet access to our lab and test VMs. Our favorite routers are the Vyatta and VyOS (Vyatta community fork) routers, but you can use a Windows Server 2012 R2 virtual machine with routing configured, as well.

> **Note:** For detailed guidance on setting up a virtual router for your lab environment, see this article: http://tinyurl.com/usingvirtualrouter.

Software

The following list describe the various applications used by ViaMonstra. To be able to follow all the step-by-step guides and configurations in the book, you must download the following software or collect it from vendor stores like the Microsoft Store. They can be either trial or full versions.

- Notepad LOB custom ViaMonstra application

- Windows Assessment and Deployment Toolkit (ADK)

- ConfigMgr

- ConfigMgr 2012 R2 Toolkit

- SQL Server 2012 SP1 Express

- SQL Server 2014 SP1

- Windows 10

- Windows Server 2012 R2

Servers (Detailed Information)

We are using a specific set of servers in our environment. We use a concept called *hydration* (automated build of entire labs and production environments) when creating the servers.

As mentioned earlier in this chapter, for detailed step-by-step guidance on how to deploy the servers, please review Appendix A, "Using the Hydration Kit to Build the PoC Environment." And, speaking of getting the environment up and running, now is actually a good point to build it. You don't need it until Chapter 5, but it takes a few hours to build, and in the meantime, you can work with the other preparations.

To set up a virtual environment with all the servers and clients, you need a host with at least 16 GB of RAM (32 GB RAM is recommended). Make sure you are using SSD drives for your storage. A single 480 GB SSD is enough to run all the scenarios in this book.

> **Real World Note:** If using a laptop or desktop when doing the step-by-step guides in this book, please do use a SSD drive for your virtual machines. Normal spindle-based disks are just too slow for decent lab and test environments. Also, please note that most laptops support at least 16 GB of RAM these days, even if many vendors do not update their specifications with this information.

A detailed description of the servers follows:

- **DC01.** A **Windows Server 2012 R2** machine, fully patched with the latest security updates and configured as Active Directory Domain Controller, DNS Server, and DHCP Server in the **corp.viamonstra.com** domain.
  - Server name: **DC01**
  - IP Address: **192.168.1.200**
  - Roles: **DNS**, **DHCP**, and **Domain Controller**

- **GW01.** A **Windows Server 2012 R2** machine, fully patched with the latest security updates, and configured as a workgroup server. This server is used as an optional virtual router that enables having all the other virtual machines on an isolated network, but still having Internet access.
  - Server name: **GW01**
  - IP Address: **192.168.1.1**
  - Roles: **Routing and Remote Access (RRAS)**

- **ADFS01.** A **Windows Server 2012 R2** machine fully patched with the latest security updates and configured as a member server in the **corp.viamonstra.com** domain. The server has been configured with the AD FS role. The server also has SQL Server 2012 SP1 Express installed.
  - Server name: **ADFS01**
  - IP Address: **192.168.1.244**
  - Roles: **AD FS**
  - Software: **SQL Server 2012 SP1 Express**

- **WAP01.** A **Windows Server 2012 R2** machine fully patched with the latest security updates and configured as a workgroup server. This is the web application proxy server used for controlling access to internal resources based on conditions like network, device, group membership, and so forth.
  - Server name: **WAP01**
  - IP Address: **192.168.1.6**
  - Software: None
  - Workgroup Server

- **NDES01:** A **Windows Server 2012 R2** machine fully patched with the latest security updates and configured as a member server in the **corp.viamonstra.com** domain.
  - Server name: **NDES01**
  - IP Address: **192.168.1.209**
  - Software: None

- **CM01.** A **Windows Server 2012 R2** machine fully patched with the latest security updates and configured as a member server in the **corp.viamonstra.com** domain. The server has SQL Server 2014 SP1 and ConfigMgr installed.
  - o   Server name: **CM01**
  - o   IP Address: **192.168.1.214**
  - o   Roles: **WDS** and **IIS**
  - o   Software: **SQL Server 2014 SP1** and **ConfigMgr**

.

Chapter 3

Identity Management

The identity is key and the powerful center of the Microsoft Enterprise Mobility Suite, so let's start by identifying what is necessary to execute a securely managed EMS PoC.

Understanding Identity Management

Identity Management is the key component of EMS. Before you start configuring EMS's components, you need to identify where you want your identity to live and where you need to authenticate to get access to resources.

Regarding the identity and authentication, there are three scenarios:

- Identity in the cloud, authentication in the cloud

- Identity in the cloud and on premises, authentication in the cloud

- Identity in the cloud and on premises, authentication on premises via AD FS

To be able to make the right decision before you move forward, you need to go a bit deeper into the three scenarios.

Identity in the Cloud, Authentication in the Cloud

This scenario is valid when you don't have an Active Directory on premises. You can then use Azure Active Directory as the source for your identity and use it for authenticating access, for instance, to Microsoft Intune or Office 365.

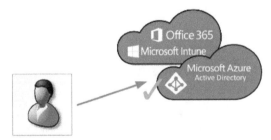

Identity in the cloud.

This scenario is not valid for ViaMonstra because the company has an on-premise Active Directory that you want to synchronize with the Azure Active Directory.

Identity in the Cloud and on Premises, Authentication in the Cloud

The second scenario involves an on-premise Active Directory that is synchronized to the Azure Active Directory. With Azure Active Directory Connect, you are able to set up the synchronization of your Active Directory accounts and enable the password synchronization and password writeback options.

By enabling the password synchronization option, the hash of the password is together with the account synchronized to the Azure Active Directory. This way, users can use the same password on premises and for accessing resources like Office 365 and Microsoft Intune. Enabling the password writeback option allows you to let your users change their passwords via the Azure Active Directory Premium edition.

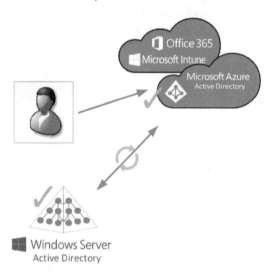

Identity managed on premises and synced including the password to Azure.

This scenario is not valid for ViaMonstra because management demands that AD FS be set up as an extra security layer.

Identity in the Cloud and on Premises, Authentication on Premises via AD FS

The third scenario is almost the same as the second, but in this case, you don't set up password synchronization and password writeback. Instead, you federate your on-premises Active Directory with the Azure Active Directory. Federating your Active Directory allows you to authenticate at your own on-premises Active Directory when accessing resources in the cloud. When accessing Microsoft Intune, for instance, a user is redirected to the on-premises AD FS proxy server where the user is able to authenticate. Then, after the authentication is successful, the user is redirected back to Microsoft Intune with a token that the authentication was successful.

With the Azure Active Directory Connect tool, you are able to set up directory synchronization and the AD FS servers.

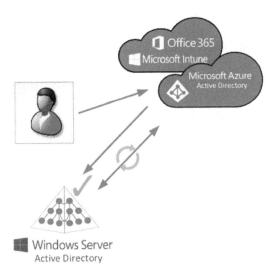

Identity without the password synced with Azure.

This third scenario matches the requirements of ViaMonstra's management. To prove whether your PoC is successful, you want to check your requirements before closing the PoC. The following table can help when you gather your requirements:

Requirement	Result	Satisfying
Commitment from management to synchronize accounts to Azure Active Directory		
Authentication on premises / cloud can be done		

Azure Active Directory Connect

In each of the solution chapters (Chapter 4 for the EMS standalone solution and Chapter 5 for the EMS hybrid solution), you install and configure Azure Active Directory Synchronization service, which is part of Azure Active Directory Connect. The configuration involves the following:

- Enabling directory synchronization in Microsoft Azure

- Configuring the synchronization service accounts

- Installing Azure Active Directory Synchronization Service

- Configuring the on-premises user principal name for the users that will be synchronized to Azure Active Directory

- Configuring Azure Active Directory Synchronization Service to synchronize only the required on-premises user and group objects

Azure Active Directory Synchronization

Before you start using any of the Microsoft cloud services, you first need to create and maintain a resource directory in the cloud. For most IT pros, maintaining a resource directory is not a new task as they have been managing Active Directory on-premises for years. With the cloud services, however, you need to manage a cloud directory alongside your on-premises directory. Before you start working with the cloud directory, you need to ask yourself a few questions like these:

- **Who is going to own the service internally?** To answer that question, ask yourself another question: Who owns the on-premises directory service? Failure to define the service owner will result in chaos when your organization tries to sign up for a new cloud service at Microsoft. Too often, we have seen the Intune administrator become owner of Azure Active Directory because Intune was the first cloud service introduced in the organization, and that is *so* wrong. Just imagine if the System Center Configuration Manager administrator also had to install, configure, and own the on-premises directory service.

- **What do you want to synchronize?** It is highly unlikely that you want to synchronize the entire on-premises directory including all users and groups. Often you want to control the process and only select resources from a specific organizational unit.

- **Which accounts are you going to use to run the synchronization between your on-premises and cloud-based directories?** Another common mistake is using a non-service account for the purpose. You should create specific service accounts on-premises and in the cloud that are used only for this purpose.

- **Which tool are you going to use to synchronize the directories?** Microsoft has released several tools, so selecting the correct one is important if you don't want to spend days troubleshooting the synchronization process. The latest and greatest tool as this writing is *Microsoft Azure Active Directory Connect*, which you can download from http://ref.ms/Azureconnect.

Azure Rights Management (RMS)

Part of the Microsoft Enterprise Mobility Suite is also Azure Rights Management (RMS). You can us Azure RMS to protect your data against data leakage, for instance an employee who sends a business-sensitive Excel sheet to the competitor. In the old days, you were able to secure document locations with just NTFS permissions because the document stayed on the share, but nowadays users share documents very quickly via mail, cloud services, and solutions like SharePoint. Because the world has changed, there is a growing need to protect the data itself. Protection can be configured by the document owner or automatically, and it follows the document nowhere it travels.

So, based on the identity of the user, the document can, for instance, be edited, printed, emailed, or only viewed. All actions with the document are logged and can be emailed automatically to the document owner.

> **Real World Note**: You might not think that your colleagues send email messages to competitors or other business associates. The fact is that most of such email messages are sent unintentionally to the wrong recipient. Just think about the number of "Joes" you have in your address book.

Planning Azure Rights Management

Before enabling the feature of Azure Active Directory, a solid plan needs to be the basis of Azure RMS. Without a plan, the implementation of Azure RMS is likely to fail, or the lack of user acceptance result in the feature not being used at all.

What Do We Want to Achieve?

Planning the Azure RMS feature is the most important phase of the Azure RMS PoC. The goals of the PoC needs to be clear. ViaMonstra wants to protect its data against data leakage based on classifications, as well as achieving the other goals listed in the following table.

ViaMonstra Goals	Your Goals
Prevent data leakage of sensitive documents	
Access to "normal" data for all ViaMonstra employees	
Access to sensitive data for all members of the group RMS_ Sensitive	
No rights management on premises; implement only Azure rights management	

Based on these requirements, ViaMonstra will test the usability of Azure RMS.

Tenant Key

By default, Azure RMS generates a tenant key. This tenant key is used to decrypt the license that is part of an RMS-protected document. In the document license, information is stored about which user (identity) has which kind of access to the document.

Another option is *bring your own key* (BYOK). With this option, the company creates its own security key that needs to be transferred securely to Microsoft. The transfer can be in person or via a support call with Microsoft Support. This second scenario can be used when a company is using RMS on premises also, or when the regulations of the company do not allow that Microsoft creates and manages the tenant key.

ViaMonstra trusts Microsoft and uses the cloud-only solution, so the default tenant key deployment will be used.

Azure Active Directory Premium Features

The list of features in Azure Active Directory Premium is long and growing fast these days. Listing the features in a book makes no sense as new features continue to flow in, so instead we highlight the features that we see as "game changing." Some features are new, whereas others replace existing services that companies had to purchase separately and thus save the organization money.

Multi-Factor Authentication (MFA)

Many might consider a password to be secure because it never travels unencrypted on the network between the device and Active Directory. Instead, a one-way irreversible password hash is generated and compared with the password hash stored in the password attribute for the user account. A match between the two hashes and the password is considered correct.

Although this might sound like a secure authentication method, we strongly recommend reading articles about attacks like pass-the-hash as described in this blog post: http://ref.ms/pass-the-hash. A password is something the user knows. ViaMonstra wants to combine that authentication method with something that *proves* who the user is. That second authentication method must be provided by a device possessed by the user.

Microsoft Multi-Factor Authentication (MFA) comes in two flavors: as a cloud-based service and as an on-premises solution. Your company goals will determine whether you need both or you can do with a single service.

With Azure Active Directory, multi-factor authentication can be configured using a text message, receiving a phone call, or installing the Azure Multi-Factor Authentication application on a device. Combining one of these methods with the password fulfills the authentication goal.

What Do We Want to Achieve?

Planning how, where, and why you want to use MFA is crucial to your project. *A clearly defined goal is the best way to measure success* and should include what you are trying to secure and whom you are trying secure. The ViaMonstra goals are listed in the first column of the following table, use those goals as a reference for your own goals.

ViaMonstra Goals	Your Goals
MFA must be enforced when accessing any SaaS application.	
Users must use MFA when enrolling devices into the organization.	
The Mobile Mobile-Factor Auth app must be available to all users and should be used as the primary authentication source.	
MFA will be configured only for ViaMonstra users.	

Branding Azure AD

Branding and personalizing Azure AD helps to establish trust between your users and Azure AD. Never underestimate the value of presenting users with a familiar logo and text. You can customize most elements of the sign-in page, such as adding a custom logo, sign-in illustration, and sign-in text.

Branding the Azure user experience.

Self-Service Password Reset with On-Premises Writeback

It is the same everywhere and every time: users return from vacation and have forgotten their password. For many organizations, this requires a call to a service desk and a ticket in the service management system. All in all, this is a costly affair, in which the user loses valuable time their first day back to work and the organization is burdened with an unnecessary cost.

Active Directory Premium supports self-service password reset with on-premises writeback (SSPR) to your on-premises Active Directory. The feature has a few moving parts that must be configured correctly before you can get it to work, but configured properly, it's one of those features that will make you look great in the eyes of management.

In order to enable SSPR, you need to ensure the following requirements are met:

- Infrastructure
    - Azure Active Directory sync tool with version number 1.0.0419.0911 or higher
    - Password reset configured in the Azure Active Directory sync tool
    - The correct edition of Azure Active Directory (You are covered with EMS and Azure Active Directory Premium.)
    - Password reset enabled in Azure Active Directory
    - Firewall rules
- End users
    - Must be enabled for password reset
    - Must be configured with Multi-Factor Authentication

> **Real World Note**: Did you know that 25–50 percent of all service desk calls pertain to password resets? Implementing SSPR will save your organization up to $637 per user per year, according to some studies. Search for "password reset ROI" on Google/Bing and check out one of the ROI calculators to estimate your savings.

Azure AD Join

For many years, we have been used to adding devices to a domain or making them a member of a workgroup. With Azure AD Premium, you get one additional option: joining the device to Azure through a feature called Azure AD Join. When you join a device to Azure, the Azure Device Registration Service creates the computer object in Azure. The object is not exactly the same as the traditional on-premises computer object. One of the differences is that the device is always *associated with a user* unlike on-premises computer objects that are stored and treated as individual objects. You need to perform a few configuration steps in Azure AD premium before you can start enrolling the devices. The solution chapters detail these steps.

Software as a Service (SaaS)

SaaS applications are applications you run from a cloud provider or from a company-hosted resource. You have probably been using SaaS applications without even realizing it. Salesforce is a good example, as are Facebook and Twitter. With Azure AD Premium, you can configure SaaS applications to offer a single sign-on experience to your users. After Azure AD Premium has authenticated the user, single sign-on is a reality!

ViaMonstra has several SaaS applications for which users expect single sign-on experiences, among them Office 365, SharePoint Online, and Twitter. The marketing department uses the same Twitter account several times a day. Instead of giving the password to all members in the marketing department, you use the password rollover feature through which the password is unknown to all users. That way if one leaves the company, you do not have to worry about changing the password for your Twitter account. The solution chapters detail the configuration steps for setting up SaaS.

Reporting and Dashboard

The Azure Active Directory Premium service comes with a wealth of reports that can be used to track user activity like suspicious login attempts, use of failed password reset attempts, use of SaaS applications, and much more. The dashboard feature can be seen as the "sum of all activity." Like any other dashboard, you are presented with an informative overview of the current and historical activities.

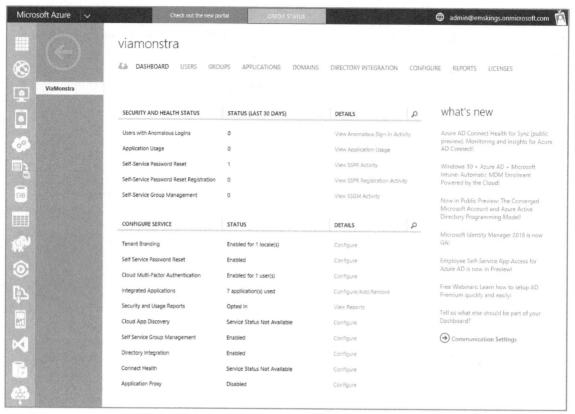

The Azure dashboard is a great cockpit for most of the premium services

The reports are all accessible by clicking Reports while connected to your domain. Reports are not customizable and most of them show you activity from the last 30 days. *We strongly encourage you to go through all the reports*, especially the reports in the Anomalous Activity category.

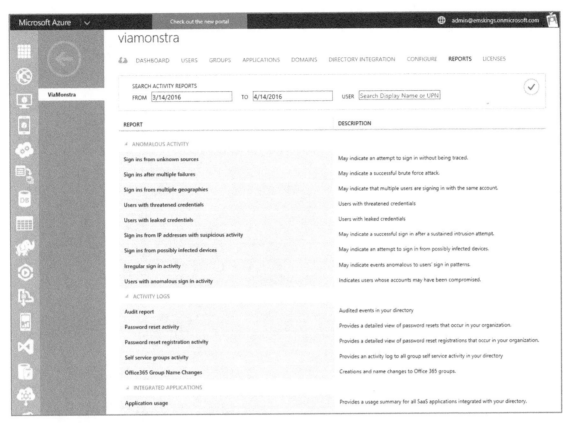

Overview of the built-in Azure Premium reports.

Chapter 4

EMS Standalone Solution

For years, IT pros have been installing and managing resource directories on-premises using tools like Active Directory Users and Computers. For most organizations, managing on-premises resources is still an integral part of the IT pro job description. With the new cloud services, IT pros must become familiar with managing resource directories in the cloud.

> **Note:** This chapter is about the EMS standalone solution only. If you want to do the EMS hybrid scenario, integrating Microsoft Intune with ConfigMgr, you find that information in Chapter 5. Also, please note that the administration portal used to configure the standalone solution changes frequently, so the step-by-step guides provided in this book may not match exactly.

Azure Active Directory is a service offered in three flavors: Free, Basic and Premium. Some of the features are the same, but services like Multi-Factor Authentication, advanced anomaly security reports, and self-service password reset with on-premises writeback are available only in the Premium edition. For a full list of features in the three editions, read https://msdn.microsoft.com/en-us/library/Azure/dn532272.aspx.

Your next step is to configure Microsoft Intune so users are able to enroll their devices and get access to corporate resources. This configuration involves the following steps:

1. Creating a Microsoft subscription
2. Configuring Azure Active Directory Connect
3. Setting up licensing
4. Setting up Azure Active Directory Premium features
5. Configuring Mobile Device Management in Microsoft Intune

Microsoft Subscriptions

In order to follow the exercises in this chapter, you need to establish a 30-day Microsoft EMS trial account. Included in the Microsoft EMS license, you get a subscription to Microsoft Intune, Azure Rights Management, and Azure Active Directory Premium services.

Create the EMS Trial Environment

In this guide, you create the EMS trial environment for the EMS standalone solution:

1. Go to **http://ref.ms/ems**, select **Get Started**, and click **Try Now**.

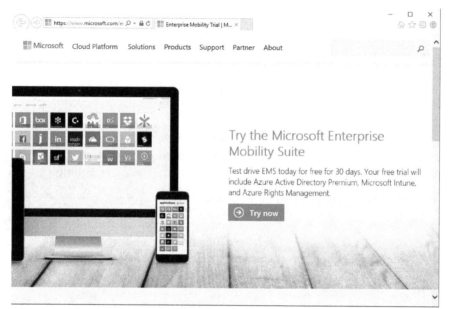

The Microsoft Enterprise Mobility Suite landing page for setting up the subscriptions.

2. In order to start the setup of the **Microsoft Intune** trial, click **Try Now**.

3. You are prompted to fill out your company information:

Setting	Your Value
Country or region	
First name	
Last name	
Business email address	
Business phone number	
Company name	
Your organization size	

4. Click **Next** after supplying the information.

5. Enter the information as shown here:

Setting	ViaMonstra Value	Your Value
Enter a user name	admin	
Your company	emskings.onmicrosoft.com	

6. Supply the password twice and click **Next**.

7. Choose **Text me**, supply a phone number to prove your identity, and click **Text me**.

8. Supply the **verification code** and click **Create my account** to set up the EMS trial account.

9. Click **You're ready to go** to access the new tenant via https://portal.office365.com and stay there for the next steps.

Set Up an Azure Subscription

To be able to use the EMS licenses, you need to create a Microsoft Azure subscription:

1. In the **Office 365 admin center** (https://portal.office.com/admin/default.aspx), browse to the **Admin** section and click **Azure AD**.

2. On the **Oops! Access to Azure Active Directory Is Not Available** window, click **Azure Subscription** to activate a subscription.

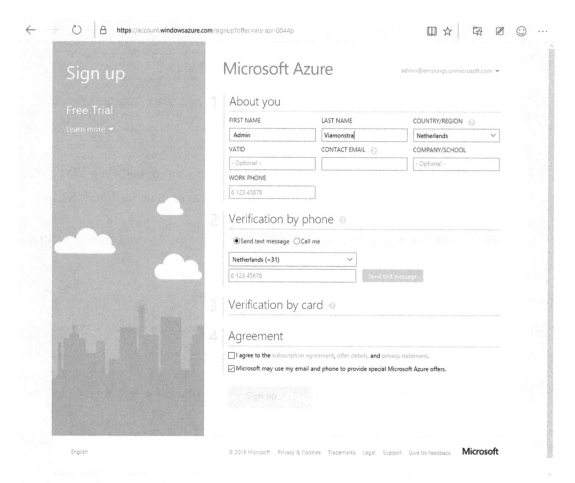

Configuring the Microsoft Azure subscription.

3. Supply information about yourself, verify your mobile phone, agree to the terms, and verify your credit card.

Real World Note: During this trial, your credit card will not be used, but Microsoft wants to verify your identity. Your credit card will be charged only after you explicitly remove the spending limit.

4. Click **Sign up** to get access to Microsoft Azure. Click **Start managing my service** to get access to the new Microsoft Azure portal (https://portal.azure.com).

5. Click **Browse** and select the **white star** next to **Active Directory**. Notice that the star changes color after you select it.

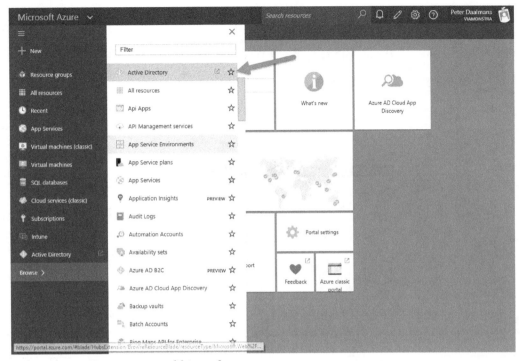

Select Active Directory to add it to the menu.

6. Click **Active Directory** in the menu. the Azure Device Registration Service. Navigate through the tour, and the newly created Azure Active Directory then opens in the Dashboard.

> **Real World Note:** Microsoft is in the process of moving all services to the new Azure Portal, which is accessible via http://portal.azure.com. Until all services are moved, there will be two portals, but all services are accessible via the new portal.

Set Up DNS

Initially, the new domain needs to be configured for Microsoft Intune, but before the domain can be added, verification of the ownership of the domain name must be done:

1. After the subscription is active, you need to configure the primary domain name. Configuring your public DNS name for Microsoft Intune is required to prove that you own the public domain. Go to the **Office 365 admin center** (https://portal.office.com/admin/default.aspx) and click **Domains**.

2. Click **Add domain**, and then click **Let's get started**.

3. Supply the domain name and click **Next**.

4. Next, you need to prove that you are the owner of the domain name supplied. You can do this by adding a TXT record that is supplied to your domain or adding an MX record to the same public domain that you want to add to Microsoft Intune.

41

Verifying domain ownership.

5. Before you click **Okay, I've added the record**, launch the **Admin portal** of the DNS provider, in this case GoDaddy (www.godaddy.com).

Real World Note: If GoDaddy is not used, you can ignore the following steps, but make sure that you manually add the TXT or MX and CNAME records following the process of your ISP.

---

6. After logging in, click **My Account** and **Manage** in the **Domain** section of the screen.

7. Select your domain, click the **wheel** to access the domain menu, and click **Manage DNS**.

8. In **Domain Details**, select the **DNS ZONE FILE** tab.

9. Scroll down to the **TXT (Text)** section and click **Add Record**.

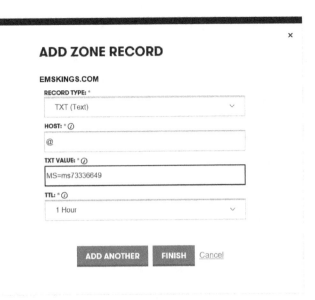

Adding TXT records to prove you own the public domain.

> **Real World Note:** Depending on your hosting provider, you may need to contact its support staff to add these records. Some providers don't allow you to enter all this information in their control panels. For example, you may not be able to specify the TTL value.

10. Supply the following values and click **Finish**:

Setting	Your Value
Record Type	TXT (Text)
Host	@
TXT Value	MS=ms*xxxxxxxx*
TTL	1 Hour

11. The DNS registration to prove that you are the owner of the public domain name is finished. You have two more public DNS registrations to do in order to enroll devices in Intune. These are technically not requirements, but they make life easier for the persons enrolling devices. Click **Add Record**, and select **CNAME (Alias)** as the record type.

12. Create two CNAME records with the following values:

Record 1:

Setting	Your Value
Record Type	CNAME (Alias)
Host	enterpriseenrollment
Points to	manage.microsoft.com
TTL	1 Hour

Record 2:

Setting	Your Value
Record Type	CNAME (Alias)
Host	enterpriseregistration
Points to	enterpriseregistration.windows.net
TTL	1 Hour

13. Click **Finish** after creating the two records and save the changes in the GoDaddy admin portal.

14. Go back to the **Office 365 admin center** and click **Okay, I've added the record** to check whether the domain you want to add is yours.

Real World Note: Be aware that it can take up to 72 hours before changes in your DNS zone have been replicated to the DNS servers used by Microsoft Intune.

Under normal circumstances, the verification process is quick, but sometimes it can take several hours.

15. Click **Next** to optionally update the current users in Office 365 with the new domain:

    a. Select the just created **admin@emskings.onmicrosoft.com** user and click **Update selected users**.

    b. Click **Next** and then click **Sign out** to log on again with the **admin@emskings.com** user.

> **Real World Note:** It might take a couple of minutes before the user information is updated and can be used.

16. Click **skip this step** (twice) on the **Add new users** page.

17. Click **Next**, select **No, I have an existing website or prefer to manage my own DNS records**, and click **Next** again.

18. Clear all the option check boxes, click **Next**, and then click **Finish** to finish the initial DNS setup.

In the next section, you further configure the DNS for Office 365.

Set Up Office 365

At ViaMonstra, you are planning to use the Office 365 and want to integrate conditional access to your Exchange and SharePoint services in the EMS PoC.

1. Browse to **http://portal.office.com** and log in with your admin credentials. The Welcome screen displays a message that no subscription is active.

2. Click **Purchase**, choose a trial version of **Office 365**, and then click **Start free trial**.

> **Real World Note:** For ViaMonstra, with 6000 users, we signed up for the Enterprise Office 365 Enterprise E3. If you are with a smaller organization, you may look into other services like the Office 365 Business Premium.

3. Click **Try now** on the checkout screen and then click **Continue** to go back to the Office 365 admin center.

4. Next you need to set up the domain to be able accept email and service other Office 365 components like Skype for Business. Click **Domains** and select **Complete setup** for the domain you configured earlier (emskings.com).

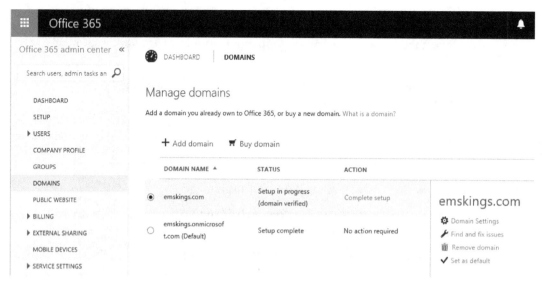

Completing the setup of the domain.

5. On the **Add a new domain in Office 365** page, click **Next**.

6. Click **skip this step twice** and then click **Next** to set up the domain for Office 365.

7. Next, you need to identify the services you want to use with your domain:

    a. In this case, select the following:

        ▪ **Outlook on the web for email, calendar and contacts**

        ▪ **Skype for Business for instant messaging and online meetings**

    b. You also need to clear the **Mobile Device Management for Office 365** check box because you are going to use Microsoft Intune as your mobile device management solution.

> **Real World Note:** If for some reason the MDM Authority is already set to Office 365 and you do not want to use Office 365 MDM, contact Microsoft Technical Support to reverse the setting. Note that it can take up to five days. Check this blog for more info: http://ref.ms/mdmauthblog.

8. Click **Next**.

> **Note**: Appendix B covers the basic Office 365 services configuration like Exchange Online and SharePoint Online.

9. Click **Add records**. Because you are using GoDaddy, you can allow Office 365 to configure automatically the DNS records needed for Office 365.

    a. In the pop-up, log in to the **GoDaddy portal** and click **Accept** to allow the creation of the DNS records for Office 365.

Confirm Access

Office 365 is requesting permission to make changes to your domain **emskings.com** at GoDaddy.

Click **Accept** to allow Office 365 to make these changes to **emskings.com**.

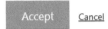

You can configure Office 365 to update automatically all required DNS records in a GoDaddy-hosted domain.

b. Click **Finish** to complete the DNS setup for Office 365.

If you are not using GoDaddy, you need to add the records yourself. If you are not allowed to do this, contact your DNS admin to configure the following DNS records for your domain:

o Use the following settings for **Exchange Online**:

Type	Priority	Host Name	Points to Address / Value	TTL
MX	0	@	emskings-com.mail.protection.outlook.com	1 Hour
CNAME	-	autodiscover	autodiscover.outlook.com	1 Hour
TXT	-	@	v=spf1 include:spf.protection.outlook.com -all	1 Hour

o Use the following settings for **Skype for Business**:

Type	Service	Proto-col	Port	Weight	Prior-ity	TTL	Name	Target
SRV	_sip	_tls	443	1	100	1 Hour	@	sipdir.online.lync.com
SRV	_sipfederationtls	_tcp	5061	1	100	1 Hour	@	sipfed.online.lync.com

Type	Host Name	Points to Address	TTL	Type
CNAME	sip	sipdir.online.lync.com	1 Hour	CNAME
CNAME	lyncdiscover	webdir.online.lync.com	1 Hour	CNAME

10. After the domain is set up, select the domain you added (**emskings.com**) and click **Set as default**.

Azure Active Directory Connect

In this section, you install and configure Azure Active Directory Synchronization service, which is part of Azure Active Directory Connect. As you learned in the preceding chapter, the configuration involves the following:

- Enabling directory synchronization in Microsoft Azure

- Configuring the synchronization service accounts

- Installing Azure Active Directory Synchronization Service

- Configuring the on-premises user principal name for the users that will be synchronized to Azure Active Directory

- Configuring Azure Active Directory Synchronization Service to synchronize only the required on-premises user and group objects

Configure the Azure Active Directory Connect Service Account

In the following steps, you enable directory synchronization in Microsoft Azure, creating the synchronization service account and installing Microsoft Azure Active Directory Connect on the domain controller. Notice that installing the application on the domain controller is not a requirement. You simply use DC01 to limit the number of virtual machines in the pilot environment.

1. Start **DC01** and log in as **VIAMONSTRA\Administrator**.

2. From an Internet browser, connect to **https://portal.Azure.com** (the old portal, https://manage.windowsazure.com, was still available when this book was written). **https://portal.Azure.com** is the latest Azure dashboard, from which you can connect to the Azure portal, view your billing information, get support, and much more.

3. To access the portal, click **Active Directory** in the menu of the Azure portal.

4. In the new tab, with the Default Active Directory active, select **Directory Integration**, and enable **Directory Sync** by clicking **Activated**.

5. When prompted, click **SAVE** to save the configuration, and then click **Yes** to confirm.

6. Keep the **Azure Portal** open, as you will need it to create the cloud synchronization service account. Click **Users**.

7. Click **ADD USER**.

8. On the first page of the **Add User** wizard, select **New user in your organization**, type **AzureAD_SVC**, and click the arrow to move to the next page.

9. On the second page, fill out the following user information and then click the arrow to move to the next page:

    a. First Name: **AzureAD_SVC**

    b. Display Name: **AzureAD_SVC**

    c. Role: **Global Admin**

10. As the **Alternate Email Address**, type your admin recovery email address, we used **emskings@outlook.com**. Then click the arrow to move to the next page.

11. On the **Get Temporary Password** page, click **Create**.

12. While still on the **Get Temporary Password** page, click the **check mark** to finish the creation of the account. Notice you need the temporary password in subsequent steps.

13. Open a new instance of the Internet browser in private browsing mode. You start InPrivate Browsing in Internet Explorer and Microsoft Edge by pressing **Ctrl + Shift +P**.

14. Connect to **https://portal.Azure.com/** and log in as **AzureAD_SVC@emskings.onmicrosoft.com** with the temporary password.

15. When prompted, change the password and make sure you document it.

16. The final step in configuring the service account is to configure the password never to expire. You can configure that process using Microsoft PowerShell:

    a. On **DC01**, launch **PowerShell** as **Administrator**.

    b. Type **Connect-MsolService** and press **Enter**.

    c. Enter the Service Account login information and click **OK**:

        i. User Name: AzureAD_SVC@emskings.onmicrosoft.com

        ii. Password: **Your new password**

Real World Note: Use Get-MsolUser in PowerShell to get a list of your users in the Microsoft Online directory. This is a great way to start and verify that you are connected to the correct directory. To get the cmdlets, download and install:

Microsoft Online Services Sign-In Assistant for IT Professionals Beta: http://ref.ms/msolsignin/

Azure Active Directory Module for Windows PowerShell: http://ref.ms/azureposh

---

    d. To configure the service account password never to expire, type this command (one line) and press **Enter**:

```
Set-MsolUser -UserPrincipalName
AzureAD_SVC@emskings.onmicrosoft.com
-PasswordNeverExpires $True
```

17. The on-premises account AAD_SVC is already created during the build of the machines in Appendix A. If you didn't use our demo kit to build your machines, then go ahead and create an Active Directory user account named **AAD_SVC**.

Configure the User Principal Name (UPN)

The user principal name, also known as the UPN, is an Active Directory user attribute. It must match the public domain name that you registered in the preceding chapter. By default, all users inherit the UPN from the on-premises Active Directory domain name. Changing the UPN on each user is a two-step process: creating the new domain name and then changing the attribute on each user account.

Real World Note: You need to change the UPN only when it differs from the external domain name. The script that follows connects to the local Active Directory (corp.viamonstra.com), adds a UPN with the public domain name, and sets it as the default.

You can use the following script to configure the new UPN domain name and all users in the Cloud Users organizational unit with the new UPN.

```
$LocalDomainName = 'corp.viamonstra.com'

$PublicDomainName = emskings.com'

Set-ADForest -identity "$LocalDomainName" -UPNSuffixes
@{Add="$PublicDomainName "}

$CloudUsers = 'OU=Cloud
Users,OU=Users,OU=Viamonstra,DC=corp,DC=viamonstra,DC=com'

Get-ADUser -SearchBase $CloudUsers -Filter * | ForEach-Object
-Process {

    $NewUPN =
$PSItem.userPrincipalName.Replace($LocalDomainName,$PublicDomainN
ame)

    $PSItem | Set-ADUser -UserPrincipalName $NewUPN -EmailAddress
$NewUPN

}
```

You can use Active Directory Users and Computers to open the properties for one of the users in the Cloud Users organization unit to verify the new UPN.

Using PowerShell to configure the UPN to match to the public domain name.

Install and Configure Microsoft Azure Active Directory Connect

The final step in the process is to install and configure the Microsoft Azure Active Directory Connect tool. The tool is the latest version of what is also known as DirSync. However, we will emphasize that it has come a long way since the first version of DirSync. You can use the tool to do much more than just configure directory synchronization. You also can use it to install and configure Active Directory Federation Services.

1. Start **DC01** and log in as **VIAMONSTRA\Administrator**.

2. Download the **Microsoft Azure Active Directory Connec**t tool to **C:\Tools** from **http://ref.ms/Azureconnect**.

3. Run **C:\Tools\AzureADConnect.msi**, and when prompted by the Open File – Security Warning, click **Run** and **Yes** in the User Account Control window.

4. On the **Welcome** page, enable **I agree to the license terms and privacy notice** and click **Continue**.

5. On the **Express Settings** page, click **Express Settings** to start the process.

6. On the **Connect to Azure AD** page, for **USERNAME**, enter **AzureAD_SVC@emskings.onmicrosoft.com** and the password. Then click **Next**.

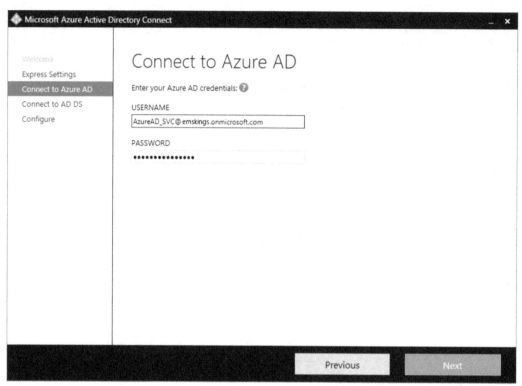

Specifying the Azure AD synchronization account.

7. On the **Connect to AD DS** page, for **USERNAME**, type **VIAMONSTRA\Administrator**, and for **PASSWORD**, type **P@ssw0rd**. Then click **Next**.

8. On the **Configure** page, clear the **Start the synchronization process as soon as the configuration completes** check box and click **Install**.

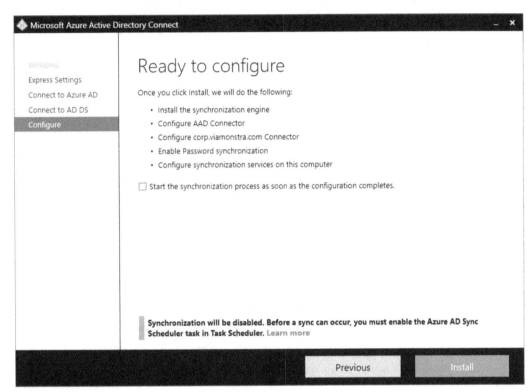

Configuring Azure Active Directory Connect.

9. On the **Configure** page, when the installation is complete, click **Exit**.

The reason for disabling automatic synchronization is control. You want to control the unique part of your on-premises directory that you will be synchronizing to the Azure. Control comes with a cost, which is having to configure the synchronization partition and enable the scheduled task in Windows. ViaMonstra has decided to control users and groups on-premises as much as possible and create Azure resources only if required by any of the cloud services. The following steps guide you through the process, starting with configuring the Cloud Users and Security Groups organizational units as the only object to synchronize.

1. While still on **DC01**, open **File Explorer** and run **miisclient.exe** as administrator from **C:\Program Files\Microsoft Azure AD Sync\UIShell**.

Note: The Azure Active Directory Connect synchronization UI is also available on the start menu, in the Azure AD Connect section, named Synchronization Service.

2. From the toolbar, select **Connectors**, right-click the **corp.viamonstra.com** Active Directory Domains Services connector and select **Properties**.

3. In **Properties**, select **Configure Directory Partitions** and click **Containers**

4. In the **Credentials** dialog box, fill in the information about your on-premises synchronization account and click **OK**:

    a.   User name: **AAD_SVC**

    b.   Password: **P@ssw0rd**

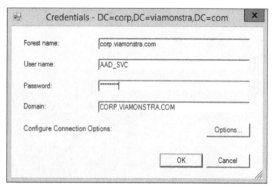

Specifying the service password.

5. From the **Select Containers** window, clear the check box of the domain name (**Root Domain**) listed at the top. This disables synchronization of the entire domain.

6. Expand **ViaMonstra / Users**, and then select **Cloud Users**, expand **Groups** and select **Cloud Security Groups** and click **OK** twice.

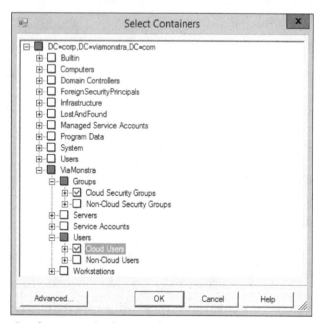

Configuring which OUs to synchronize.

Start the Azure Active Directory Connect Synchronization

Once the Azure Active Directory Connect setup is completed, you need to start the synchronization.

1. On **DC01**, using the **Synchronization Services Manager Tool**, in the **Connectors** tab, right-click the **corp.viamonstra.com** connector, and select **Run**.

2. In the **Run Connector** dialog box, select **Full synchronization**, and click **OK**.

You can also use PowerShell to start the synchronization by using the below cmdlet.

```
Start-ADSyncSyncCycle -PolicyType Initial
```

Verify the Azure Active Directory Connect Synchronization

A very easy way to verify that users and groups are being synchronized is to launch PowerShell and run the commands following this paragraph. It takes a while before the sync runs because Microsoft removed the scheduled task. The first command connects to your online directory. Then, when prompted, enter your Azure account and password. The second command lists all the users in your directory. You should memorize these cmdlets, as you will use them over and over again.

```
Connect-MsolService

Get-MsolUser
```

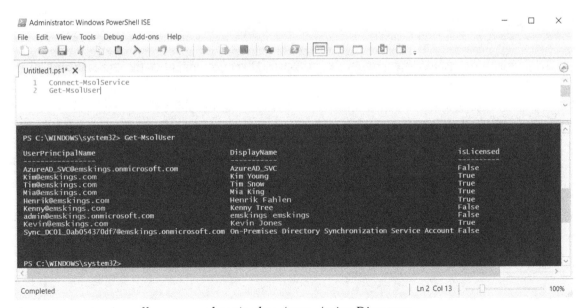

An easy way to view all users synchronized to Azure Active Directory.

To view members of a user group, you can use two PowerShell cmdlets. First, run the following cmdlet:

```
Get-MsolGroup
```

After running Get-MsolGroup, make a note of the ObjectId and add that to the second cmdlet:

```
Get-MsolGroupMember -GroupObjectId 3cd02398-2ed0-4153-94eb-
64b16177278d
```

Real World Note: You can force a synchronization by running DirectorySyncClientCmd.exe from C:\Program Files\Microsoft Azure AD Sync\Bin. Monitor the Azure Active Directory synchronization process by reading the application.log in Event Viewer.

Setting Up Licensing

Without the licenses assigned, users do not have access to the features of EMS.

Assign EMS Licenses to a Synced AAD Group

The EMS licenses can be assigned to a user or a group of users. ViaMonstra does not want to assign the license based on users, but rather use an Active Directory security group that can be managed via the on-premises Active Directory.

To assign the licenses to a security group, follow this procedure:

1. Browse to **https://manage.windowsAzure.com** and sign in with the admin account (**admin@emskings.com**).

2. In the Azure management portal, select **Active Directory** and click the domain (directory) that you created earlier.

3. Click **Licenses** and select the **Enterprise Mobility Suite** licenses.

4. Click **Assign users**, expand the **SHOW** pull-down menu (1), and change it to **Groups**. Click the **checkmark** (2).

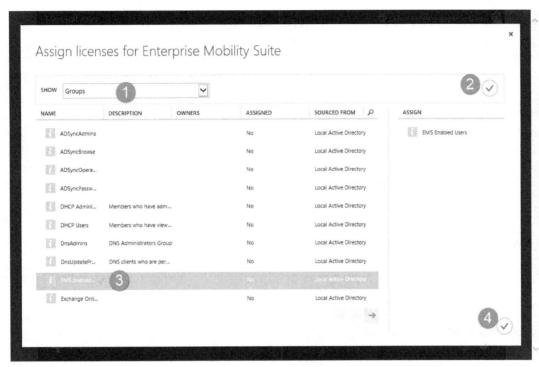

Assigning licenses.

5. Select the group created for the **EMS Enabled Users** (3) and click the **checkmark** (4) in the lower right corner.

Now all users who are members of the security group have access to the EMS features and resources like Azure RMS, Azure Active Directory, and Azure Remote App.

Setting Up Azure Active Directory Premium Features

In this section, you set up four of the Active Directory Premium features you learned about in Chapter 3:

- Multi-Factor Authentication (MFA)

- Self-Service Password Reset with On-Premises Writeback

- Azure AD Join

- Software as a Service (SaaS)

Multi-Factor Authentication (MFA)

With Azure Active Directory, the multi-factor authentication can be configured using a text message, receiving a phone call, or installing the Azure Multi-Factor Authentication application on a device. Combining one of these methods with the password fulfills the authentication goal.

What Do We Want to Achieve?

Planning how, where, and why you want to use MFA is crucial to your project. *A clearly defined goal is the best way to measure success* and should include what you are trying to secure and whom you are trying secure. The following table lists the ViaMonstra goals in the first column. Use those goals as a reference for your own goals.

ViaMonstra Goals	Your Goals
MFA must be enforced when accessing any SaaS application.	
Users must use MFA when enrolling devices into the organization.	
The Mobile Mobile-Factor Auth app must be available to all users and should be used as the primary authentication source.	
MFA will be configured only for ViaMonstra users.	

Enable MFA for a Cloud-Enabled User Account

You can configure MFA in the Azure management portal or through PowerShell. In order to enable MFA in the UI, follow these steps:

1. Open **https://manage.windowsAzure.com** and sign in with the Azure admin account.

2. In the Azure management portal, select **Active Directory** and click the **ViaMonstra** directory name to open the domain properties.

3. Click **Configure**, navigate to the **multi-factor authentication** section, and click **Manage service settings**.

4. In the **multi-factor authentication** portal, on the **service settings** page, select the **users** page.

5. From the list of users, select **Henrik Fahlen** and click **Enable** in the right pane. When prompted, click **enable multi-factor auth** and then **Close**.

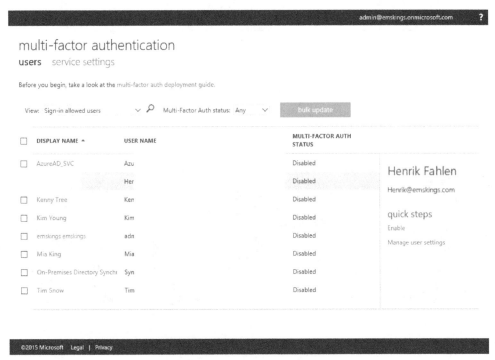

Configuring MFA for a single user.

Real World Note: You can perform most actions either from the Azure portal or with PowerShell using the MSOnline module. To view all the MSOnline PowerShell cmdlets, open PowerShell and type Get-Command -Module MSOnline.

Verify MFA

A common troubleshooting scenario is verifying the Multi-Factor Authorization settings for a given account. Instead of using the Azure portal, you will find it is much quicker to familiarize yourself with a few PowerShell cmdlets. To verify, disable, and enable MFA using PowerShell, follow these steps. (Notice that the listed result of the steps requires that MFA be already enabled for the user Henrik Fahlen.)

1. Open **PowerShell ISE** as administrator.

2. Type the following lines and press **F5** to run the script. When prompted, log in as the global Azure administrator.

   ```
   #Establish the connection to Azure

   Connect-MsolService

   # List the MFA settings

   $f = Get-MsolUser -UserPrincipalName henrik@emskings.com

   $f.StrongAuthenticationRequirements
   ```

> **Note:** In this step, you need to replace the emskings.com domain with your domain name.

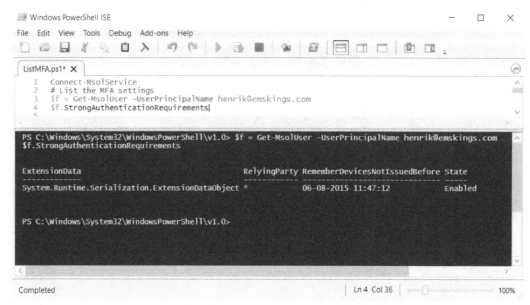

Using PowerShell to verify the user MFA settings.

Enable and Disable MFA Using PowerShell

After a while, you will build a rock solid library of PowerShell cmdlets and learn quickly that managing Azure Active Directory with PowerShell is in many ways much easier than playing around in the user interface. You can use the two examples that follow first to disable and then to enable MFA for a given user. In both examples, we recommend that you use PowerShell ISE.

```
#Disable MFA for a specific user

$sta = @()

Set-MsolUser -UserPrincipalName henrik@emskings.com
-StrongAuthenticationRequirements $sta

# Enable MFA for a specific user

$st = New-Object -TypeName
Microsoft.Online.Administration.StrongAuthenticationRequirement

$st.RelyingParty = "*"

$st.State = "Enabled"
```

```
$sta = @($st)

Set-MsolUser -UserPrincipalName henrik@emskings.com
-StrongAuthenticationRequirements $sta
```

Configure MFA for Joining Devices

One of the ViaMonstra business requirements is enforcing MFA for users when they enroll devices into a cloud service. You enable the feature in the Azure portal following these steps:

1. Open **https://manage.windowsAzure.com** and sign in with the Azure admin account.

2. In the management console, select **Active Directory** and click the **ViaMonstra** directory name to open the domain properties.

3. Click **Configure**, navigate to the **devices** section, and click **Yes** in **require multi-factor auth to join devices**.

4. Click **Save** to update the ViaMonstra directory.

MFA Exclusions

Although MFA is a great security enhancement, it can be very annoying if the feature is enabled for all applications and networks. ViaMonstra does not want to frustrate users who are working in the office by having them use MFA. To configure that, you add the company IP information to an exclusions list:

1. Open **https://manage.windowsAzure.com** and sign in with the Azure admin account.

2. In the management console, select **Active Directory** and click the **ViaMonstra** directory name to open the domain properties.

3. Click **Users** and then click **Manage Multi-factor auth** on the ribbon.

4. On the **multi-factor authentication** page, click **service settings**.

5. In **Trusted IPs**, enable **skip multi-factor authentication for request from federated users on my intranet**, type the IP address subnets in the form of 192.168.1.0/24, and click **Save**.

The MFA End-User Experience

End users quickly learn how MFA works. As administrator, you just need to provide them with a few links to the Azure end-user portal (myapps.microsoft.com) and the Azure Authenticator application from one of the stores. In the following example, Henrik uses his iOS device to install and configure the Azure Authenticator application.

Note: For testing the MFA end-user experience, make sure the device is not connected to the network excluded in the preceding guide, such as by using 4G instead of local wireless.

1. On the iOS device, open the **App Store** and then search for and install the **Azure Authenticator**.

The Azure Authenticator app.

2. Launch the **Azure Authenticator** application on the device.

3. From a web browser (on any computer/device), connect to **http://myapps.microsoft.com** and sign in as **henrik@emskings.com** using **P@ssw0rd** as the password. Notice that the sign-in process is unsuccessful due to the multi-factor auth requirements.

Note: Again, please replace the emskings.com domain with your domain.

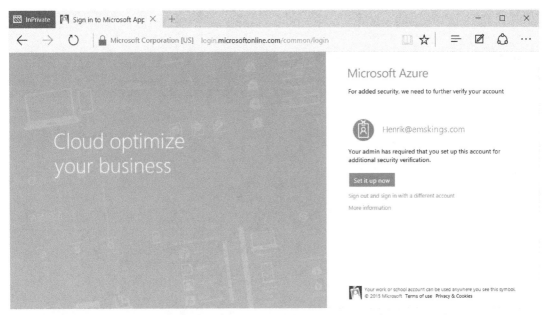

Multi-factor auth preventing the user from signing in with a single password.

4. Click **Set it up now**.

5. On the **Additional Security Verification** page, in **Step 1** select **Mobile app** and click **Setup**. This displays a QR code on the webpage that you need to scan using the device.

6. On your device, open the **Azure Authenticator** application and tap **Scan Barcode**.

7. Scan the **QR code** in the **Azure portal** and click **Done**. On your mobile device, note that the Azure Authenticator application is being associated with the user.

8. In the **Azure portal**, click **Contact me** to start **Step 2** of the process.

9. On your device, you should receive a verification, click **Verify** and **Close** to finish the setup process.

10. Close the **Azure portal**, and sign in to **http://myapps.microsoft.com** again. This time use the Azure Authenticator application to verify that you are Henrik; otherwise, the sign-in process will not finish.

You can use the Microsoft Azure end user portal to access applications, reset password, work with security groups, and configure end-user settings like additional MFA settings. There are two links: applications and profile. From the profile link, you can configure additional security verification settings and change the current MFA settings. Before you start adding phone and text verification settings, you should be aware that local cell provider charges might apply.

Adding Authentication Phone settings to MFA Profile

MFA App Passwords

One of the first phone calls you will get after enabling MFA in your organization will be colleagues complaining about not being able to access applications such as Microsoft Skype for Business. Certain applications do not support MFA and prevent the user from accessing the application. In order to mitigate that problem, MFA has a feature called App password that enables users to generate a password automatically per user at http://myapps.microsoft.com. Typically, users generate the password the first time an application prompts the user for a password. To generate the app password, follow these instructions:

1. Open a browser and sign in as **henrik@emskings.com** to **http://myapps.microsoft.com**.

2. From the **profile** link, click **Additional security verification**. This takes you to the **Additional security verification** page.

3. Click the **app passwords** link.

4. Click **create**, and a page opens on which you can enter a name. You can use the same password for all applications on a single device. For that reason, ViaMonstra recommends that users enter the name of the device on which the password is to be used.

5. Enter the device name and click **Next**.

6. Memorize the password, or if you are not Rain Man, click **copy password to clipboard** and click **close**.

7. Use the password when prompted in Skype for Business and the other applications.

Branding Azure AD

Branding and personalizing Azure AD helps to establish trust between your users and Azure AD. Never underestimate the value of presenting users with a familiar logo and text. You can customize most elements of the sign-in page, and the following example is what you will experience after you add a custom logo, sign-in illustration, and sign-in text.

Branding the Azure user experience.

The following steps require that you have downloaded and extracted the book sample files to C:\Setup.

1. Open a browser, go to **https://manage.windowsAzure.com**, and sign in with the Azure admin account.

2. Select **Active Directory**, and click **Default Directory / Configure**.

3. Click **customize branding** to start the process.

4.   On the **customize branding** page, click **Next**.

5.   On the **customize default branding** page, configure the following settings and click **Next**:

    a.   In **Banner logo**, click **browse**, and then from **C:\Setup\Branding**, select **banner logo.png** and click **Open**.

    b.   In **SQUARE logo**, click **browse**, and from **C:\Setup\Branding**, select **Tile Logo - 120x120.png** and click **Open**.

    c.   In **SIGN-IN page text heading**, type **ViaMonstra sign-in**.

    d.   In **SIGN-IN page text**, type **Please sign-in to ViaMonstra and prepare to learn!**

6.   On the second **customize branding** page, configure these settings and click **complete**:

    a.   In **SIGN-IN page illustration**, click **browse**, and from **C:\Setup\Branding**, select **Sign In Page Illustration - 1420x1200.jpg** and click **Open**.

    b.   In **post logout link label**, type **ViaMonstra**.

    c.   In **post logout link URL**, type **http://viamonstra.com/**.

Self-Service Password Reset with On-Premises Writeback

As you learned in chapter 3, Active Directory Premium supports self-service password reset with on-premises writeback (SSPR) to your on-premises Active Directory. The feature has a few moving parts that must be configured correctly before you can get it to work, but configured properly, it's one of those features that will make you look great in the eyes of management.

In order to enable SSPR, you need to ensure the following requirements are met:

- Infrastructure
  - Azure Active Directory sync tool with version number 1.0.0419.0911 or higher
  - Password reset configured in the Azure Active Directory sync tool
  - The correct edition of Azure Active Directory (You are covered with EMS and Azure Active Directory Premium.)
  - Password reset enabled in Azure Active Directory
  - Firewall rules
- End users
  - Must be enabled for password reset
  - Must be configured with Multi-Factor Authentication

Configure Infrastructure Requirements

With the latest version of Azure AD Sync and Azure AD Premium, you are already covered on some of the requirements. Most organizations also are compliant with the firewall rules, as the only requirement is an outbound rule using port TCP port 443 to https://ssprsbprodncu-sb.accesscontrol.windows.net/. To configure the remaining infrastructure requirements, complete the steps in the next two guides.

Configure Password Reset in the Azure AD Sync Tool

1. Log in to **DC01** as **VIAMONSTRA\Administrator** and launch the **Azure AD Connect tool** (a shortcut should be on the desktop).

2. On the **Tasks** page, click **Customize synchronization options** and click **Next**.

3. On the **Connect to Azure AD** page, fill in the Azure Active Directory account (**admin@mdmhybrid.onmicrosoft.com**) and password, and then click **Next**.

4. On the **Connect Directories** page, in **Username**, type **VIAMONSTRA\Administrator**, and in **Password**, type **P@ssw0rd**. Then click **Next**.

5. On the **Optional Features** page, enable **Password writeback** and click **Next**.

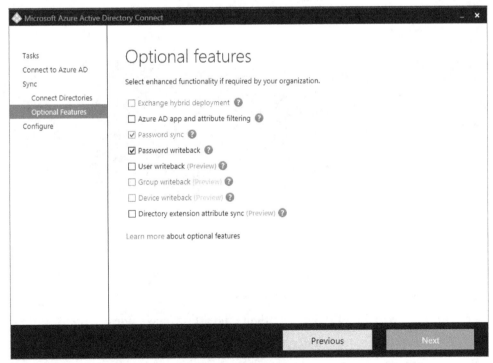

Enable Password writeback in Azure AD Connect.

6. On the **Configure** page, click **Install** and then click **Exit** when the installation is finished. Notice that you might have the enable to the Azure AD Sync scheduled task in Task Scheduler again.

Configure Password Reset in Azure AD Premium Using PowerShell

1. From **DC01**, start a new instance of **PowerShell ISE** as administrator, type the following command, and note the Azure AD connector name:

```
Get-ADSyncConnector | Where-Object ConnectorTypeName -eq
Extensible2 | Select-Object -Property Name
```

2. Type the following **PowerShell** command to enable the Password Reset Writeback feature where **mdmhybrid.onmicrosoft.com – AAD** must be replaced with your Azure AD connector name:

```
Set-ADSyncAADPasswordResetConfiguration -Connector
"emskings.onmicrosoft.com - AAD" -Enable $True -Verbose
```

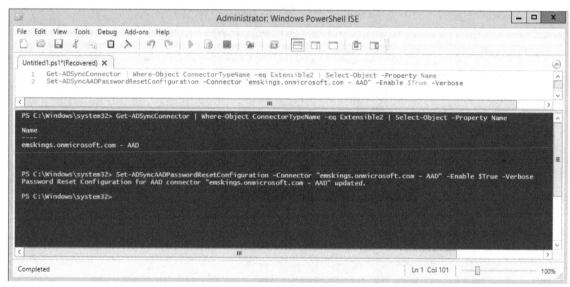

Enabling Password Reset Writeback using PowerShell.

3. Log in to the **Azure portal** using **Internet Explorer**: **https://portal.Azure.com/**.

4. Select **Active Directory**, and click **ViaMonstra / Configure**.

5. Under **User Password Reset Policy**, configure the following settings:

    a. Users enabled for password reset: **YES**

    b. Restrict access to password reset: **NO**

    c. Authentication Methods Available to Users:

        ▪ **Mobile Phone**

        ▪ **Alternate Email Address**

     d.   Number of Authentication Methods Required: **1**

     e.   Require users to register when signing in to the Access Panel: **YES**

     f.   Write back passwords to on-premises active directory: **YES**

     g.   Password writeback service status: **Configured**

6. Click **Save**.

Configure User Requirements

In an ideal world, users would sign up for password resets in advance. ViaMonstra knows that we not always live in the ideal world and that you need to assist your users to get them moving towards self-service. So you email all your users (several times during a period of one month) telling them to register for password reset using this link: aka.ms/ssprsetup. In the email message, you also inform them that about 35–40 percent of all the calls you get at the service desk pertain to password resets. The following steps explain how the user can register and perform password reset:

1. Launch your Internet browser and open **https://passwordreset.microsoftonline.com/** or **http://outlook.com/emskings.com**. If you use http://outlook.com/emskings.com, then click **Can't access your account**.

2. From the **Get back into your account** page, notice that the user ID is filled out if you began the processes from http://outlook.com/emskings.com. Type the characters in the picture and click **Next**.

3. On the **verification step 1** page, type your mobile phone number and click **Text**.

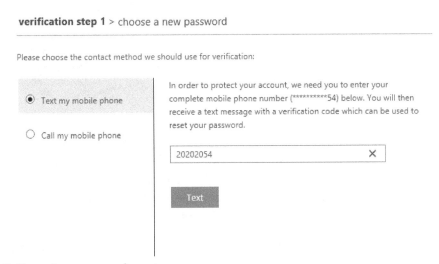

Self-service password reset.

4. While still on the **verification step 1** page, enter the code from your text message and click **Next**.

5. Enter your new password and click **Finish**. Note that you still have to comply with the internal password rules.

    After a successful change, the user is able to access the cloud services once again.

Password reset information is written to the Application log on your on-premises domain controllers and available in the Azure AD reports. You can track both successful and failed attempts.

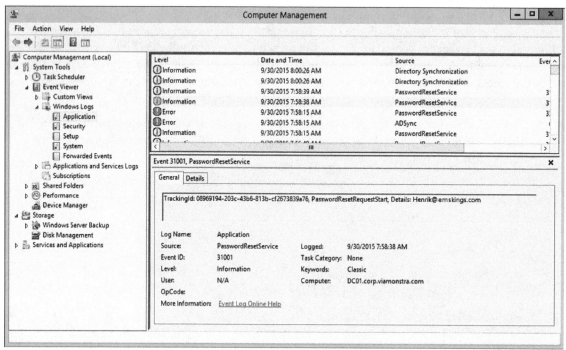

Viewing the Application log for password reset information. Notice the error. This information is from a password reset attempt that failed due to password restrictions.

Azure AD Join

For many years, we have been used to adding devices to a domain or making them a member of a workgroup. With Azure AD Premium, you get one additional option: joining the device to Azure through a feature called Azure AD Join. When you join a device to Azure, the Azure Device Registration Service creates the computer object. The object is not exactly the same as the traditional on-premises computer object. One of the differences is that the device is always *associated with a user* unlike on-premises computer objects that are stored and treated as individual objects. You need to configure a few things in Azure AD premium before you can start enrolling the devices:

1. Log in to **Azure portal** using **Internet Explorer**: **https://portal.Azure.com/**.

2.   Select **Active Directory**, and click **ViaMonstra / Configure**.

3.   Scroll down to the **devices** section and configure these settings:

   a.   USERS MAY JOIN DEVICES TO AZURE AD: **ALL**

   b.   ADDITIONAL ADMINISTRATOR ON AZURE AD JOINED DEVICES: Click **Add**, select **Mia King** and **Tim Snow**, and then click the **Complete** button to add the users.

   c.   REQUIRE MULTI-FACTOR AUTH TO JOIN DEVICES: **Yes**

   d.   Click **Save**.

Device registration configured with two local administrators.

One of the many benefits of using EMS is automatic enrollment of AD-joined devices into Microsoft Intune. By default, Azure AD adds Microsoft Intune to the list of SaaS applications and configures the enrollment URL. To change or view the settings, follow these steps:

1.   Open an Internet browser, go to **https://manage.windowsAzure.com**, and sign in with the Azure admin account.

2.   Select **Active Directory**, and click **Default Directory / Applications**.

3.   From the list of applications, click **Microsoft Intune**.

4. Click **Configure**. Notice that both the MDM DISCOVERY URL and MDM COMPLIANCE URL are configured to enroll the device into Microsoft Intune. You can change these values if you are using another MDM platform.

5. For **MDM TERMS OF USE URL**, type **http://viamonstra.com/?page_id=47.**

6. Select **APPLY TO: ALL**, and then click **Save**.

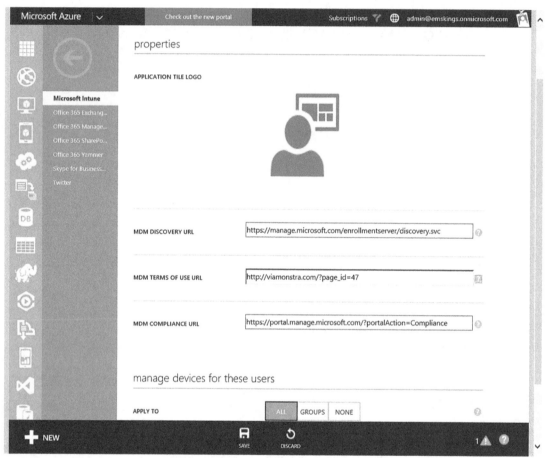

Configuring Intune MDM enrollment as part of the Azure AD join.

Software as a Service (SaaS)

In Chapter 3, you learned about the SaaS feature. In order to configure Twitter as a SaaS application with automatic password rollover, follow the steps in the next section. You start by creating an Azure-based group to which users can request membership and that way be granted access without having to call the service desk. Note that this requires you to have an existing Twitter account.

Configure Azure Active Directory Groups

1. Open a browser, go to **https://manage.windowsAzure.com**, and sign in with the Azure admin account.

2. Select **Active Directory**, and click **Default Directory / Groups**.

3. Click **ADD GROUP**, and then in **NAME**, type **Twitter**, and in **DESCRIPTION**, type **Enable access to corporate Twitter account**. Click **OK.**

4. From the list of groups, select the newly created **Twitter** group and click **OWNERS**.

5. Click **ADD OWNERS**, and from the list of users, select **Henrik Fahlen**. Click **OK.**

6. Open a browser, go to **https://manage.windowsAzure.com**, and sign in as **henrik@emskings.com** (who is the member of the group).

7. Select **groups**. Notice that you see only the newly created Twitter group.

8. Click the **Twitter** group to open the properties.

9. Click **Edit**, and from the **Group policy** drop-down list, select **This group requires owner approval**. Click **Update**. Don't close the browser; a user is about to request membership.

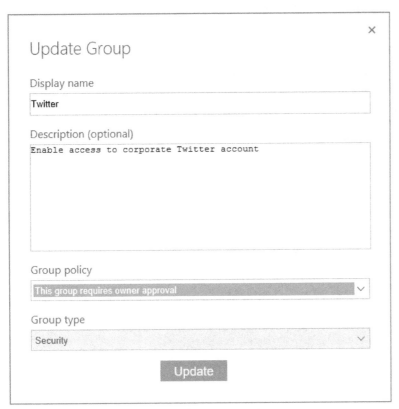

Configuring security group self-service in Azure.

Users can request group membership from http://myapps.microsoft.com/. After the request is made, the owner grants or denies access, when approval for the group is configured. In the following example, tim@emskings.com requests and is granted access to the newly created Twitter group.

1.   Open a browser, go to **https://manage.windowsAzure.com**, and sign in as **tim@emskings.com**.

2.   Select **groups**, click **list all groups**, and type **twitter** in the **search** field.

3.   Open the **Twitter** group properties and click **Join group**. For the business justification, write something nice, please, and click **Request**. Don't close the browser. Wait until the request has been approved by the manager. Don't leave the browser, as you will shortly get access to Twitter.

4.   The approval request shows up in the browser belonging to the group owner. As group owner, click **approvals**, select **approval request**, and click **Approve**.

After the membership is approved, the requesting user is able to see the group by selecting My memberships from the drop-down list on the groups page.

Real World Note: You can view the group self-service activity in Azure Active Directory. Open the group properties and click SELF SERVICE ACTIVITY.

Configure SaaS Apps

1.   Open a browser, go to **https://manage.windowsAzure.com**, and sign in with the Azure admin account.

2.   Select **Active Directory**, and click **Default Directory / Applications**.

3.   Click **Add**, and in **What do you want to do?**, select **Add an application from the gallery**.

4. In **search**, type **twitter** and press **Enter**.

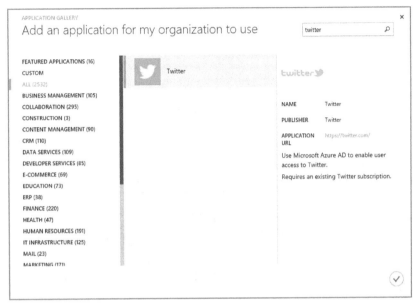

The Application Gallery with more than 2500 applications.

5. Select **Twitter** and click the **OK** button (the checkmark).

6. Click **Configure Single sign-on**, select **Password Single Sign-On**, and click **OK**.

7. Click **Assign accounts** and make sure groups are listed. If no groups are listed, click **Show Groups** and click **OK**. From the list of groups, select **Twitter** and click **Assign**.

8. In the **Assign Groups** window, enable **I want to enter Twitter credentials to be shared among all group members**.

9. Enter your Twitter account information, enable **I want to enable automatic password rollover**, and click **OK**. With automatic password rollover, no one knows the password. In order to restore the password, you have to go through the normal "I forgot my Twitter password" experience.

10. After you have configured the application, shift to the browser where you have logged in as Tim. Select the **applications** tab and notice you have access to Twitter. (If you don't, refresh the browser page.)

What Happens Behind the Scenes

It might look like magic when you access Office 365 or another SaaS application without being prompted for sign-on credentials. Behind the scenes, your sign-on request is similar to what happens on-premises with Kerberos tickets and Kerberos granting tickets. The following list describes the process and what takes place behind the scenes:

1. When a user is authenticated, Azure AD passes down an object called the *primary refresh token*, which is stored in the local .NET ADAL (Azure Directory Authentication Library) cache on the device. You can think of the primary refresh token as being the cloud-based version of a Kerberos ticket.

> **Real World Note**: Azure Directory Authentication Library (ADAL) for .NET enables client application developers to easily authenticate users to cloud or on-premises Active Directory.

2. When the user tries to connect to a SaaS application like Office 365, the Windows 10 device, for instance, sends single sign-on request to Azure AD using the primary refresh token.

3. Azure AD verifies that the primary refresh token is still valid and passes down a single sign-on token to the device.

4. The device now has two tokens, the single sign-on token and the primary refresh token. This process might seem familiar and very similar to on-premises AD where you have your Kerberos ticket-granting token and your Kerberos ticket.

5. With the single sign-on token, the user accesses the SaaS applications and is signed in.

Azure Cloud App Discovery

Most people simply do not know about all of the local applications installed in the organization. This is true not only for traditional applications like .exe and .msi, but also for SaaS applications. Often administrators have no or very little clue about what and how many SaaS applications are being used. With Azure Cloud App Discovery, administrators can collect information about where applications are in use and who is using them. The information is collected through the Azure Cloud App Discovery.

Azure Cloud App Discovery is an agent that can be installed (the traditional way) on your computers. The agent analyzes network traffic and uploads information about the usage of SaaS applications to Azure AD. In Azure, you can use the dashboard to view the collected information. To get started with Cloud App Discovery, follow these steps:

1. In your favorite browser, navigate to **https://appdiscovery.Azure.com/** and click **Get Started**.

2. From the **Cloud App Discovery** pane, click **Create**.

3. Click **Settings / Management Agent** and then click the **User consent** option. Select one of the options for user warnings and click **Update**.

4. Click **Download**. This downloads the agent.

5. You can deploy the agent through ConfigMgr or any other software-distribution method. In **ConfigMgr**, you can create a legacy package/program with the command line **/quiet /norestart**.

    Log files for the installation and scanning are created in the %temp% folder in files named Cloud_App_Discovery_-_Endpoint_Agent_*.

Configuring Mobile Device Management in Microsoft Intune

After you have configured all the mobile device management (MDM) prerequisites, you need to configure the MDM authority to be Microsoft Intune so you can enable the platform support in Microsoft Intune.

Configure Mobile Device Management Authority

To configure the MDM authority, you need to follow this procedure:

1. Go to the webpage **http://manage.microsoft.com** and log in with your administrative account.

2. In the **Microsoft Intune console**, select **Admin / Mobile Device Management**.

3. On the **Mobile Device Management** page, click **Set Mobile Device Management Authority**.

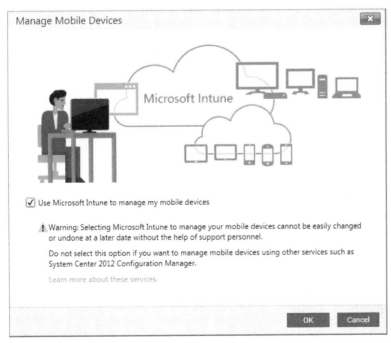

Setting the MDM authority to Microsoft Intune.

> **Real World Note:** After setting the MDM authority to Microsoft Intune, you cannot undo this yourself if, for example, you want to switch to a hybrid configuration. Technical support needs to be contacted to reverse this setting, which can take up to five days.

4. In the pop-up window shown in the preceding figure, select **Use Microsoft Intune to manage my mobile devices** and click **OK**.

Next, you see the list of platforms Microsoft Intune supports, some of which need extra configuration. In the following sections, you configure all the platforms used within ViaMonstra.

Configure Windows

ViaMonstra needs to be able to manage Windows 10 devices, so you need to be sure that employees are able to enroll their Windows (10) devices into Microsoft Intune.

1. Go to the webpage **http://manage.microsoft.com** and log in with your administrative account.

2. In the **Microsoft Intune console**, select **Admin / Mobile Device Management and Windows**.

3. Supply the domain name you configured in Chapter 2 and click **Test Auto-Detection**.

Testing that all DNS records are set to support auto detection for enrollment.

If all CNAME DNS records are in place, your domain name should be able to pass the auto-detection so that you are able to enroll your Windows devices.

The DNS records are configured correctly.

Configure Windows Phone

In ViaMonstra, only Windows Phone 8.1 or later is supported, so there is not much to set up. If you want, however, you can check the DNS settings as described in the preceding Windows section.

Configure Passport for Work

Microsoft Passport for Work is an alternate sign-in *method for Windows 10 that uses* Active Directory or an Azure Active Directory account to replace *a* password, smart *card, or virtual smart card.* The behavior can be managed:

Setting	ViaMonstra Value	Your Value
Enable Passport for Work	Enabled	
Use a Trusted Platform Module (TPM)	Required	
Require minimum PIN length	6	
Require maximum PIN length:	127	
Require lowercase letters in PIN:	Allowed	
Require uppercase letters in PIN:	Allowed	
Require special characters in PIN:	Not allowed	
PIN expiration (days):	41	
Remember PIN history:	5	
Allow biometric authentication:	Yes	
Use enhanced anti-spoofing, when available	Yes	
Use Remote Passport:	Yes	

Configure iOS

To be able to enroll and manage an iOS device with Microsoft Intune, you need to configure an Apple Push Notification service certificate.

1. Go to the webpage **http://manage.microsoft.com** and log in with your administrative account.

2. In the **Microsoft Intune console**, select **Admin / Mobile Device Management / iOS and Mac OS X**.

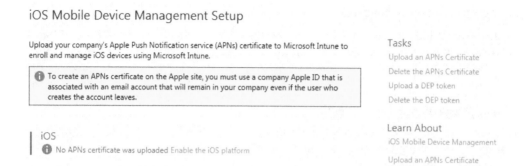

For iOS support, you need to upload an Apple Push Notification service certificate.

3. Click **Enable the iOS platform** to start the procedure to get the Apple Push Notification service (APNs) certificate.

4. On the next screen, click **Download the APNs Certificate Request**.

5. Supply the file name **APNRequest.csr** and save it to your computer's desktop.

6. Next, you need to create the actual APNs:

    a. Click the **Apple Push Certificates portal** link.

    b. On the **Apple Push Certificates portal**, log in with the Apple ID that you created in Chapter 2.

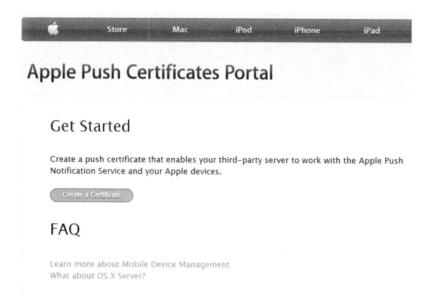

Creating the Apple push certificate.

7. After logging in, click **Create a Certificate**. Read the **Terms of Use**, select the check box confirming than **I have read and agree to these terms and conditions**, and click **Accept** to be able to upload the CSR file you created earlier.

8. On the **Create a New Push Certificate** page, browse for the CSR file stored on the desktop. Click **Upload** to upload the CSR file so that the APNs certificate can be created.

Real World Note: If you are using Internet Explorer, you will likely be prompted about a .JSON file that can be downloaded. Ignore this message about downloading the .JSON file and refresh the page to see the certificate you can use in Microsoft Intune. Unfortunately, the Apple Push Certificates Portal is not compatible with Internet Explorer.

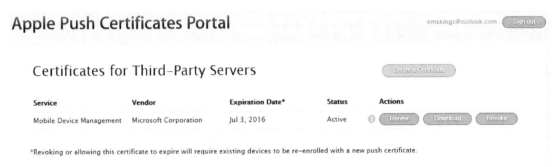

Downloading the certificate.

9. Click **Download** and store the file **MDM_ Microsoft Corporation_Certificate.pem**, for instance, on the desktop.

10. Move back to the **Microsoft Intune console** and click **Upload the APNs Certificate**.

11. On the **Upload the APNs Certificate** page, click **Browse**, select the **MDM_ Microsoft Corporation_Certificate.pem** file, and supply the **Apple ID** before clicking **Upload**.

Upload the certificate to Microsoft Intune

The iOS platform support is now configured.

Configure Microsoft Exchange

To use the Service to Service Connector, the user who is logged on must have Exchange admin rights.

1. Go to the webpage **http://manage.microsoft.com** and log in with your administrative account.

2. In the **Microsoft Intune console**, select **Admin / Mobile Device Management / Microsoft Exchange / Set Up Exchange Connection**.

3. Click **Set Up Service to Service Connector**, and then click **OK** to configure the Service to Service Connector with the account that is currently logged on.

Configure Enrollment Rules

Microsoft Intune allows up to five devices to be enrolled for each user. You can configure the number of devices that can be enrolled as follows:

1. Go to the webpage **http://manage.microsoft.com** and log in with your administrative account.

2. In the **Microsoft Intune console**, select **Admin / Mobile Device Management / Enrollment Rules**.

3. Select a value between **1** and **5** to set the maximum number of devices a user can enroll and click **Save**.

Configure the Company Portal

The Company Portal is the place where the user needs to access to request and install apps, access company resources, and contact the IT DEPARTMENT. The legal department of ViaMonstra requires that the users be notified about the terms and conditions that are valid when a user enrolls a device into Microsoft Intune.

1. Go to the webpage **http://manage.microsoft.com** and log in with your administrative account.

2. In the **Microsoft Intune console**, select **Admin / Mobile Device Management / Company Portal**.

3. In the Company Portal, information can be added about the company, the following table can be used as a reference:

Company Portal

Specify company name, company contact information and privacy statement
The company name is displayed as the title of the Microsoft Intune company portal. The contact
information and details are displayed to users in the Contact IT screen of the Microsoft Intune
company portal. The privacy statement is displayed when user clicks on the privacy link.

Company name:

ViaMonstra

IT department contact name:

Service Desk ViaMonstra

IT department phone number:

+000-00000000

IT department email address:

support@viamonstra.com

Additional information:

[Save] [Cancel]

Company Portal information.

Setting	ViaMonstra Value	Your Value
Company name	ViaMonstra Inc.	
IT department contact name	Service Desk ViaMonstra	
IT department phone number	+000-00000000	
IT department email address	support@viamonstra.com	
Additional information		
Company privacy statement URL		
Support website URL (not displayed)		
Website name (displayed to user)	http://viamonstra.com	
Theme color		
Include company logo	Yes	

4. Click **Save** to store the supplied values.

Terms and Conditions

ViaMonstra does not make a distinction between personally owned and company-owned devices. To access corporate resources, the user needs to comply with the terms and conditions of ViaMonstra. It is very important that users know that limitations can occur while enrolling the device into Microsoft Intune.

1. Go to the webpage **http://manage.microsoft.com** and log in with your administrative account.

2. In the **Microsoft Intune console**, select **Policy / Terms And Conditions**.

3. Click **Add** and supply the information listed in the following table:

Setting	ViaMonstra Value	Your Value
Name	Bring Your Own Device Terms & Conditions	
Description		
Title	Bring Your Own Device Terms & Conditions	
Text for terms	Access only to persons explicitly authorized by ViaMonstra.	
Text to explain what it means if the user accepts	Access only to persons explicitly authorized by ViaMonstra.	

4. Click **Save** to store the changes.

5. Select the created terms and conditions and click **Manage Deployment**.

6. Select **All Users** and click **Add**. Then click **OK** to deploy the new terms and conditions.

Setting Up Groups

With Microsoft Intune, you are not able to deploy apps and policies to devices, users, or Active Directory groups directly. To deploy apps and policies, you need to create Intune groups. After creating the Intune groups, you need to add the synchronized AD security groups as a member of the Intune group to include the users that are member of the security groups.

Microsoft Intune is a solution that is user centric, which means that you deploy policies and applications to users or groups of users instead of devices.

For special kiosk devices, device groups are created to deploy policies and apps that are specific to those devices.

1. Go to the webpage **http://manage.microsoft.com** and log in with your administrative account.

2. In the **Microsoft Intune console**, select **Groups / Create Group**.

3. Supply the group name **SW_Office_Install**, select the parent group **All Users**, and click **Next**.

4. On the **Define Membership Criteria** page, click **Browse** next to **Include members from these security groups**.

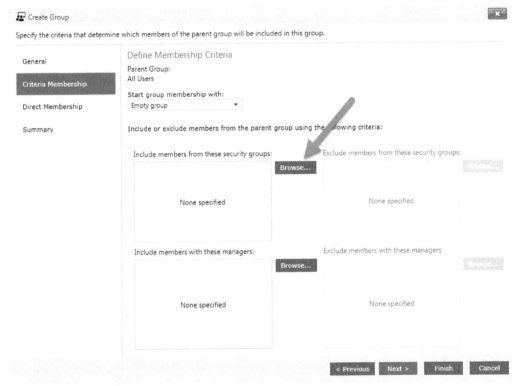

Selecting the option to include security group members.

5. Select the **SW_Office_Install** security group, click **Add**, and then click **OK** to add the members of this security group to the Intune group.

6. Click **Finish**.

7. Repeat steps 2–6 to create each of the Microsoft Intune groups listed in the following table using the security groups as their members.

Intune Group Name	Member (Security Group)
SW_Office_Uninstall	SW_Office_Uninstall
SW_Managed_Viewers_Install	SW_Managed_Viewers_Install
SW_Managed_Viewers_Uninstall	SW_Managed_Viewers_Uninstall
SW_Notepad_Install	SW_Notepad_Install
SW_Notepad_Uninstall	SW_Notepad_Uninstall
SW_Adobe_Reader_Install	SW_Adobe_Reader_Install
SW_Adobe_Reader_Uninstall	SW_Adobe_Reader_Uninstall
SW_Preferred_Apps	EMS Enabled Users

Chapter 5

EMS Hybrid Solution

In this chapter, you learn about the Windows services in Active Directory and how to implement the required ConfigMgr features to support the hybrid scenario:

- Configure discovery methods
- Adding the reporting services point
- Create collections

In addition to learning about the EMS hybrid solution in the next section, this chapter takes you through the following configurations:

- Creating a Microsoft subscription
- Configuring Azure Active Directory Connect
- Setting up licensing
- Setting up Azure Active Directory Premium features
- Setting up the ConfigMgr infrastructure
- Preparing for mobile device management
- Configuring hybrid platform support

Real World Note: The administration portal used to configure the standalone solution changes frequently, so the step-by-step guides provided in this book may not match exactly.

Microsoft Intune Connected with ConfigMgr (Hybrid Solution)

Mobile device management integration between ConfigMgr and Microsoft Intune has come a long way since the release of Microsoft System Center SP1. With ConfigMgr Current Branch, organizations receive almost the same MDM support as organizations that choose to install a standalone Microsoft Intune solution. ConfigMgr CB offers support for iOS, Windows, Windows Phone, and Android devices. The first release of ConfigMgr 2012 offered only MDM management support via the Exchange Connector. With ConfigMgr Current Branch, you achieve MDM support by integrating ConfigMgr and Microsoft Intune.

Why Choose a Hybrid Solution?

Choosing a hybrid solution makes sense for all of the thousands of organizations on the globe that already manage Microsoft devices with ConfigMgr and at the same time have the need for a MDM environment. ViaMonstra already uses ConfigMgr to manage Windows computers and has a high level of organizational knowledge about managing the environment. Some of the main benefits for choosing a hybrid solution include the following:

- **Single pane of glass management.** You do not have to learn a new interface in order to manage mobile devices.

- **A common database.** You use the same database to collect information about users, computers, and mobile devices.

- **SQL Reporting Services.** With all the data in the same database, it's easy to create custom reports that suit your needs.

- **PowerShell.** Using PowerShell and a little pixie dust, your internal team can automate many MDM processes such as finding all jailbroken devices and placing them in quarantine.

- **Log files and CMTrace.** As a ConfigMgr administrator, you are familiar with some of the many log files. Mobile device management introduces new log files that are very helpful when troubleshooting.

Microsoft Subscriptions

In order to follow the exercises in this chapter, you need to establish a 30-day Microsoft EMS trial account. Included in the Microsoft EMS license, you get a subscription to Microsoft Intune, Azure Rights Management, and Azure Active Directory Premium services.

Create the EMS Trial Environment

1.   Go to **http://ref.ms/ems**, select **Get Started**, and click **Try Now**.

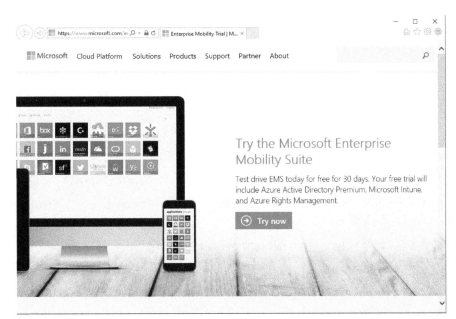

The Microsoft Enterprise Mobility Suite landing page for setting up the subscriptions.

2. In order to start the setup of the **Microsoft Intune** trial, click **Try Now**.

3. You are prompted to fill out your company information:

Setting	Your Value
Country or region	
First name	
Last name	
Business email address	
Business phone number	
Company name	
Your organization size	

4. Click **Next** after supplying the information.

5. Enter the information as shown here:

Setting	ViaMonstra Value	Your Value
Enter a user name	admin	
Your company	mdmhybrid.onmicrosoft.com	

6. Supply the password twice and click **Next**.

7. Choose **Text me**, supply a phone number to prove your identity, and click **Text me**.

8. Supply the **verification code** and click **Create my account** to set up the EMS trial account.

9. Click **You're ready to go** to access the new tenant via https://portal.office365.com and stay there for the next steps.

Set Up an Azure Subscription

To be able to use the EMS licenses, you need to create a Microsoft Azure subscription:

1. In the **Office 365 admin center** (https://portal.office.com/admin/default.aspx), browse to the **Admin** section and click **Azure AD**.

2. On the **Oops! Access to Azure Active Directory Is Not Available** window, click **Azure Subscription** to activate a subscription.

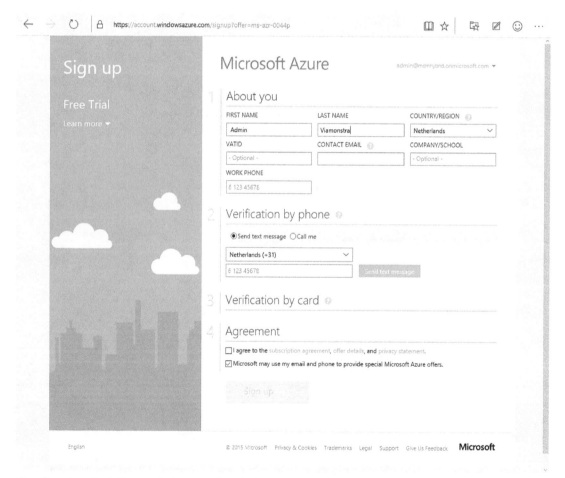

Configuring the Microsoft Azure subscription.

3. Supply information about yourself, verify your mobile phone, agree to the terms, and verify your credit card.

Real World Note: During this trial, your credit card will not be used, but Microsoft wants to verify your identity. Your credit card will be charged only after you explicitly remove the spending limit.

4. Click **Sign up** to get access to Microsoft Azure. Click **Start managing my service** to get access to the new Microsoft Azure portal (https://portal.azure.com).

5. Click **Browse** and select the **white star** next to **Active Directory**. Notice that the star changes color after you select it.

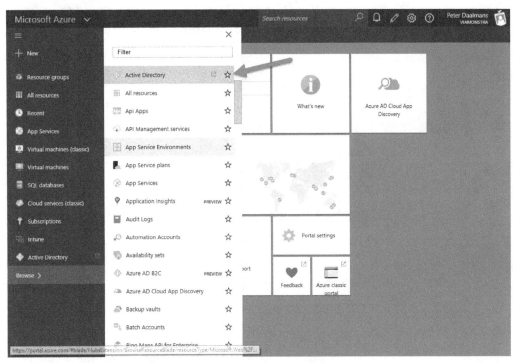

Select Active Directory to add it to the menu.

6. Click **Active Directory** in the menu. A new tab with the (old) Microsoft Azure portal opens and introduces you to Windows Azure with a tour of the service. Navigate through the tour, and the newly created Azure Active Directory then opens in the Dashboard.

Real World Note: Microsoft is in the process of moving all services to the new Azure Portal, which is accessible via http://portal.azure.com. Until all services are moved, there will be two portals, but all services are accessible via the new portal.

Set Up DNS

Initially, the new domain needs to be configured for Microsoft Intune, but before the domain can be added, verification of the ownership of the domain name must be done:

1. After the subscription is active, you need to configure the primary domain name. Configuring your public DNS name for Microsoft Intune is required to prove that you own the public domain. Go to the **Office 365 admin center** (https://portal.office.com/admin/default.aspx) and click **Domains**.

2. Click **Add domain**, and then click **Let's get started**.

3. Supply the domain name and click **Next**.

4. Next, you need to prove that you are the owner of the domain name supplied. You can do this by adding a TXT record that is supplied to your domain or adding an MX record to the same public domain that you want to add to Microsoft Intune.

Verifying domain ownership.

5. Before you click **Okay, I've added the record**, launch the **Admin portal** of the DNS provider, in this case GoDaddy (www.godaddy.com).

Real World Note: If you do not use GoDaddy, you can ignore the following steps, but make sure that you manually add the TXT or MX and CNAME records following the process of your ISP.

---

6. After logging in, click **My Account** and **Manage** in the **Domain** section of the screen.

7. Select your domain, click the **wheel** to access the domain menu, and click **Manage DNS**.

8. In **Domain Details**, select the **DNS ZONE FILE** tab.

9. Scroll down to the **TXT (Text)** section and click **Add Record**.

ADD ZONE RECORD   ×

MDMHYBRID.COM

RECORD TYPE: *

| TXT (Text)   ⌄ |

HOST: * ⓘ

| @ |

TXT VALUE: * ⓘ

| MS=ms73336649 |

TTL: * ⓘ

| 1 Hour   ⌄ |

[ADD ANOTHER]   [FINISH]   Cancel

Adding TXT records to prove you own the public domain.

> **Real World Note:** Depending on your hosting provider, you may need to contact its support staff to add these records. Some providers don't allow you to enter all this information in their control panels. For example, you may not be able to specify the TTL value.

10. Supply the following values and click **Finish**:

Setting	Your Value
Record Type	TXT (Text)
Host	@
TXT Value	MS=ms*xxxxxxxx*
TTL	1 Hour

11. The DNS registration to prove that you are the owner of the public domain name is finished. You have to do two additional public DNS registrations to enroll devices in Intune. These are technically not requirements, but they make life easier for the persons enrolling devices. Click **Add Record**, and select **CNAME (Alias)** as the record type.

12. Create two CNAME records with the following values:

Record 1:

Setting	Your Value
Record Type	CNAME (Alias)
Host	enterpriseenrollment
Points to	manage.microsoft.com
TTL	1 Hour

Record 2:

Setting	Your Value
Record Type	CNAME (Alias)
Host	enterpriseregistration
Points to	enterpriseregistration.windows.net
TTL	1 Hour

13. Click **Finish** after creating the two records and save the changes in the GoDaddy admin portal.

14. Go back to the **Office 365 admin center** and click **Okay, I've added the record** to check whether the domain you want to add is yours.

Real World Note: Be aware that it can take up to 72 hours before changes in your DNS zone are replicated to the DNS servers used by Microsoft Intune.

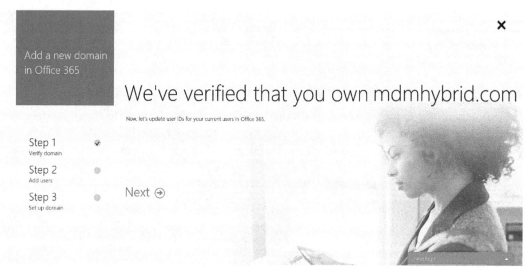

Under normal circumstances, the verification process is quick, but sometimes it can take several hours.

15. Click **Next** to optionally update the current users in Office 365 with the new domain:

    a.   Select the just created **admin@ mdmhybrid.onmicrosoft.com** user and click **Update selected users**.

    b.   Click **Next** and then click **Sign out** to log on again with the **admin@mdmhybrid.com** user.

> **Real World Note:** It might take a couple of minutes before the user information is updated and can be used.

16. Click **skip this step** (twice) on the **Add new users** page.

17. Click **Next**, select **No, I have an existing website or prefer to manage my own DNS records**, and click **Next** again.

18. Clear all the option check boxes, click **Next**, and then click **Finish** to finish the initial DNS setup.

In the next section, you further configure the DNS for Office 365.

Set Up Office 365

At ViaMonstra, you are planning to use the Office 365 and want to integrate conditional access to your Exchange and SharePoint services in the EMS PoC.

1. Browse to **http://portal.office.com** and log in with your admin credentials. The Welcome screen displays a message that no subscription is active.

2. Click **Purchase**, choose a trial version of **Office 365**, and then click **Start free trial**.

> **Real World Note:** For ViaMonstra, with 6000 users, we signed up for the Enterprise Office 365 Enterprise E3. If you are with a smaller organization, you may look into other services like the Office 365 Business Premium.

3. Click **Try now** on the checkout screen and then click **Continue** to go back to the Office 365 admin center.

4. Next you need to set up the domain to be able accept email and service other Office 365 components like Skype for Business. Click **Domains** and select **Complete setup** for the domain you configured earlier (mdmhybrid.com).

Completing the setup of the domain.

5. On the **Add a new domain in Office 365** page, click **Next**.

6. Click **skip this step twice** and then click **Next** to set up the domain for Office 365.

7. Next, you need to identify the services you want to use with your domain:

    a. In this case, select the following:

        ▪ **Outlook on the web for email, calendar and contacts**

        ▪ **Skype for Business for instant messaging and online meetings**

    b. You also need to clear the **Mobile Device Management for Office 365** check box because you are going to use Microsoft Intune as your mobile device management solution.

Real World Note: If for some reason the MDM Authority is already set to Office 365 and you do not want to use Office 365 MDM, contact Microsoft Technical Support to reverse the setting. Note that it can take up to five days. Check this blog for more info: http://ref.ms/mdmauthblog.

---

8. Click **Next**.

Note: Appendix B covers the basic Office 365 services configuration like Exchange Online and SharePoint Online.

---

9. Click **Add records**. Because you are using GoDaddy, you can allow Office 365 to configure automatically the DNS records needed for Office 365.

    a. In the pop-up, log in to the **GoDaddy portal** and click **Accept** to allow the creation of the DNS records for Office 365.

Confirm Access

Office 365 is requesting permission to make changes to your domain **mdmhybrid.com** at GoDaddy.

Click **Accept** to allow Office 365 to make these changes to **mdmhybrid.com**

Accept   Cancel

You can configure Office 365 to automatically update all required DNS records in a GoDaddy-hosted domain.

    b.   Click **Finish** to complete the DNS setup for Office 365.

If you are not using GoDaddy, you need to add the records yourself. If you are not allowed to do this, contact your DNS admin to configure the following DNS records for your domain:

- Use the following settings for **Exchange Online**:

Type	Priority	Host Name	Points to Address / Value	TTL
MX	0	@	mdmhybrid-com.mail.protection.outlook.com	1 Hour
CNAME	-	autodiscover	autodiscover.outlook.com	1 Hour
TXT	-	@	v=spf1 include:spf.protection.outlook.com -all	1 Hour

- Use the following settings for **Skype for Business**:

Type	Service	Proto-col	Port	Weight	Prior-ity	TTL	Name	Target
SRV	_sip	_tls	443	1	100	1 Hour	@	sipdir.online.lync.com
SRV	_sipfederationtls	_tcp	5061	1	100	1 Hour	@	sipfed.online.lync.com

Type	Host Name	Points to Address	TTL	Type
CNAME	sip	sipdir.online.lync.com	1 Hour	CNAME
CNAME	lyncdiscover	webdir.online.lync.com	1 Hour	CNAME

10. After the domain is set up, select the domain you added (**mdmhybrid.com**) and click **Set as default**.

Azure Active Directory Connect

In this section, you install and configure Azure Active Directory Synchronization service, which is part of Azure Active Directory Connect. As you learned in the preceding chapter, the configuration involves the following:

- Enabling directory synchronization in Microsoft Azure

- Configuring the synchronization service accounts

- Installing Azure Active Directory Synchronization Service

- Configuring the on-premises user principal name for the users that will be synchronized to Azure Active Directory

- Configuring Azure Active Directory Synchronization Service to synchronize only the required on-premises user and group objects

Configure the Azure Active Directory Connect Service Account

In the following steps, you enable directory synchronization in Microsoft Azure, creating the synchronization service account and installing Microsoft Azure Active Directory Connect on the domain controller. Notice that installing the application on the domain controller is not a requirement. You simply use DC01 to limit the number of virtual machines in the pilot environment.

1. Start **DC01** and log in as **VIAMONSTRA\Administrator**.

2. From an Internet browser, connect to **https://portal.Azure.com** (the old portal, https://manage.windowsazure.com, was still available when this book was written). **https://portal.Azure.com** is the latest Azure dashboard, from which you can connect to the Azure portal, view your billing information, get support, and much more.

3. To access the portal, click **Active Directory** in the menu of the Azure portal.

4. In the new tab, with the Default Active Directory active, select **Directory Integration**, and enable **Directory Sync** by clicking **Activated**.

5. When prompted, click **SAVE** to save the configuration, and click **Yes** when asked to confirm.

6. Keep the **Azure Portal** open, as you will need it to create the cloud synchronization service account. Click **Users**.

7. Click **ADD USER**.

8. On the first page of the **Add User** wizard, select **New user in your organization**, type **AzureAD_SVC**, and click the arrow to move to the next page.

9. On the second page, fill out the following user information and then click the arrow to move to the next page:

    a. First Name: **AzureAD_SVC**

    b. Display Name: **AzureAD_SVC**

    c. Role: **Global Admin**

10. As the **Alternate Email Address**, type your admin recovery email address, we used **mdmhybrid @outlook.com**. Then click the arrow to move to the next page.

11. On the **Get Temporary Password** page, click **Create**.

12. While still on the **Get Temporary Password** page, click the **check mark** to finish the creation of the account. Notice you need the temporary password in subsequent steps.

13. Open a new instance of the Internet browser in private browsing mode. You start InPrivate Browsing in Internet Explorer and Microsoft Edge by pressing **Ctrl + Shift +P**.

14. Connect to **https://portal.Azure.com/** and log in as **AzureAD_SVC@mdmhybrid.onmicrosoft.com** with the temporary password.

15. When prompted, change the password and make sure you document it.

16. The final step in configuring the service account is to configure the password never to expire. You can configure that process using Microsoft PowerShell:

    a. On **DC01**, launch **PowerShell** as **Administrator**.

    b. Type **Connect-MsolService** and press **Enter**.

    c. Enter the Service Account login information and click **OK**:

        i.   User Name: AzureAD_SVC@mdmhybrid.onmicrosoft.com

        ii. Password: **Your new password**

Real World Note: Use Get-MsolUser in PowerShell to get a list of your users in the Microsoft Online directory. This is a great way to start and verify that you are connected to the correct directory. To get the cmdlets, download and install:

Microsoft Online Services Sign-In Assistant for IT Professionals Beta: http://ref.ms/msolsignin/

Azure Active Directory Module for Windows PowerShell: http://ref.ms/azureposh

---

    d. To configure the service account password never to expire, type this command (one line) and press **Enter**:

```
Set-MsolUser -UserPrincipalName
AzureAD_SVC@mdmhybrid.onmicrosoft.com
-PasswordNeverExpires $True
```

17. The on-premises account AAD_SVC is already created during the build of the machines in Appendix A. If you didn't use our demo kit to build your machines, then go ahead and create an Active Directory user account named **AAD_SVC**.

Configure the User Principal Name (UPN)

The user principal name, also known as the UPN, is an Active Directory user attribute. It must match the public domain name that you registered in the preceding chapter. By default, all users inherit the UPN from the on-premises Active Directory domain name. Changing the UPN on each user is a two-step process: creating the new domain name and then changing the attribute on each user account.

Real World Note: You need to change the UPN only when it differs from the external domain name. The script that follows connects to the local Active Directory (corp.viamonstra.com), adds a UPN with the public domain name, and sets it as the default.

You can use the following script to configure the new UPN domain name and all users in the Cloud Users organizational unit with the new UPN.

```
$LocalDomainName = 'corp.viamonstra.com'

$PublicDomainName = mdmhybrid.com'

Set-ADForest -identity "$LocalDomainName" -UPNSuffixes
@{Add="$PublicDomainName "}

$CloudUsers = 'OU=Cloud
Users,OU=Users,OU=Viamonstra,DC=corp,DC=viamonstra,DC=com'

Get-ADUser -SearchBase $CloudUsers -Filter * | ForEach-Object
-Process {

    $NewUPN =
$PSItem.userPrincipalName.Replace($LocalDomainName,$PublicDomainN
ame)

    $PSItem | Set-ADUser -UserPrincipalName $NewUPN -EmailAddress
$NewUPN

}
```

You can use Active Directory Users and Computers to open the properties for one of the users in the Cloud Users organization unit to verify the new UPN.

Using PowerShell to configure the UPN to match to the public domain name.

Install and Configure Microsoft Azure Active Directory Connect

The final step in the process is to install and configure the Microsoft Azure Active Directory Connect tool. The tool is the latest version of what is also known as DirSync. However, we will emphasize that it has come a long way since the first version of DirSync. You can use the tool to do much more than just configure directory synchronization. You also can use it to install and configure Active Directory Federation Services.

1. Start **DC01** and log in as **VIAMONSTRA\Administrator**.

2. Download the **Microsoft Azure Active Directory Connect** tool to **C:\Tools** from **http://ref.ms/Azureconnect**.

3. Run **C:\Tools\AzureADConnect.msi**, and when prompted by the Open File – Security Warning, click **Run** and **Yes** in the User Account Control window.

4. On the **Welcome** page, enable **I agree to the license terms and privacy notice** and click **Continue**.

5. On the **Express Settings** page, click **Express Settings** to start the process.

6. On the **Connect to Azure AD** page, for **USERNAME**, enter **AzureAD_SVC@mdmhybrid.onmicrosoft.com** and the password. Then click **Next**.

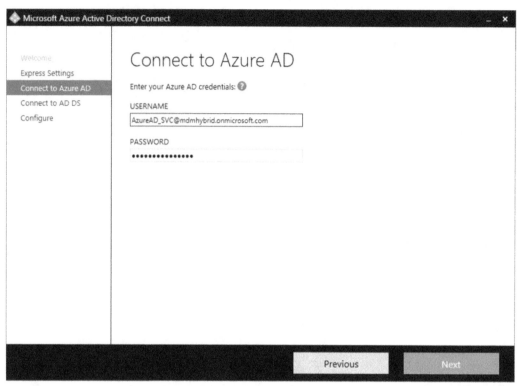

Specifying the Azure AD synchronization account.

7. On the **Connect to AD DS** page, for **USERNAME**, type
    VIAMONSTRA\Administrator, and for **PASSWORD**, type **P@ssw0rd**. Then click
    Next.

8. On the **Configure** page, clear the **Start the synchronization process as soon as the configuration completes** check box and click **Install**.

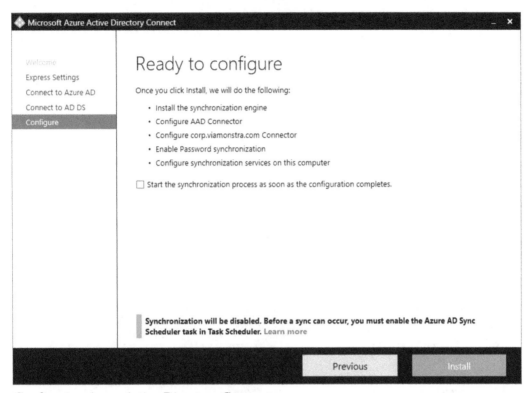

Configuring Azure Active Directory Connect.

9. On the **Configure** page, when the installation is complete, click **Exit**.

The reason for disabling automatic synchronization is control. You want to control the unique part of your on-premises directory that you will be synchronizing to the Azure. Control comes with a cost, which is having to configure the synchronization partition and enable the scheduled task in Windows. ViaMonstra has decided to control users and groups on-premises as much as possible and create Azure resources only when required by any of the cloud services. The following steps guide you through the process, starting with configuring the Cloud Users and Security Groups organizational units as the only object to synchronize.

1. While still on **DC01**, open **File Explorer** and run **miisclient.exe** as administrator from **C:\Program Files\Microsoft Azure AD Sync\UIShell**.

Note: The Azure Active Directory Connect synchronization UI is also available on the start menu, in the Azure AD Connect section, named Synchronization Service.

2. From the toolbar, select **Connectors**, right-click the **corp.viamonstra.com** Active Directory Domains Services connector and select **Properties**.

3. In **Properties**, select **Configure Directory Partitions** and click **Containers**

4. In the **Credentials** dialog box, fill in the information about your on-premises synchronization account and click **OK**:

    a. User name: **AAD_SVC**

    b. Password: **P@ssw0rd**

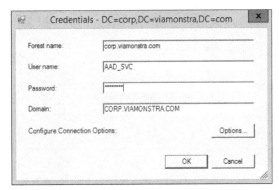

Specifying the service password.

5. From the **Select Containers** window, clear the check box of the domain name (**Root Domain**) listed at the top. This disables synchronization of the entire domain.

6. Expand **ViaMonstra / Users**, and then select **Cloud Users**, expand **Groups** and select **Cloud Security Groups** and click **OK** twice.

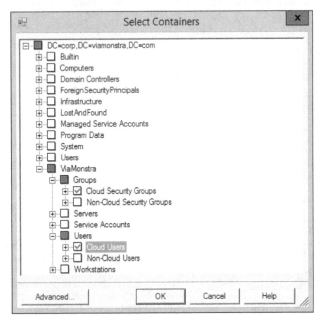

Configuring which OUs to synchronize.

Start the Azure Active Directory Connect Synchronization

Once the Azure Active Directory Connect setup is completed, you need to start the synchronization.

1. On **DC01**, using the **Synchronization Services Manager Tool**, in the **Connectors** tab, right-click the **corp.viamonstra.com** connector, and select **Run**.

2. In the **Run Connector** dialog box, select **Full synchronization**, and click **OK**.

You can also use PowerShell to start the synchronization by using the below cmdlet.

```
Start-ADSyncSyncCycle -PolicyType Initial
```

Verify the Azure Active Directory Connect Synchronization

A very easy way to verify that users and groups are being synchronized is to launch PowerShell and run the commands following this paragraph. It takes a while before the sync runs because Microsoft removed the scheduled task. The first command connects to your online directory. Then, when prompted, enter your Azure account and password. The second command lists all the users in your directory. You should memorize these cmdlets, as you will use them over and over again.

```
Connect-MsolService

Get-MsolUser
```

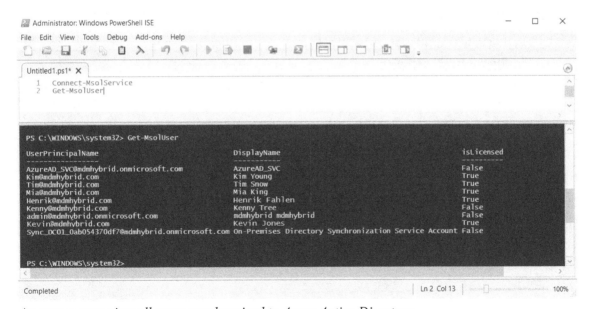

An easy way to view all users synchronized to Azure Active Directory.

To view members of a user group, you can use two PowerShell cmdlets. First, run the following cmdlet:

```
Get-MsolGroup
```

After running Get-MsolGroup, make a note of the ObjectId and add that to the second cmdlet:

```
Get-MsolGroupMember -GroupObjectId 3cd02398-2ed0-4153-94eb-
64b16177278d
```

Real World Note: You can force a synchronization by running DirectorySyncClientCmd.exe from C:\Program Files\Microsoft Azure AD Sync\Bin. Monitor the Azure Active Directory synchronization process by reading the application.log in Event Viewer.

Setting Up Licensing

Without the licenses assigned, users do not have access to the features of EMS.

Assign EMS Licenses to a Synced AAD Group

You can assign the EMS license to a user or a group of users. ViaMonstra does not want to assign the license based on users, but rather use an Active Directory security group that can be managed via the on-premises Active Directory.

To assign the licenses to a security group, follow this procedure:

1. Browse to **https://manage.windowsAzure.com** and sign in with the admin account (**admin@mdmhybrid.com**).

2. In the Azure management portal, select **Active Directory** and click the domain (directory) that you created earlier.

3. Click **Licenses** and select the **Enterprise Mobility Suite** licenses.

4. Click **Assign users**, expand the **SHOW** pull-down menu (1), and change it to **Groups**. Click the **checkmark** (2).

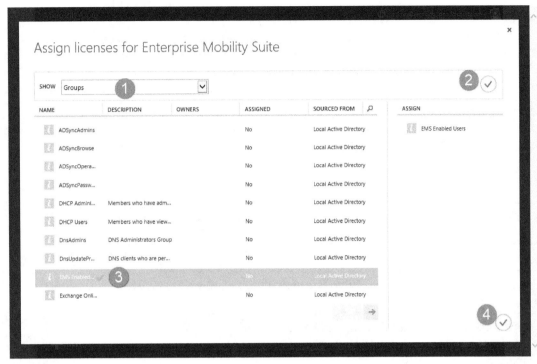

Assigning licenses.

5. Select the group created for the **EMS Enabled Users** (3) and click the **checkmark** (4) in the lower right corner.

Now all users who are members of the security group have access to the EMS features and resources like Azure RMS, Azure Active Directory, and Azure Remote App.

Setting Up Azure Active Directory Premium Features

In this section, you set up four of the Active Directory Premium features you learned about in Chapter 3:

- Multi-Factor Authentication (MFA)

- Self-Service Password Reset with On-Premises Writeback

- Azure AD Join

- Software as a Service (SaaS)

Multi-Factor Authentication (MFA)

With Azure Active Directory, the multi-factor authentication can be configured using a text message, receiving a phone call, or installing the Azure Multi-Factor Authentication application on a device. Combining one of these methods with the password fulfills the authentication goal.

What Do We Want to Achieve?

Planning how, where, and why you want to use MFA is crucial to your project. *A clearly defined goal is the best way to measure success* and should include what you are trying to secure and whom you are trying secure. The following table lists the ViaMonstra goals in the first column. Use those goals as a reference for your own goals.

ViaMonstra Goals	Your Goals
MFA must be enforced when accessing any SaaS application.	
Users must use MFA when enrolling devices into the organization.	
The Mobile Mobile-Factor Auth app must be available to all users and should be used as the primary authentication source.	
MFA will be configured only for ViaMonstra users.	

Enable MFA for a Cloud-Enabled User Account

You can configure MFA in the Azure management portal or through PowerShell. In order to enable MFA in the UI, follow these steps:

1. Open **https://manage.windowsAzure.com** and sign in with the Azure admin account.

2. In the Azure management portal, select **Active Directory** and click the **ViaMonstra** directory name to open the domain properties.

3. Click **Configure**, navigate to the **multi-factor authentication** section, and click **Manage service settings**.

4. In the **multi-factor authentication** portal, on the **service settings** page, select the **users** page.

5. From the list of users, select **Henrik Fahlen** and click **Enable** in the right pane. When prompted, click **enable multi-factor auth** and then **Close**.

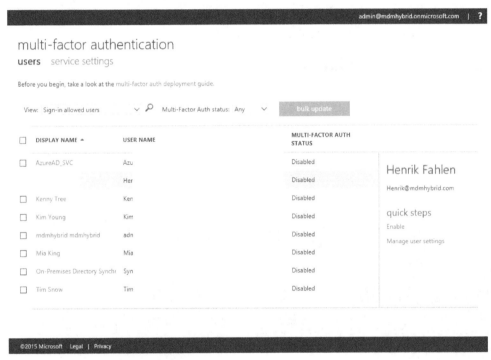

Configuring MFA for a single user.

Real World Note: You can perform most actions from the Azure portal or with PowerShell using the MSOnline module. To view all the MSOnline PowerShell cmdlets, open PowerShell and type Get-Command -Module MSOnline.

Verify MFA

A common troubleshooting scenario is verifying the Multi-Factor Authorization settings for a given account. Instead of using the Azure portal, you will find it is much quicker to familiarize yourself with a few PowerShell cmdlets. To verify, disable, and enable MFA using PowerShell, follow these steps. (Notice that the listed result of the steps requires that MFA be already enabled for the user Henrik Fahlen.)

1. Open **PowerShell ISE** as administrator.

2. Type the following lines and press **F5** to run the script. When prompted, log in as the global Azure administrator.

    ```
    #Establish the connection to Azure

    Connect-MsolService

    # List the MFA settings

    $f = Get-MsolUser -UserPrincipalName henrik@mdmhybrid.com

    $f.StrongAuthenticationRequirements
    ```

Note: In this step, you need to replace the mdmhybrid.com domain with your domain name.

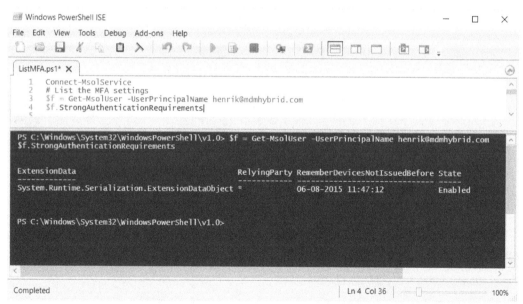

Using PowerShell to verify the user MFA settings.

Enable and Disable MFA Using PowerShell

After a while, you will build a rock solid library of PowerShell cmdlets and learn quickly that managing Azure Active Directory with PowerShell is in many ways much easier than playing around in the user interface. You can use the two examples that follow first to disable and then to enable MFA for a given user. In both examples, we recommend that you use PowerShell ISE.

```
#Disable MFA for a specific user

$sta = @()

Set-MsolUser -UserPrincipalName henrik@mdmhybrid.com
-StrongAuthenticationRequirements $sta

# Enable MFA for a specific user

$st = New-Object -TypeName
Microsoft.Online.Administration.StrongAuthenticationRequirement

$st.RelyingParty = "*"

$st.State = "Enabled"

$sta = @($st)

Set-MsolUser -UserPrincipalName henrik@mdmhybrid.com
-StrongAuthenticationRequirements $sta
```

Configure MFA for Joining Devices

One of the ViaMonstra business requirements is enforcing MFA for users when they enroll devices into a cloud service. You enable the feature in the Azure portal following these steps:

1. Open **https://manage.windowsAzure.com** and sign in with the Azure admin account.

2. In the management console, select **Active Directory** and click the **ViaMonstra** directory name to open the domain properties.

3. Click **Configure**, navigate to the **devices** section, and click **Yes** in **require multi-factor auth to join devices**.

4. Click **Save** to update the ViaMonstra directory.

MFA Exclusions

Although MFA is a great security enhancement, it can be very annoying if the feature is enabled for all applications and networks. ViaMonstra does not want to frustrate users who are working in the office by having them use MFA. To configure that, you add the company IP information to an exclusions list:

1. Open **https://manage.windowsAzure.com** and sign in with the Azure admin account.

2. In the management console, select **Active Directory** and click the **ViaMonstra** directory name to open the domain properties.

3. Click **Users** and then click **Manage Multi-factor auth** on the ribbon.

4. On the **multi-factor authentication** page, click **service settings**.

5. In **Trusted IPs**, enable **skip multi-factor authentication for request from federated users on my intranet**, type the IP address subnets in the form of 192.168.1.0/24, and click **Save**.

The MFA End-User Experience

End users quickly learn how MFA works. As administrator, you just need to provide them with a few links to the Azure end-user portal (myapps.microsoft.com) and the Azure Authenticator application from one of the stores. In the following example, Henrik uses his iOS device to install and configure the Azure Authenticator application.

Note: For testing the MFA end-user experience, make sure the device is not connected to the network excluded in the preceding guide, such as by using 4G instead of local wireless.

---

1. On the iOS device, open the **App Store** and then search for and install the **Azure Authenticator**.

The Azure Authenticator app.

2. Launch the **Azure Authenticator** application on the device.

3. From a web browser (on any computer/device), connect to **http://myapps.microsoft.com** and sign in as **henrik@mdmhybrid.com** using **P@ssw0rd** as the password. Notice that the sign-in process is unsuccessful due to the multi-factor auth requirements.

Note: Again, please replace the emskings.com domain with your domain.

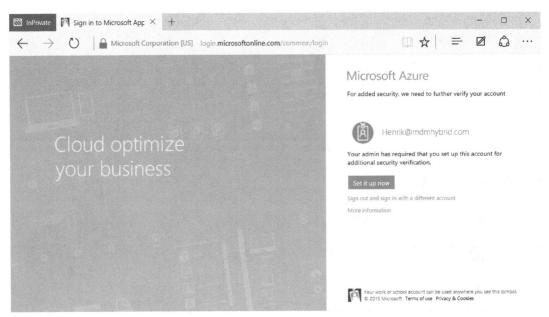

Multi-factor auth preventing the user from signing in with a single password.

4. Click **Set it up now**.

5. On the **Additional Security Verification** page, in **Step 1** select **Mobile app** and click **Setup**. This displays a QR code on the webpage that you need to scan using the device.

6. On your device, open the **Azure Authenticator** application and tap **Scan Barcode**.

7. Scan the **QR code** in the **Azure portal** and click **Done**. On your mobile device, note that the Azure Authenticator application is being associated with the user.

8. In the **Azure portal**, click **Contact me** to start **Step 2** of the process.

9. On your device, you should receive a verification, click **Verify** and **Close** to finish the setup process.

10. Close the **Azure portal**, and sign in to **http://myapps.microsoft.com** again. This time use the Azure Authenticator application to verify that you are Henrik; otherwise, the sign-in process will not finish.

You can use the Microsoft Azure end user portal to access applications, reset password, work with security groups, and configure end-user settings like additional MFA settings. There are two links: applications and profile. From the profile link, you can configure additional security verification settings and change the current MFA settings. Before you start adding phone and text verification settings, you should be aware that local cell provider charges might apply.

Henrik@mdmhybrid.com | ?

Additional security verification app passwords

When you sign in with your password, you are also required to respond from a registered device. This makes it harder for a hacker to sign in with just a stolen password.
View video

what's your preferred option?

We'll use this verification option by default.

Notify me through app ⌄

how would you like to respond?

Set up one or more of these options. Learn more

☑ Authentication phone	Denmark (+45)	⌄	26262626 ✕
☐ Office phone	Select your country or region	⌄	
			Extension
☐ Alternate authentication phone	Select your country or region	⌄	

☑ Azure Authenticator app   Configure   Mobile app has been configured.

Save   cancel

Your phone numbers will only be used for account security. Standard telephone and SMS charges will apply.

©2015 Microsoft   Legal | Privacy

Adding Authentication Phone settings to MFA Profile

MFA App Passwords

One of the first phone calls you will get after enabling MFA in your organization will be colleagues complaining about not being able to access applications such as Microsoft Skype for Business. Certain applications do not support MFA and prevent the user from accessing the application. In order to mitigate that problem, MFA has a feature called App password that enables users to generate a password automatically per user at http://myapps.microsoft.com. Typically, users generate the password the first time an application prompts the user for a password. To generate the app password, follow these instructions:

1. Open a browser and sign in as **henrik@mdmhybrid.com** to **http://myapps.microsoft.com**.

2. From the **profile** link, click **Additional security verification**. This takes you to the **Additional security verification** page.

3. Click the **app passwords** link.

4. Click **create**, and a page opens on which you can enter a name. You can use the same password for all applications on a single device. For that reason, ViaMonstra recommends that users enter the name of the device on which the password is to be used.

5. Enter the device name and click **Next**.

6. Memorize the password, or if you are not Rain Man, click **copy password to clipboard** and click **close**.

7. Use the password when prompted in Skype for Business and the other applications.

Branding Azure AD

Branding and personalizing Azure AD helps to establish trust between your users and Azure AD. Never underestimate the value of presenting users with a familiar logo and text. You can customize most elements of the sign-in page, and the following example is what you will experience after you add a custom logo, sign-in illustration, and sign-in text.

Branding the Azure user experience.

The following steps require that you have downloaded and extracted the book sample files to C:\Setup.

1. Open a browser, go to **https://manage.windowsAzure.com**, and sign in with the Azure admin account.

2. Select **Active Directory**, and click **Default Directory / Configure**.

3. Click **customize branding** to start the process.

4. On the **customize branding** page, click **Next**.

5. On the **customize default branding** page, configure the following settings and click **Next**:

   a. In **Banner logo**, click **browse**, and then from **C:\Setup\Branding**, select **banner logo.png** and click **Open**.

   b. In **SQUARE logo**, click **browse**, and from **C:\Setup\Branding**, select **Tile Logo - 120x120.png** and click **Open**.

   c. In **SIGN-IN page text heading**, type **ViaMonstra sign-in**.

   d. In **SIGN-IN page text**, type **Please sign-in to ViaMonstra and prepare to learn!**

6. On the second **customize branding** page, configure these settings and click **complete**:

   a. In **SIGN-IN page illustration**, click **browse**, and from **C:\Setup\Branding**, select **Sign In Page Illustration - 1420x1200.jpg** and click **Open**.

   b. In **post logout link label**, type **ViaMonstra**.

   c. In **post logout link URL**, type **http://viamonstra.com/**.

Self-Service Password Reset with On-Premises Writeback

As you learned in chapter 3, Active Directory Premium supports self-service password reset with on-premises writeback (SSPR) to your on-premises Active Directory. The feature has a few moving parts that must be configured correctly before you can get it to work, but configured properly, it's one of those features that will make you look great in the eyes of management.

In order to enable SSPR, you need to ensure the following requirements are met:

- Infrastructure
  - Azure Active Directory sync tool with version number 1.0.0419.0911 or higher
  - Password reset configured in the Azure Active Directory sync tool
  - The correct edition of Azure Active Directory (You are covered with EMS and Azure Active Directory Premium.)
  - Password reset enabled in Azure Active Directory
  - Firewall rules
- End users
  - Must be enabled for password reset
  - Must be configured with Multi-Factor Authentication

Configure Infrastructure Requirements

With the latest version of Azure AD Sync and Azure AD Premium, you are already covered on some of the requirements. Most organizations also are compliant with the firewall rules, as the only requirement is an outbound rule using port TCP port 443 to https://ssprsbprodncu-sb.accesscontrol.windows.net/. To configure the remaining infrastructure requirements, complete the steps in the next two guides.

Configure Password Reset in the Azure AD Sync Tool

1. Log in to **DC01** as **VIAMONSTRA\Administrator** and launch the **Azure AD Connect tool** (a shortcut should be on the desktop).

2. On the **Tasks** page, click **Customize synchronization options** and click **Next**.

3. On the **Connect to Azure AD** page, fill in the Azure Active Directory account (**admin@mdmhybrid.onmicrosoft.com**) and password, and then click **Next**.

4. On the **Connect Directories** page, in **Username**, type **VIAMONSTRA\Administrator**, and in **Password**, type **P@ssw0rd**. Then click **Next**.

5. On the **Optional Features** page, enable **Password writeback** and click **Next**.

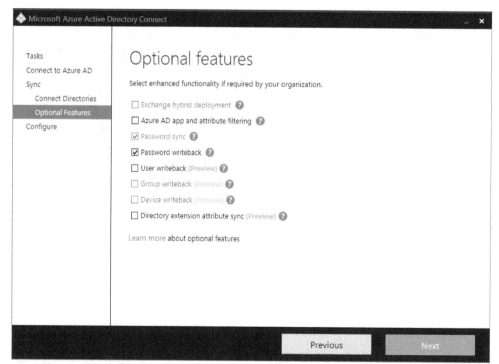

Enable password writeback in Azure AD Connect.

6. On the **Configure** page, click **Install** and then click **Exit** when the installation is finished. Notice that you might have the enable to the Azure AD Sync scheduled task in Task Scheduler again.

Configure Password Reset in Azure AD Premium Using PowerShell

1. From **DC01**, start a new instance of **PowerShell ISE** as administrator, type the following command, and note the Azure AD connector name:

```
Get-ADSyncConnector | Where-Object ConnectorTypeName -eq
Extensible2 | Select-Object -Property Name
```

2. Type the following **PowerShell** command to enable the Password Reset Writeback feature where **mdmhybrid.onmicrosoft.com – AAD** must be replaced with your Azure AD connector name:

```
Set-ADSyncAADPasswordResetConfiguration -Connector
"mdmhybrid.onmicrosoft.com - AAD" -Enable $True -Verbose
```

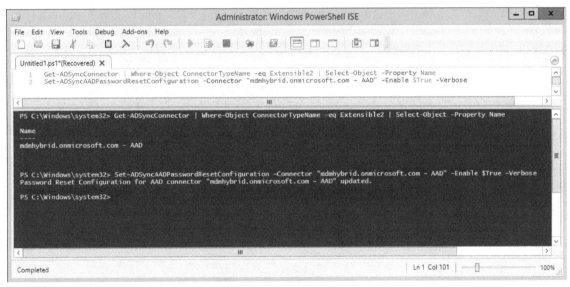

Enabling Password Reset Writeback using PowerShell.

3. Log in to the **Azure portal** using **Internet Explorer**: **https://portal.Azure.com/**.

4. Select **Active Directory**, and click **ViaMonstra / Configure**.

5. Under **User Password Reset Policy**, configure the following settings:

   a. Users enabled for password reset: **YES**

   b. Restrict access to password reset: **NO**

      c.   Authentication Methods Available to Users:

- **Mobile Phone**
- **Alternate Email Address**

      d.   Number of Authentication Methods Required: **1**

      e.   Require users to register when signing in to the Access Panel: **YES**

      f.   Write back passwords to on-premises active directory: **YES**

      g.   Password writeback service status: **Configured**

6. Click **Save**.

Configure User Requirements

In an ideal world, users would sign up for password resets in advance. ViaMonstra knows that we not always live in the ideal world and that you need to assist your users to get them moving towards self-service. So you email all your users (several times during a period of one month) telling them to register for password reset using this link: aka.ms/ssprsetup. In the email message, you also inform them that about 35–40 percent of all the calls you get at the service desk pertain to password resets. The following steps explain how the user can register and perform password reset:

1. Launch your Internet browser and open **https://passwordreset.microsoftonline.com/** or **http://outlook.com/mdmhybrid.com**. If you use http://outlook.com/mdmhybrid.com, then click **Can't access your account**.

2. From the **Get back into your account** page, notice that the user ID is filled out if you began the processes from http://outlook.com/mdmhybrid.com. Type the characters in the picture and click **Next**.

3. On the **verification step 1** page, type your mobile phone number and click **Text**.

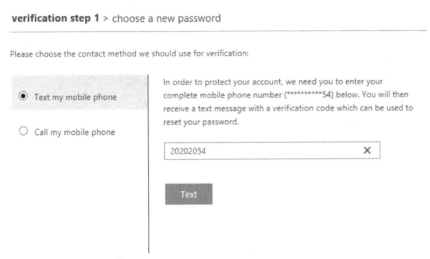

Get back into your account

verification step 1 > choose a new password

Please choose the contact method we should use for verification:

⦿ Text my mobile phone	In order to protect your account, we need you to enter your complete mobile phone number (**********54) below. You will then receive a text message with a verification code which can be used to reset your password.
◯ Call my mobile phone	

| 20202054   ✕ |

[Text]

Self-service password reset.

4. While still on the **verification step 1** page, enter the code from your text message and click **Next**.

5. Enter your new password and click **Finish**. Note that you still have to comply with the internal password rules.

   After a successful change, the user is able to access the cloud services once again.

Password reset information is written to the Application log on your on-premises domain controllers and available in the Azure AD reports. You can track both successful and failed attempts.

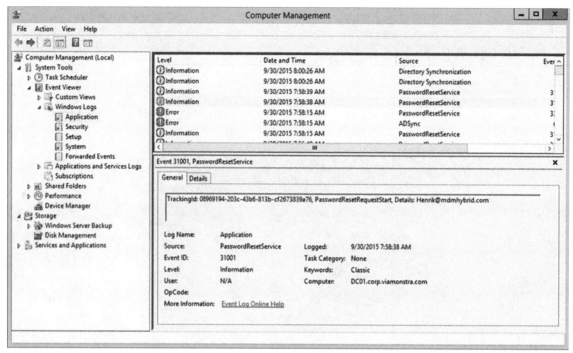

Viewing the Application log for password reset information. Notice the error. This information is from a password reset attempt that failed due to password restrictions.

Azure AD Join

For many years, we have been used to adding devices to a domain or making them a member of a workgroup. With Azure AD Premium, you get one additional option: joining the device to Azure through a feature called Azure AD Join. When you join a device to Azure, the Azure Device Registration Service creates the computer object. The object is not exactly the same as the traditional on-premises computer object. One of the differences is that the device is always *associated with a user* unlike on-premises computer objects that are stored and treated as individual objects. You need to configure a few things in Azure AD Premium before you can start enrolling the devices:

1. Log in to **Azure portal** using **Internet Explorer**: **https://portal.Azure.com/**.

2. Select **Active Directory**, and click **ViaMonstra / Configure**.

3. Scroll down to the **devices** section and configure these settings:

    a. USERS MAY JOIN DEVICES TO AZURE AD: **ALL**

    b. ADDITIONAL ADMINISTRATOR ON AZURE AD JOINED DEVICES: Click **Add**, select **Mia King** and **Tim Snow**, and then click the **Complete** button to add the users.

    c. REQUIRE MULTI-FACTOR AUTH TO JOIN DEVICES: **Yes**

    d. Click **Save**.

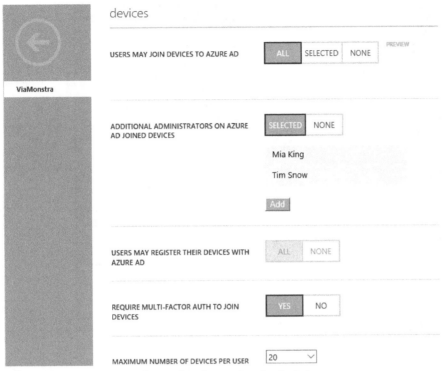

Device registration configured with two local administrators.

One of the many benefits of using EMS is automatic enrollment of AD-joined devices into Microsoft Intune. By default, Azure AD adds Microsoft Intune to the list of SaaS applications and configures the enrollment URL. To change or view the settings, follow these steps:

1. Open an Internet browser, go to **https://manage.windowsAzure.com**, and sign in with the Azure admin account.

2. Select **Active Directory**, and click **Default Directory / Applications**.

3. From the list of applications, click **Microsoft Intune**.

4. Click **Configure**. Notice that both the MDM DISCOVERY URL and MDM COMPLIANCE URL are configured to enroll the device into Microsoft Intune. You can change these values if you are using another MDM platform.

5. For **MDM TERMS OF USE URL**, type **http://viamonstra.com/?page_id=47.**

6. Select **APPLY TO: ALL**, and then click **Save**.

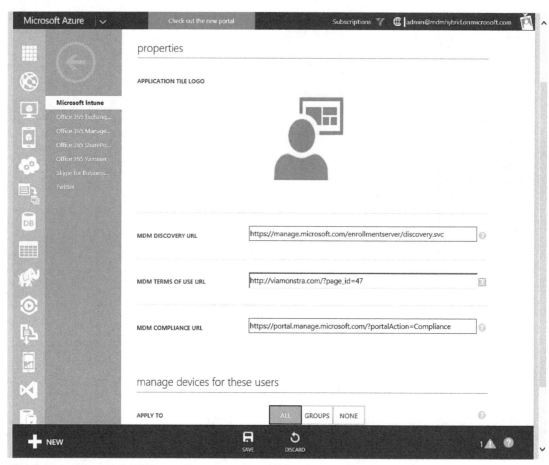

Configuring Intune MDM enrollment as part of the Azure AD join.

Software as a Service (SaaS)

In Chapter 3, you learned about the SaaS feature. In order to configure Twitter as a SaaS application with automatic password rollover, follow the steps in the next section. You start by creating an Azure-based group to which users can request membership and that way be granted access without having to call the service desk. Note that this requires you to have an existing Twitter account.

Configure Azure Active Directory Groups

1. Open a browser, go to **https://manage.windowsAzure.com**, and sign in with the Azure admin account.

2. Select **Active Directory**, and click **Default Directory / Groups**.

3. Click **ADD GROUP**, and then in **NAME**, type **Twitter**, and in **DESCRIPTION**, type **Enable access to corporate Twitter account**. Click **OK.**

4. From the list of groups, select the newly created **Twitter** group and click **OWNERS**.

5. Click **ADD OWNERS**, and from the list of users, select **Henrik Fahlen**. Click **OK**.

6. Open a browser, go to **https://manage.windowsAzure.com**, and sign in as **henrik@mdmhybrid.com** (who is the member of the group).

7. Select **groups**. Notice that you see only the newly created Twitter group.

8. Click the **Twitter** group to open the properties.

9. Click **Edit**, and from the **Group policy** drop-down list, select **This group requires owner approval**. Click **Update**. Don't close the browser; a user is about to request membership.

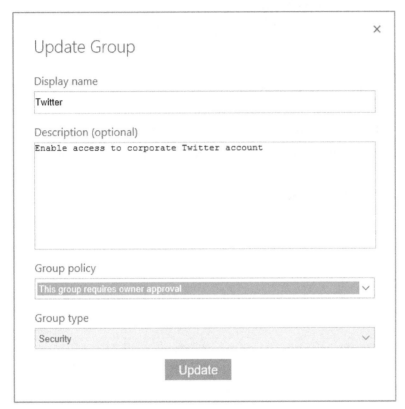

Configuring security group self-service in Azure.

Users can request group membership from http://myapps.microsoft.com/. After the request is made, the owner grants or denies access, when approval for the group is configured. In the following example, tim@mdmhybrid.com requests and is granted access to the newly created Twitter group.

1. Open a browser, go to **https://manage.windowsAzure.com**, and sign in as **tim@mdmhybrid.com**.

2. Select **groups**, click **list all groups**, and type **twitter** in the **search** field.

3. Open the **Twitter** group properties and click **Join group**. For the business justification, write something nice, please, and click **Request**. Don't close the browser. Wait until the manager has approved the request. Don't leave the browser, as you will shortly get access to Twitter.

4. The approval request shows up in the browser belonging to the group owner. As group owner, click **approvals**, select **approval request**, and click **Approve**.

    After the membership is approved, the requesting user is able to see the group by selecting My memberships from the drop-down list on the groups page.

Real World Note: You can view the group self-service activity in Azure Active Directory. Open the group properties and click SELF SERVICE ACTIVITY.

Configure SaaS Apps

1. Open a browser, go to **https://manage.windowsAzure.com**, and sign in with the Azure admin account.

2. Select **Active Directory**, and click **Default Directory / Applications**.

3. Click **Add**, and in **What do you want to do?**, select **Add an application from the gallery**.

4. In **search**, type **twitter** and press **Enter**.

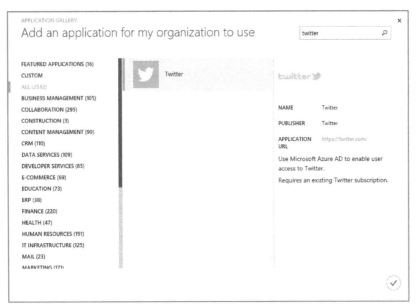

The Application Gallery with more than 2500 applications.

5. Select **Twitter** and click the **OK** button (the checkmark).

6. Click **Configure Single sign-on**, select **Password Single Sign-On**, and click **OK**.

7. Click **Assign accounts** and make sure groups are listed. If no groups are listed, click **Show Groups** and click **OK**. From the list of groups, select **Twitter** and click **Assign**.

8. In the **Assign Groups** window, enable **I want to enter Twitter credentials to be shared among all group members**.

9. Enter your Twitter account information, enable **I want to enable automatic password rollover**, and click **OK**. With automatic password rollover, no one knows the password. In order to restore the password, you have to go through the normal "I forgot my Twitter password" experience.

10. After you have configured the application, shift to the browser where you have logged in as Tim. Select the **applications** tab and notice you have access to Twitter. (If you don't, refresh the browser page.)

What Happens Behind the Scenes

It might look like magic when you are accessing Office 365 or another SaaS application without being prompted for sign-on credentials. Behind the scenes, your sign-on request is a little similar to what happens on-premises with Kerberos tickets and Kerberos granting tickets. The following list describes the process and what takes place behind the scenes:

1. When a user is authenticated, Azure AD passes down an object called the *primary refresh token*, which is stored in the local .NET ADAL (Azure Directory Authentication Library) cache on the device. You can think of the primary refresh token as being the cloud-based version of a Kerberos ticket.

> **Real World Note**: Azure Directory Authentication Library (ADAL) for .NET enables client application developers to easily authenticate users to cloud or on-premises Active Directory.

2. When the user tries to connect to a SaaS application like Office 365, the Windows 10 device, for instance, sends single sign-on request to Azure AD using the primary refresh token.

3. Azure AD verifies that the primary refresh token is still valid and passes down a single sign-on token to the device.

4. The device now has two tokens, the single sign-on token and the primary refresh token. This process might seem familiar and very similar to on-premises AD where you have your Kerberos ticket-granting token and your Kerberos ticket.

5. With the single sign-on token, the user accesses the SaaS applications and is signed in.

Azure Cloud App Discovery

Most people simply do not know about all of the local applications installed in the organization. This is true not only for traditional applications like .exe and .msi, but also for SaaS applications. Often administrators have no or very little clue about what and how many SaaS applications are being used. With Azure Cloud App Discovery, administrators can collect information about where applications are in use and who is using them. The information is collected through the Azure Cloud App Discovery.

Azure Cloud App Discovery is an agent that can be installed (the traditional way) on your computers. The agent analyzes network traffic and uploads information about the usage of SaaS applications to Azure AD. In Azure, you can use the dashboard to view the collected information. To get started with Cloud App Discovery, follow these steps:

1. In your favorite browser, navigate to **https://appdiscovery.Azure.com/** and click **Get Started**.

2. From the **Cloud App Discovery** pane, click **Create**.

3. Click **Settings / Management Agent** and then click the **User consent** option. Select one of the options for user warnings and click **Update**.

4. Click **Download**. This downloads the agent.

5. You can deploy the agent through ConfigMgr or any other software-distribution method. In **ConfigMgr**, you can create a legacy package/program with the command line **/quiet /norestart**.

   Log files for the installation and scanning are created in the %temp% folder in files named Cloud_App_Discovery_-_Endpoint_Agent_*.

Setting Up the ConfigMgr Infrastructure

In this section, you set up a base ConfigMgr server for hybrid mobile device management. In these guides, you use the CM01 virtual machine you configured as part of the hydration kit. The base configuration involves the following:

- Configuring discovery methods

- Adding the reporting services point

If you want to run the step-by-step guides from now on in this chapter, you need a lab environment configured as outlined in Appendix A. In the remaining guides in this chapter, you use the following virtual machines:

DC01

CM01

The VMs used in this section.

For more detailed information about how to configure and use Configuration Manager, please check out this book: *System Center 2012 R2 Configuration Manager: Mastering the Fundamentals* (http://ref.ms/CMMasteringFundamentals).

Review the Service Accounts in Active Directory

ConfigMgr uses several service accounts for the setup. The hydration kit creates these accounts (Appendix A).

1. On **DC01**, log in as **VIAMONSTRA\Administrator** using a password of **P@ssw0rd**.

2. Using **Active Directory Users and Computers**, review which service accounts were created by the hydration kit.

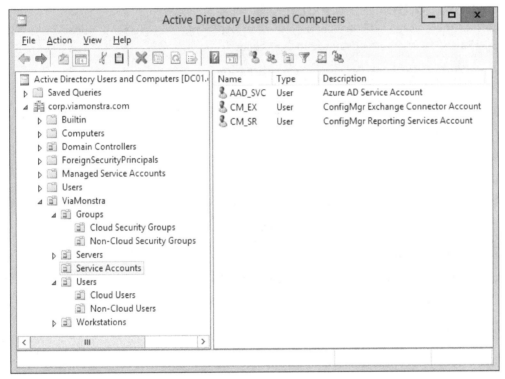

ViaMonstra service accounts.

Configure Discovery Methods

1. On **CM01**, log in as **VIAMONSTRA\Administrator** using a password of **P@ssw0rd**.

2. From the **Start screen**, select the **Configuration Manager Console**.

3. In the **Administration** workspace, expand **Hierarchy Configuration / Discovery Methods**.

4. In the **Administration** workspace, in the **Discovery Methods** node, enable **Active Directory User Discovery**, add the **ViaMonstra / Users** OU, and run the discovery.

5. Using **CMTrace**, review the **D:\Program Files\Microsoft Configuration Manager\Logs\adusrdis.log** file.

Note: CMTrace is available in the E:\Program Files\Microsoft Configuration Manager\Tools folder. Run CMTrace once, and click Yes to Associate CMTrace to log files.

---

6. **In** the **Assets and Compliance** workspace, select **Users**. Press **F5** or click the **Refresh** button to refresh the view. You should now see two members.

Add the Reporting Services Point

Reports in ConfigMgr are very useful for keeping track of deployments, both for applications and task sequences. You also can create custom reports if needed.

1. Using the **ConfigMgr console**, in the **Administration** workspace, expand **Site Configuration** and select **Sites**.

2. On the ribbon, select **Add Site System Roles**, and use the following settings for the **Add Site System Roles Wizard**:

   a. General: **<default>**

   b. Proxy: **<default>**

   c. System Role Selection: **Reporting services point**

   d. Reporting Services Point: Click **Verify**.

   e. User name: Click Set, New account:

      ▪ User name: **VIAMONSTRA\CM_SR**

      ▪ Password: **P@ss0wrd**

   f. Summary: **<default>**

Configuring Reporting Services settings.

3. Using **CMTrace**, review the **D:\Program Files\Microsoft Configuration Manager\Logs\srsrpsetup.log** and **D:\Program Files\Microsoft Configuration Manager\Logs\srsrp.log** files.

Note: It will take a short while for the log files to appear. Wait until all reports have been deployed before continuing. You don't need to worry about the red lines in the log; the target folder contains the word error in the name so you see many red lines. An easy way to check whether the reports are being deployed is by looking at the reports node in the ConfigMgr console.

4. In the **ConfigMgr console**, in the **Monitoring** workspace, expand the **Reporting /** **Reports** node, select the **Reports** node, and then review the reports available.

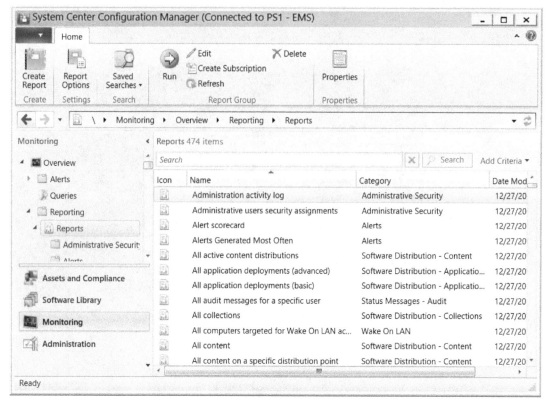

The Reports node in ConfigMgr after adding the Reporting service point role.

Verify IE Enhanced Security Configuration

Because you probably want to run the reports in a web browser (for better performance), make sure that IE Enhanced Security Configuration is disabled.

1. On **CM01**, using the **Server Manager**, select **Local Server**.

2. In the **PROPERTIES for CM01** pane, make sure the **IE Enhanced Security Configuration** is set to **Off**.

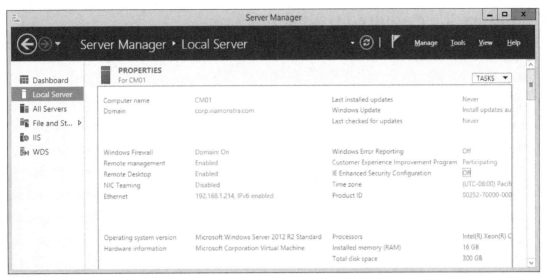

Making sure IE Enhanced Security Configuration is disabled.

Preparing for Mobile Device Management

The list of tasks you have to go through when preparing your environment for hybrid mobile device management is almost the same as a standalone Microsoft Intune. You still need to acquire a Microsoft Intune subscription, register the public domain name, and configure user principal names and directory synchronization. The following list includes the high-level steps you need to complete to configure hybrid management. The steps in bold are only required in a hybrid environment.

1. Create a Microsoft Intune trial account.

2. Configure the domain name in Microsoft Intune.

3. Configure each user's public domain user principal name (UPN) in Active Directory and **run user discovery in ConfigMgr**.

4. Configure Active Directory synchronization.

5. **Create user collection in ConfigMgr with users who can enroll devices**.

6. **Configure Microsoft Intune Subscription in the console**

7. Enroll devices.

Configure the Required User Collection

1. On **CM01**, log on as **VIAMONSTRA\Administrator** and open the **PowerShell ISE**.

2. Type and execute the following PowerShell script:

```
#Import SCCM Module

Import-Module
$env:SMS_ADMIN_UI_PATH.Replace("\bin\i386","\bin
\configurationmanager.psd1")

$SiteCode = Get-PSDrive -PSProvider CMSITE

Set-Location "$($SiteCode.Name):\"

#Collection refresh Schedules

$Schedule = New-CMSchedule -RecurCount 1 -RecurInterval Days

#Create the user collection and query all users with a
@mdmhybrid.com UPN

New-CMUserCollection -LimitingCollectionName "All Users"
-Name "All Intune Users" -Comment "Users who participate in
the Intune POC" -RefreshType Both -RefreshSchedule $Schedule

Add-CMUserCollectionQueryMembershipRule -CollectionName "All
Intune Users" -QueryExpression 'select * from SMS_R_User
where SMS_R_User.UserPrincipalName like "%mdmhybrid.com"'
-RuleName IntuneUsers
```

3. Open the **ConfigMgr console**. In the **Asset and Compliance** workspace, select **User Collections** and verify that you can see the new user collection.

4. Refresh the collection membership.

Set Up the Microsoft Intune Connector

The next step in the process is to configure the Microsoft Intune connection:

1. In the **ConfigMgr console**, in the **Administration** workspace, navigate to **Cloud Services / Microsoft Intune Subscriptions**.

2. On the ribbon, click **Add Microsoft Intune Subscription**.

3. On the **Introduction** page, click **Next**.

4. On the **Subscription** page, click **Sign In** and specify the **admin@mdmhybrid.onmicrosoft.com** account.

5. After logging on, you are prompted to accept that you will be using ConfigMgr to manage your mobile devices. Select the **I understand that after I complete the sign-in process, the mobile device management authority is permanently set to Configuration Manager and cannot be changed** check box and click **OK**.

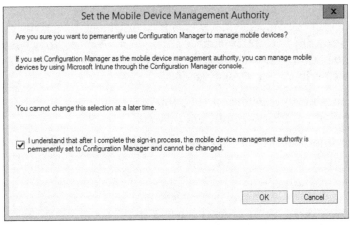

Configuring ConfigMgr as the MDM authority.

6. Log in with your Microsoft Intune administrator account. After a successful sign-in, you return to the Subscription page.

7. On the **Subscription** page, click **Next**.

8. On the **General** page, configure these settings and click **Next**:

    a. Collection: **All Intune Users**

    b. Company name: **ViaMonstra**

    c. URL to company privacy documentation: **http://viamonstra.com/privacy**

    d. Configuration Manager site code: **PS1**

9. On the **Company Contact Information** page, fill in the local IT department details and click **Next**.

10. On the **Company Logo** page, select **Include company logo**, click **Browse**, and select a company logo file. Click **Next** to continue.

11. On the **Device Enrollment Manager** page, click **Next**.

12. On the **Multi-Factor Authentication** page, click **Next**.

13. On the **Summary** page, read the summary and click **Next**. A warning appears telling you about the next steps. Click **OK** and **Close**. In the background, ConfigMgr adds a new site system role server called *manage.microsoft.com*. This is the Windows Intune distribution point. You can view the new site system in **Site Configuration / Servers and Site System Roles**.

14. On the **Completion** page, click **Close**. The next step in the process is to configure the Windows Intune Connector as a site system role.

Monitor the Intune Connection

ConfigMgr creates new log files when you install the connector. These log files are crucial when troubleshooting the connection, synchronization, and changes made to the Intune Users collection. The log files are all placed in <x>:\Program Files\Microsoft Configuration Manager\Logs where <x> is the partition where you installed ConfigMgr. As always, read your log files using CMTrace from <x>:\Program Files\Microsoft Configuration Manager\tools.

The first log file you should focus on is the Connectorsetup.log. It provides information about the installation and configuration process of the Microsoft Intune Connector.

The Cloudusersync.log file includes information about the user synchronization between your Intune Users collection and Microsoft Intune.

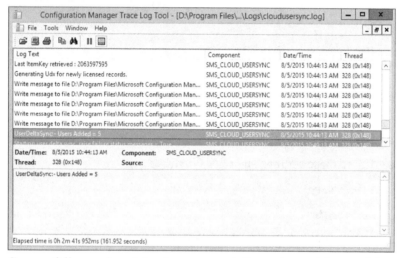

Successfully synchronizing Intune user information to Microsoft Intune.

A common mistake is manually adding users to the Intune Users collection with the wrong UPN name. That generates a synchronizing error: UserSync: Failed to perform delta sync. error = Unknown error 0x80131904, 0x80131904. To fix the error, simply remove the user(s) from the collection or add the missing UPN in Active Directory.

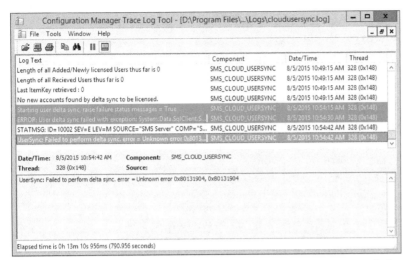

Very common mistake: adding users in the Intune collection with the wrong UPN.

Two other log files that you will find useful are Dmpdownloader.log and Dmpuploader.log. They provide information about synchronizing inventory data and policies between ConfigMgr and Microsoft Intune.

Configuring Hybrid Platform Support

To enroll and manage devices, you need to configure support for the various platforms. As mentioned earlier, ViaMonstra has a mix of iOS, Windows, and Android devices that must be supported.

Configure Android Support in a Hybrid Solution

1. In the **Administration** workspace, navigate to **Cloud Services / Microsoft Intune Subscriptions**.

2. On the ribbon, click **Configure Platforms / Android**.

3. Select **Enable Android enrollment** and click **OK**.

Configure iOS Support in a Hybrid Solution

1. In the **Administration** workspace, navigate to **Cloud Services / Microsoft Intune Subscriptions**.

2. On the ribbon, click **Create APNs certificate request**.

3. In **File Name**, type **C:\Setup\MDM\Certificates\Apple08072015.csr** and then click **Download**. (Notice that you need to create the C:\Setup\MDM\Certificates folder manually. Also notice the certificate name, which contains the date of the creation.)

4. When prompted to sign in to Intune, sign in using the
    admin@mdmhybrid.onmicrosoft.com account.

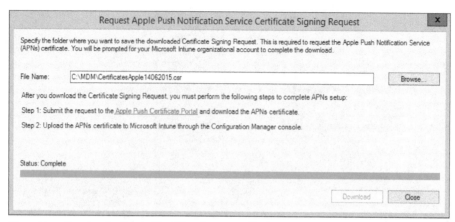

Creating the Apple Push Notification certificate.

5. After the download is complete, click the **Apple Push Certificate Portal** link to upload
    the Certificate Signing Request. This is where you need an Apple ID. You can use the
    same Apple ID to create multiple certificates.

6. Sign in to the Apple Push Certificate Portal using the **MDMhybrid@outlook.com** Apple
    ID.

7. Click **Create a Certificate** and accept the license terms. Next, you see a field where you
    can write notes about the certificate. It's a best practice to write information about who
    ordered the certificate, which service it will be used for, and the purpose.

8. Click **Browse** and upload the **C:\MDM\Certificates\Apple08072015.csr** certificate. (The
    .CSR file is used to request a trust relationship certificate from the Apple Push Certificates
    Portal.) During the process, you are prompted to save a JSON file. Simply click **Cancel**
    and refresh the web browser to see your newly created certificate.

9. In your Internet browser, go back to the **Apple Push Certificates Portal** page and
    download the Mobile Device Management certificate to
    C:\Setup\MDM\Certificates\MDM_ Microsoft Corporation_Certificate.pem.

10. Back in the **ConfigMgr console**, go to the **Administration** workspace and navigate to
    Cloud Services / Microsoft Intune Subscriptions.

11. On the ribbon, click **Configure Platforms / iOS**.

12. On the **iOS** page, select **Enable iOS enrollment**, click **Browse**, and select the
    C:\Setup\MDM\certificates\MDM_ Microsoft Corporation_Certificate.pem
    certificate.

13. Enable the APN expiry alert, configure the alert to appear **20** days before certificates
    expire, and click **OK**.

Configuring iOS and Mac OS X support.

Real World Note: If you do not upload a new iOS certificate before the old certificate expires, you are forced to re-enroll all iOS devices. Apple emails the Apple ID prior to the expiration date, but because you are using an organizational Apple ID, it is easy to miss that information.

Configure Windows 10 Mobile Support in a Hybrid Solution

1. In the **Administration** workspace, navigate to **Cloud Services / Microsoft Intune Subscriptions**.

2. On the ribbon, click **Configure Platforms / Windows Phone**.

3. Enable **Windows Phone 8.1 and Windows 10 Mobile**, click **None**, and then click **OK** twice.

Configuring support for Windows Mobile.

Configure Windows Support in a Hybrid Solution

1. In the **Administration** workspace, navigate **to Cloud Services / Microsoft Intune Subscriptions**.

2. On the ribbon, click Configure Platforms / Windows.

3. Enable **Windows enrollment** and click **OK**.

Create Mobile Device Collections

When working with mobile devices in ConfigMgr, it is a best practice to create collections for the various device platforms and user profiles. ConfigMgr uses collections as targets for various deployments, such applications, company resources, and security policies. The following PowerShell example creates a mobile device folder, several device collections, and three user collections.

```
#Import the ConfigMgr Module

Import-Module $env:SMS_ADMIN_UI_PATH.Replace("\bin\i386","\bin
\configurationmanager.psd1")

$SiteCode = Get-PSDrive -PSProvider CMSITE

Set-Location "$($SiteCode.Name):\"
```

```
#Create the MDM collection Folders

New-Item -Path PS1:\DeviceCollection -Name 'Mobile Devices'

#Adding Collection refresh Schedule

$Schedule = New-CMSchedule -RecurCount 7 -RecurInterval Days

#Creating collections for Android, iOS, Mac OS X, and Windows

$Collection1 = New-CMDeviceCollection -LimitingCollectionName
"All Mobile Devices" -Name "All Android Devices" -Comment All
-RefreshType Both -RefreshSchedule $Schedule

Add-CMDeviceCollectionQueryMembershipRule -CollectionName "All
Android Devices" -QueryExpression 'select
SMS_R_SYSTEM.ResourceID,SMS_R_SYSTEM.ResourceType,SMS_R_SYSTEM.Na
me,SMS_R_SYSTEM.SMSUniqueIdentifier,SMS_R_SYSTEM.ResourceDomainOR
Workgroup,SMS_R_SYSTEM.Client from SMS_R_System where
SMS_R_System.OperatingSystemNameandVersion like "%Android%"'
-RuleName Android

$Collection2 = New-CMDeviceCollection -LimitingCollectionName
"All Mobile Devices" -Name "All iOS Devices" -Comment All
-RefreshType Both -RefreshSchedule $Schedule

Add-CMDeviceCollectionQueryMembershipRule -CollectionName "All
iOS Devices" -QueryExpression 'select
SMS_R_SYSTEM.ResourceID,SMS_R_SYSTEM.ResourceType,SMS_R_SYSTEM.Na
me,SMS_R_SYSTEM.SMSUniqueIdentifier,SMS_R_SYSTEM.ResourceDomainOR
Workgroup,SMS_R_SYSTEM.Client from SMS_R_System where
SMS_R_System.OperatingSystemNameandVersion like "%iOS%"'-RuleName
iOS

$Collection3 = New-CMDeviceCollection -LimitingCollectionName
"All Mobile Devices" -Name "All Windows Phones" -Comment All
-RefreshType Both -RefreshSchedule $Schedule

Add-CMDeviceCollectionQueryMembershipRule -CollectionName "All
Windows Phones" -QueryExpression 'select
SMS_R_SYSTEM.ResourceID,SMS_R_SYSTEM.ResourceType,SMS_R_SYSTEM.Na
me,SMS_R_SYSTEM.SMSUniqueIdentifier,SMS_R_SYSTEM.ResourceDomainOR
Workgroup,SMS_R_SYSTEM.Client from SMS_R_System where
SMS_R_System.OperatingSystemNameandVersion like "%Windows
Phone%"' -RuleName WP
```

```
$Collection4 = New-CMDeviceCollection -LimitingCollectionName
"All Mobile Devices" -Name "All Mac OS X Devices" -Comment All
-RefreshType Both -RefreshSchedule $Schedule

Add-CMDeviceCollectionQueryMembershipRule -CollectionName "All
Mac OS X Devices" -QueryExpression 'select
SMS_R_SYSTEM.ResourceID,SMS_R_SYSTEM.ResourceType,SMS_R_SYSTEM.Na
me,SMS_R_SYSTEM.SMSUniqueIdentifier,SMS_R_SYSTEM.ResourceDomainOR
Workgroup,SMS_R_SYSTEM.Client from SMS_R_System where
SMS_R_System.OperatingSystemNameandVersion like "%os X%"'
-RuleName Mac

#Creating additional support collections for managing devices

$Collection5 = New-CMDeviceCollection -LimitingCollectionName
"All Mobile Devices" -Name "All Jailbroken" -Comment All
-RefreshType Both -RefreshSchedule $Schedule

Add-CMDeviceCollectionQueryMembershipRule -CollectionName "All
Jailbroken" -QueryExpression 'select
SMS_R_SYSTEM.ResourceID,SMS_R_SYSTEM.ResourceType,SMS_R_SYSTEM.Na
me,SMS_R_SYSTEM.SMSUniqueIdentifier,SMS_R_SYSTEM.ResourceDomainOR
Workgroup,SMS_R_SYSTEM.Client from SMS_R_System inner join
SMS_G_System_DEVICE_COMPUTERSYSTEM on
SMS_G_System_DEVICE_COMPUTERSYSTEM.ResourceId =
SMS_R_System.ResourceId where SMS_G_System_DEVICE_COMPUTERSYSTEM.
Jailbroken = 1' -RuleName Jailbroken

$Collection6 = New-CMDeviceCollection -LimitingCollectionName
"All Mobile Devices" -Name "All Company Owned" -Comment All
-RefreshType Both -RefreshSchedule $Schedule

Add-CMDeviceCollectionQueryMembershipRule -CollectionName "All
Company Owned" -QueryExpression 'select
SMS_R_SYSTEM.ResourceID,SMS_R_SYSTEM.ResourceType,SMS_R_SYSTEM.Na
me,SMS_R_SYSTEM.SMSUniqueIdentifier,SMS_R_SYSTEM.ResourceDomainOR
Workgroup,SMS_R_SYSTEM.Client from SMS_R_System where
SMS_R_System.DeviceOwner = 1' -RuleName Company

$Collection7 = New-CMDeviceCollection -LimitingCollectionName
"All Mobile Devices" -Name "All Personal Owned" -Comment All
-RefreshType Both -RefreshSchedule $Schedule
```

```
Add-CMDeviceCollectionQueryMembershipRule -CollectionName "All
Personal Owned" -QueryExpression 'select
SMS_R_SYSTEM.ResourceID,SMS_R_SYSTEM.ResourceType,SMS_R_SYSTEM.Na
me,SMS_R_SYSTEM.SMSUniqueIdentifier,SMS_R_SYSTEM.ResourceDomainOR
Workgroup,SMS_R_SYSTEM.Client from SMS_R_System where
SMS_R_System.DeviceOwner = 2' -RuleName Personal

#Adding user collections

$Collection8 = New-CMUserCollection -LimitingCollectionName "All
Users" -Name "All Jailbroken Users" -Comment "Users who have a
rooted or jailbroken device" -RefreshType Both -RefreshSchedule
$Schedule

$Collection9 = New-CMUserCollection -LimitingCollectionName "All
Users" -Name "All Sales Users" -Comment "Users who belong to
sales" -RefreshType Both -RefreshSchedule $Schedule

$Collection10 = New-CMUserCollection -LimitingCollectionName "All
Users" -Name "All Management Users" -Comment "Users who belong to
Management" -RefreshType Both -RefreshSchedule $Schedule

#move collections to the Mobile Devices folder

Move-CMObject -FolderPath '.\DeviceCollection\Mobile Devices'
-InputObject $Collection1

Move-CMObject -FolderPath '.\DeviceCollection\Mobile Devices'
-InputObject $Collection2

Move-CMObject -FolderPath '.\DeviceCollection\Mobile Devices'
-InputObject $Collection3

Move-CMObject -FolderPath '.\DeviceCollection\Mobile Devices'
-InputObject $Collection4

Move-CMObject -FolderPath '.\DeviceCollection\Mobile Devices'
-InputObject $Collection5

Move-CMObject -FolderPath '.\DeviceCollection\Mobile Devices'
-InputObject $Collection6

Move-CMObject -FolderPath '.\DeviceCollection\Mobile Devices'
-InputObject $Collection7
```

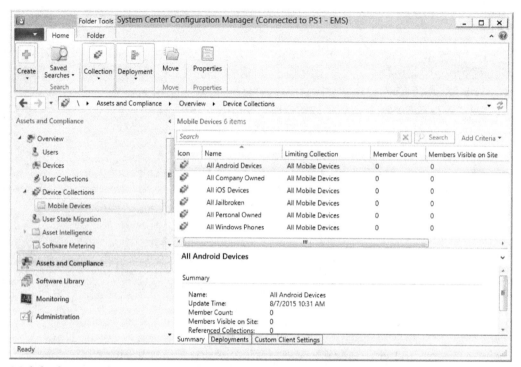

Mobile device collections created with PowerShell in ConfigMgr.

Chapter 6

Common Configurations for Standalone and Hybrid

If you ever start working with standalone Intune and hybrid device management, you will quickly realize that a lot of the settings, configurations, and processes are the same. That's not to say the entire process is the same, but preparing devices, troubleshooting devices, creating company Wi-Fi profiles, and wrapping managed applications are the same regardless of the management interface.

Enrolling the Different Devices

Enrollment of devices into Microsoft Intune differs slightly depending on the model of device that is used. For ViaMonstra, all platforms are enabled and configured to allow users to enroll their devices into Microsoft Intune.

Note that the enrollment process varies across the different platforms. It also depends on whether you have enabled Multi-Factor Authentication for the user. Finally, the implementation of AD FS affects the process.

> **Note:** In these examples, we use the emskings.com domain, the domain used for the standalone EMS scenario. If you are using the EMS hybrid scenario, replace it with the domain used for that scenario. (In this book, we used mdmhybrid.com.)

Windows Phone

Windows Phone natively supports the capability to enroll the device into an MDM solution like Microsoft Intune. You need to take the following steps to be able to enroll a Windows Phone 8.1 device:

1. On the **Windows Phone**, go to the **Store** application, search for the **Microsoft Intune Company Portal** app, and install it.

2. To start enrollment after installing the Company Portal, tap to open the app and follow the remaining steps in this guide.

Step 3	Step 4
Tap **sign in**.	Supply the email address and password, and tap **Sign in**.

Step 5	Step 6
Click **accept**.	Select **Tap to enroll this device**.

Step 7

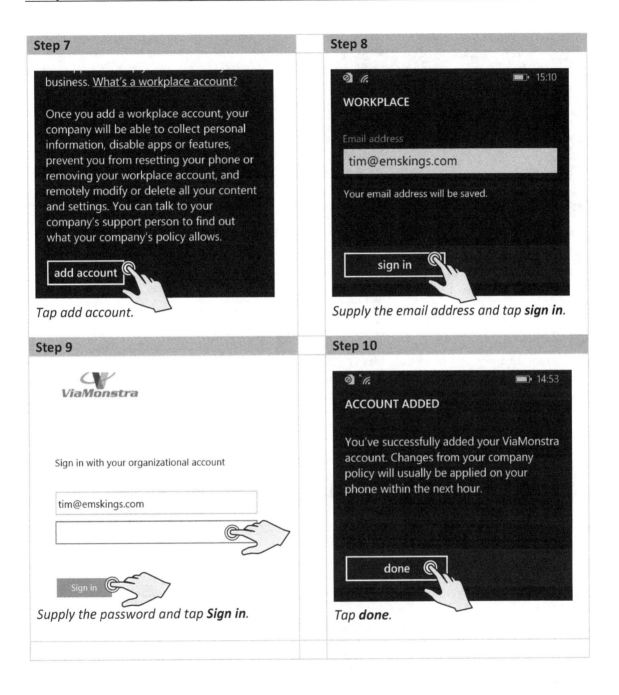

business. What's a workplace account?

Once you add a workplace account, your company will be able to collect personal information, disable apps or features, prevent you from resetting your phone or removing your workplace account, and remotely modify or delete all your content and settings. You can talk to your company's support person to find out what your company's policy allows.

add account

Tap add account.

Step 8

15:10

WORKPLACE

Email address

tim@emskings.com

Your email address will be saved.

sign in

*Supply the email address and tap **sign in**.*

Step 9

ViaMonstra

Sign in with your organizational account

tim@emskings.com

Sign in

*Supply the password and tap **Sign in**.*

Step 10

14:53

ACCOUNT ADDED

You've successfully added your ViaMonstra account. Changes from your company policy will usually be applied on your phone within the next hour.

done

*Tap **done**.*

business. What's a workplace account?

Once you add a workplace account, your company will be able to collect personal information, disable apps or features, prevent you from resetting your phone or removing your workplace account, and remotely modify or delete all your content and settings. You can talk to your company's support person to find out what your company's policy allows.

ViaMonstra
enrolled

The device is enrolled.

Real World Note: User policies apply almost instantly when enrolling the device, whereas device policies might take a few extra minutes. The reason is straightforward. Intune knows about the users from the beginning and knows which policies to apply. The device, on the other hand, is most likely unknown and requires a round trip for Intune to know which policies to apply.

Windows 10

Windows 10 for many will be a game changer. It has been a very long time since we have seen that many changes in a Microsoft operating system. Windows 10 includes a management agent you can use to manage a device that is OMA-DM compliant and can be managed through Open Mobile Alliance Uniform Resource Identifier (OMA-URI) settings. This is true for desktops or laptops as well as for phones. Although some settings apply to both platforms, there is still a fundamental difference in managing a laptop vs. a mobile phone. With the new management agent built-in, many organizations have to rethink how they want to manage the operating system. Will they still use group policies? Install the ConfigMgr agent? Install the Intune agent? Or simply use the built-in MDM agent? There are no correct answers to these questions. It's wrong to look at the new MDM agent as a replacement for the other management options. Rather, it complements them by offering you the opportunity to "light-manage" devices without installing any additional agents.

Real World Note: Some of the new Widows 10 features like Enterprise Data Protection and Device Health Attestation are not manageable with group policies.

Join Windows 10 to Azure AD

For years, we have been used to joining computers to on-premises Active Directory, but things are changing with Windows 10. When starting a Windows 10 device for the first time, you are presented with an OOBE experience in which you have to make some fundamental choices like determining the ownership of the device, personal or corporate, and deciding whether you want to join the device to on-premises Active Directory or join the device to Azure AD. ViaMonstra wants its Windows 10 devices to be joined to Azure AD.

1. From the Windows 10 out of box experience, select **Join Azure AD** and click **Next**.

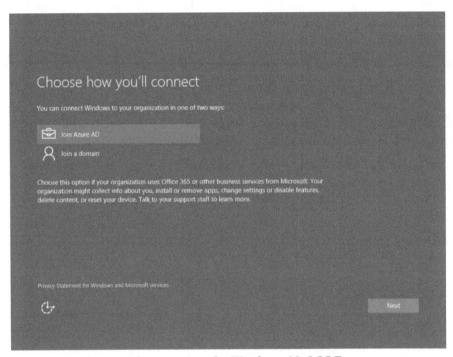

Connection choices when running the Windows 10 OOBE.

2. For **Let's get you signed in**, type **tim@emskings.com**. When using a known domain name like emskings.com, the wizard takes you to the AD FS sign-in portal, if one exists, to finish the login process.

    After a successful enrollment, the Windows 10 device is ready.

The enrollment process might prompt you to accept company policies. Those are settings coming from Microsoft Intune.

Real World Note: You can verify how the Windows 10 device is connected by using Settings / Accounts / Work access.

What Happens Behind the Scenes
The following describes what is happening behind the scenes when you are joining a Windows 10 device to Azure. The process involves three cloud services and the device.

1. When the email address is entered, Windows 10 asks for an Azure domain managing the specific user. If an Azure AD domain is found, Azure AD next performs a lookup during

which it checks for Azure AD join settings. If the Azure AD setting is enabled, the end user is prompted for authentication.

2. If the end user is authorized for Azure AD Join, several objects are passed down to the device, like the Azure device registration service single sign-on token. Local administrators are added, and if so configured, the MDM enrollment URL is passed down to the Windows 10 device. The MDM enrollment URL allows for automatic enrollment into Microsoft Intune.

3. The single sign-on token on the device is now passed from the device to the Azure Device Registration Service with a request to join the device to Azure AD.

4. The Azure Device Registration Service registers the device object in Azure AD. As part of the registration process, the Azure Device Registration Service passes down a local computer certificate that is stored in the personal computer store on the device.

5. The next step depends on the Azure AD and Intune application settings. If Intune is configured for auto-enrollment, the MDM agent on the device the MDM agent on the device connects to Azure AD and requests another single sign-on token for the MDM enrollment URL.

6. Azure AD returns a new single sign-on token to the device that is used to connect to the MDM enrollment server and start the enrollment process.

Windows 10 Mobile

You manage Windows 10 Mobile the same way you manage a Windows Phone, though the enrollment process is slightly different. Follow these steps to enroll a Windows 10 Mobile device.

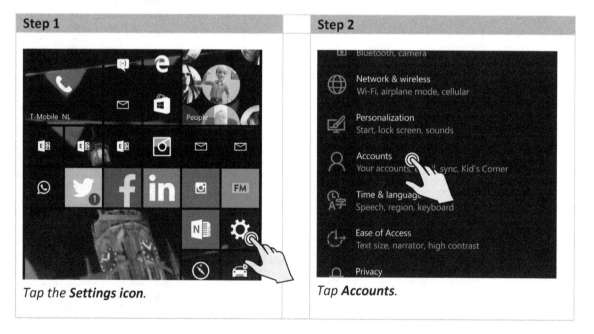

Step 1	Step 2
Tap the **Settings icon**.	Tap **Accounts**.

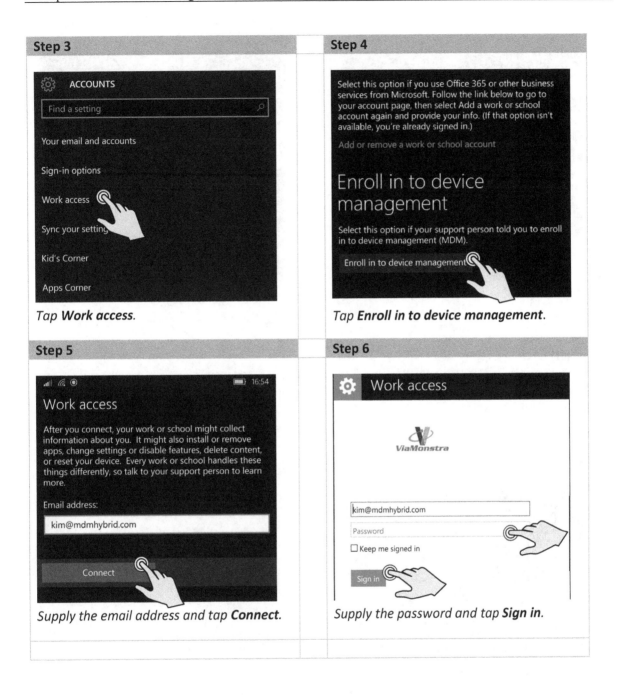

Step 3

Your email and accounts

Sign-in options

Work access

Sync your settings

Kid's Corner

Apps Corner

Tap **Work access**.

Step 4

Select this option if you use Office 365 or other business services from Microsoft. Follow the link below to go to your account page, then select Add a work or school account again and provide your info. (If that option isn't available, you're already signed in.)

Add or remove a work or school account

Enroll in to device management

Select this option if your support person told you to enroll in to device management (MDM).

Enroll in to device management

Tap **Enroll in to device management**.

Step 5

Work access

After you connect, your work or school might collect information about you. It might also install or remove apps, change settings or disable features, delete content, or reset your device. Every work or school handles these things differently, so talk to your support person to learn more.

Email address:

kim@mdmhybrid.com

Connect

Supply the email address and tap **Connect**.

Step 6

Work access

ViaMonstra

kim@mdmhybrid.com

Password

☐ Keep me signed in

Sign in

Supply the password and tap **Sign in**.

Tap **done**.

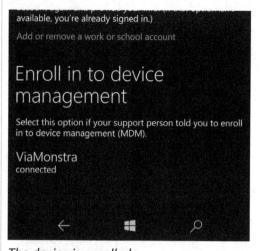

The device is enrolled.

Android

Users themselves also can enroll Android devices. Android has no native MDM support like Windows. For that reason, you need to install the Company Portal to be able to enroll the device in Microsoft Intune.

Follow the next steps to enroll the Android devices:

Step 1	Step 2
	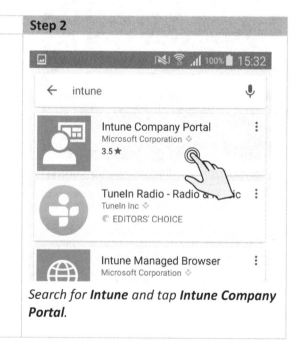
Tap on the **Play Store icon**.	Search for **Intune** and tap **Intune Company Portal**.

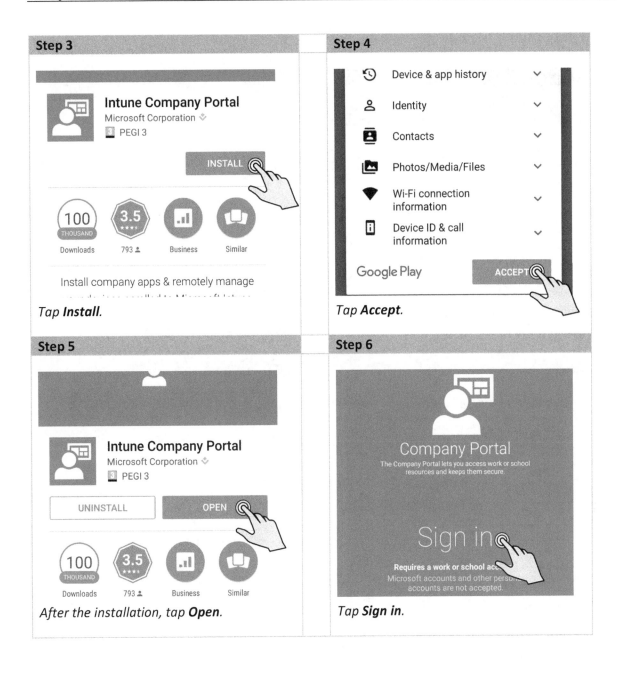

Step 3

Intune Company Portal
Microsoft Corporation
PEGI 3

INSTALL

100 THOUSAND
Downloads

3.5 ★★★★
793 ☻

Business

Similar

Install company apps & remotely manage

*Tap **Install**.*

Step 4

🕓 Device & app history   ˅

👤 Identity   ˅

☰ Contacts   ˅

🖼 Photos/Media/Files   ˅

📶 Wi-Fi connection information   ˅

📱 Device ID & call information   ˅

Google Play   ACCEPT

*Tap **Accept**.*

Step 5

Intune Company Portal
Microsoft Corporation
PEGI 3

UNINSTALL   OPEN

100 THOUSAND
Downloads

3.5 ★★★★
793 ☻

Business

Similar

*After the installation, tap **Open**.*

Step 6

Company Portal
The Company Portal lets you access work or school
resources and keeps them secure.

Sign in

Requires a work or school account
Microsoft accounts and other personal
accounts are not accepted.

*Tap **Sign in**.*

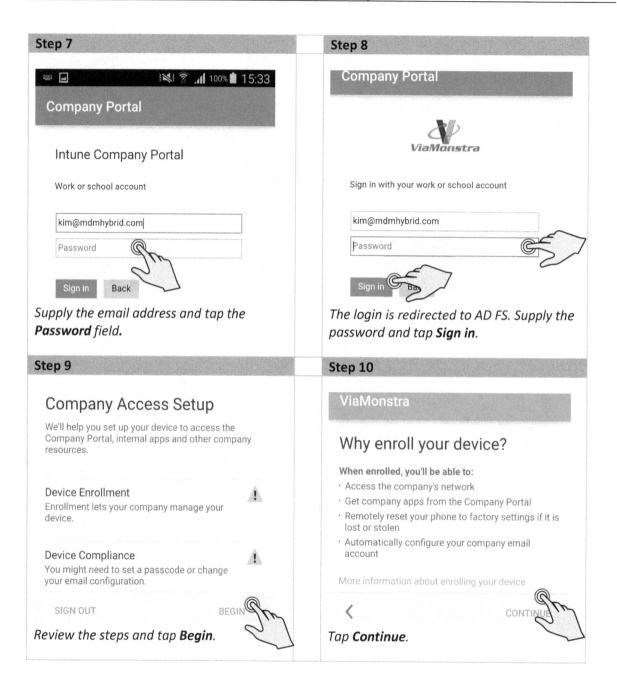

Step 7

Intune Company Portal

Work or school account

kim@mdmhybrid.com

Password

Sign in   Back

Supply the email address and tap the **Password** *field.*

Step 8

Company Portal

Sign in with your work or school account

kim@mdmhybrid.com

Password

Sign in   Back

The login is redirected to AD FS. Supply the password and tap **Sign in.**

Step 9

Company Access Setup

We'll help you set up your device to access the Company Portal, internal apps and other company resources.

Device Enrollment   ⚠
Enrollment lets your company manage your device.

Device Compliance   ⚠
You might need to set a passcode or change your email configuration.

SIGN OUT   BEGIN

Review the steps and tap **Begin.**

Step 10

ViaMonstra

Why enroll your device?

When enrolled, you'll be able to:
· Access the company's network
· Get company apps from the Company Portal
· Remotely reset your phone to factory settings if it is lost or stolen
· Automatically configure your company email account

More information about enrolling your device

‹   CONTINUE

Tap **Continue.**

154

Step 11

We care about your privacy.

🚫 **IT admin cannot see this on your device:**
- Call and Web history
- Location
- Email and text messages
- Contacts
- Passwords
- Calendar
- Camera roll

👤 **IT admin can see this on your device:**

‹   CONTINUE

*Tap **Continue.***

Step 12

ViaMonstra

What comes next?

When you tap Enroll, your device will ask you to do one or more of the following:

- **Activate** device administrator permissions
- **Confirm** the device privacy policy
- **OK** the certificate prompt
- **Allow** phone permission and other permission requests by Company Portal (This app never makes phone calls)

‹   ENROLL

*Tap **Enroll.***

Step 13

Activate device administrator?

Company Portal

🔺 Company Portal

Activating administrator will allow Company Portal to perform the following operations:

- **Erase all data**
  Erase the phone's data without warning by performing a factory data reset.

- **Change the screen-unlock**

CANCEL   ACTIVATE

*Tap **Activate.***

Step 14

and used in accordance with Samsung's Privacy Policy at [https://account.samsung.com/membership/pp].

Samsung KNOX License Key, "IMEI" or "Serial Number" or "MAC address" in

☐ I acknowledge that I have read and understood, and agree to all of the ...ns and conditions above

✕ Cancel   ✓ Confirm

*If **Samsung KNOX** is available, tap the **I acknowledge...** check box and tap **Confirm**.*

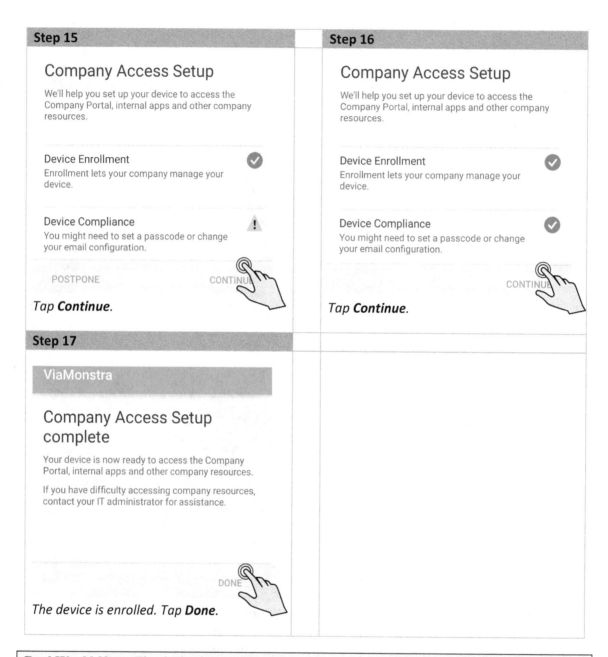

Step 15

Company Access Setup

We'll help you set up your device to access the Company Portal, internal apps and other company resources.

Device Enrollment
Enrollment lets your company manage your device.

Device Compliance
You might need to set a passcode or change your email configuration.

POSTPONE   CONTINUE

Tap **Continue.**

Step 16

Company Access Setup

We'll help you set up your device to access the Company Portal, internal apps and other company resources.

Device Enrollment
Enrollment lets your company manage your device.

Device Compliance
You might need to set a passcode or change your email configuration.

CONTINUE

Tap **Continue.**

Step 17

ViaMonstra

Company Access Setup complete

Your device is now ready to access the Company Portal, internal apps and other company resources.

If you have difficulty accessing company resources, contact your IT administrator for assistance.

DONE

The device is enrolled. Tap **Done.**

Real World Note: The device is now enrolled. Because the policies are configured and deployed, the device may not be compliant. Be sure to configure the device so it is compliant.

The Android Architecture

In order to understand what happens behind the scenes when you manage your Android, you first need to understand the architecture:

- The enrollment experience takes place from the Company Portal that you just downloaded from Google Play.
- The Intune MDM agent is the service on the device that communicates with the cloud services in order to download policies and update inventory data and compliance information.
- The Company Portal is the end-user interface that acts like an application portal.

Some applications are so-called "managed" apps; these are a special type of applications for which the administrator has much more control with the data being accessed with the application. Most of the code to control the data behavior is built into the Company Portal and not the app itself. This allows for much more flexibility when updating core features of the managed app experience.

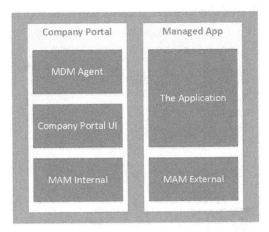

The Android architecture.

One of the very important pieces in any mobile device management scenario is the ability to apply policies and applications on a device as quickly as possible during the enrollment process. During that process, your Android device agent synchronizes five times with three-minute intervals. After the enrollment process, the next eight synchronization attempts take place every 15 minutes and after that, the service synchronizes every eight hours. The user can always manually initiate a synchronization from within the Company Portal.

Not all communication on the Android device is initiated from the device. Certain scenarios like remote wipe, retire, remote password reset, and remote lock are *pushed* to the device. Whenever a remote action is initiated from the Intune or ConfigMgr console, the following sequence takes place:

1. The administrator initiates a remote action from the console.
2. The remote action request is send to the Microsoft Intune service in the cloud.

3. Microsoft Intune does not directly connect to the Android, but instead communicates with the Google Cloud Messaging Service and asks the service to poke the device with a wake-up call.

4. When the Android is poked, it connects to the Intune service and asks for new policies.

5. Policies are downloaded and executed on the device.

iOS

Users also can enroll iOS devices themselves. Like Android, iOS has no native MDM support like Windows. For that reason, you need to install the Company Portal to be able to enroll the device in Microsoft Intune.

Follow the next steps to enroll the iOS devices:

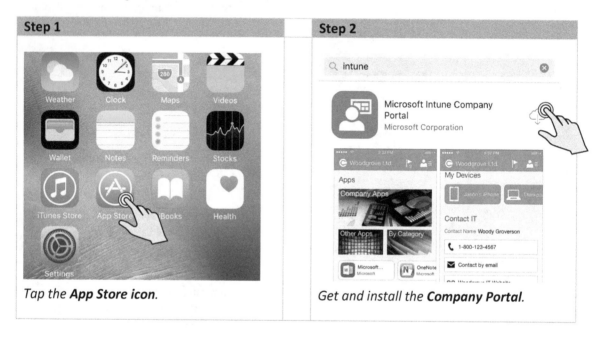

Step 1	Step 2
Tap the **App Store icon**.	Get and install the **Company Portal**.

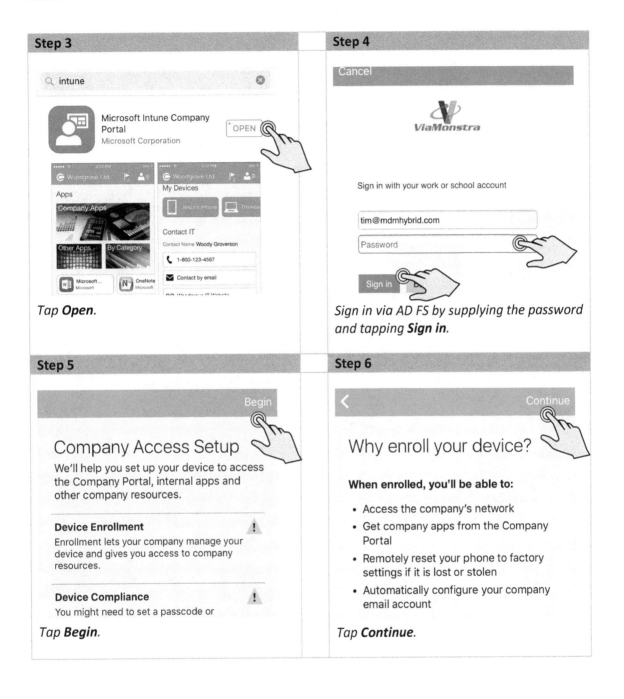

Step 3

Q intune

Microsoft Intune Company Portal
Microsoft Corporation
OPEN

Tap **Open**.

Step 4

Cancel

ViaMonstra

Sign in with your work or school account

tim@mdmhybrid.com

Password

Sign in

Sign in via AD FS by supplying the password and tapping **Sign in**.

Step 5

Begin

Company Access Setup

We'll help you set up your device to access the Company Portal, internal apps and other company resources.

Device Enrollment

Enrollment lets your company manage your device and gives you access to company resources.

Device Compliance

You might need to set a passcode or

Tap **Begin**.

Step 6

Continue

Why enroll your device?

When enrolled, you'll be able to:

- Access the company's network
- Get company apps from the Company Portal
- Remotely reset your phone to factory settings if it is lost or stolen
- Automatically configure your company email account

Tap **Continue**.

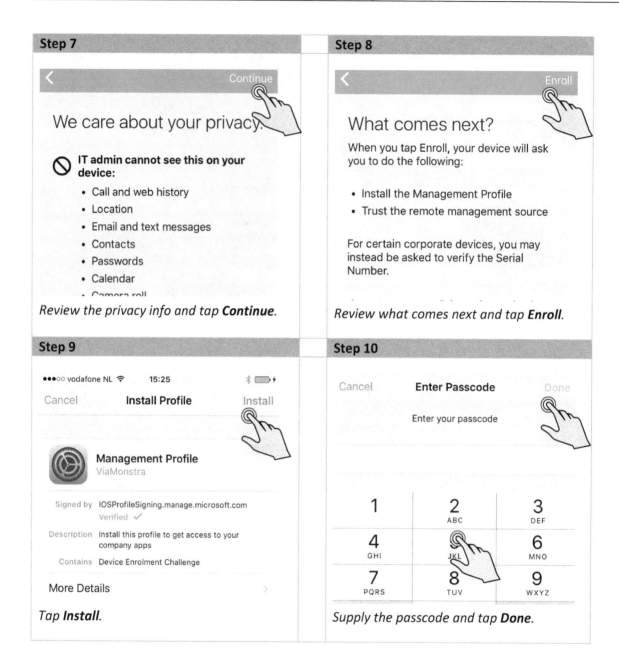

Step 7

<   Continue

We care about your privacy.

🚫 **IT admin cannot see this on your device:**

* Call and web history
* Location
* Email and text messages
* Contacts
* Passwords
* Calendar
* Camera roll

Review the privacy info and tap **Continue**.

Step 8

<   Enroll

What comes next?

When you tap Enroll, your device will ask you to do the following:

* Install the Management Profile
* Trust the remote management source

For certain corporate devices, you may instead be asked to verify the Serial Number.

Review what comes next and tap **Enroll**.

Step 9

●●●○○ vodafone NL 🛜   15:25   ✳ 🔋⚡

Cancel   **Install Profile**   Install

⚙️ **Management Profile**
ViaMonstra

Signed by   IOSProfileSigning.manage.microsoft.com
           Verified ✓

Description   Install this profile to get access to your
           company apps

Contains   Device Enrolment Challenge

More Details   >

Tap **Install**.

Step 10

Cancel   **Enter Passcode**   Done

Enter your passcode

1	2 ABC	3 DEF
4 GHI	5 JKL	6 MNO
7 PQRS	8 TUV	9 WXYZ

Supply the passcode and tap **Done**.

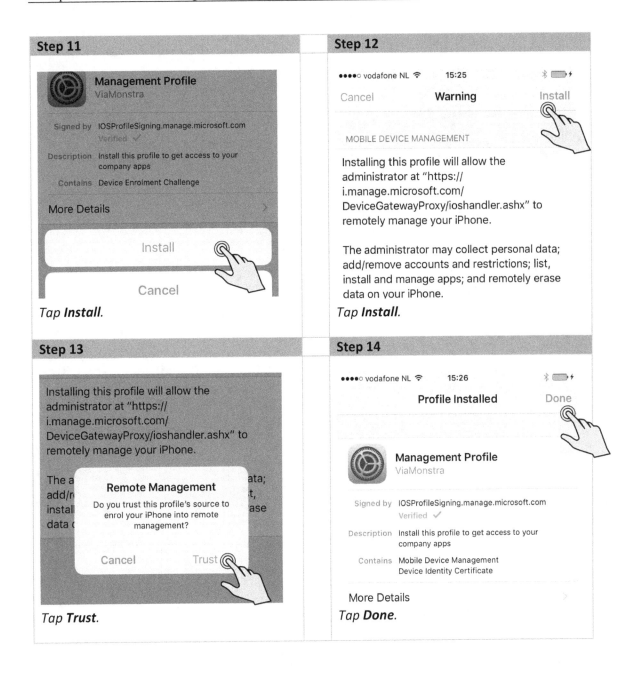

Step 11

Management Profile
ViaMonstra

Signed by IOSProfileSigning.manage.microsoft.com
Verified ✓

Description Install this profile to get access to your
company apps

Contains Device Enrolment Challenge

More Details ›

Install

Cancel

Tap Install.

Step 12

●●●●○ vodafone NL 📶   15:25   ✳ ▭✦

Cancel   **Warning**   Install

MOBILE DEVICE MANAGEMENT

Installing this profile will allow the
administrator at "https://
i.manage.microsoft.com/
DeviceGatewayProxy/ioshandler.ashx" to
remotely manage your iPhone.

The administrator may collect personal data;
add/remove accounts and restrictions; list,
install and manage apps; and remotely erase
data on your iPhone.

Tap Install.

Step 13

Installing this profile will allow the
administrator at "https://
i.manage.microsoft.com/
DeviceGatewayProxy/ioshandler.ashx" to
remotely manage your iPhone.

The a   ata;
add/r   t,
instal   ase
data o

Remote Management

Do you trust this profile's source to
enrol your iPhone into remote
management?

Cancel   Trust

Tap Trust.

Step 14

●●●●○ vodafone NL 📶   15:26   ✳ ▭✦

Profile Installed   Done

Management Profile
ViaMonstra

Signed by IOSProfileSigning.manage.microsoft.com
Verified ✓

Description Install this profile to get access to your
company apps

Contains Mobile Device Management
Device Identity Certificate

More Details ›

Tap Done.

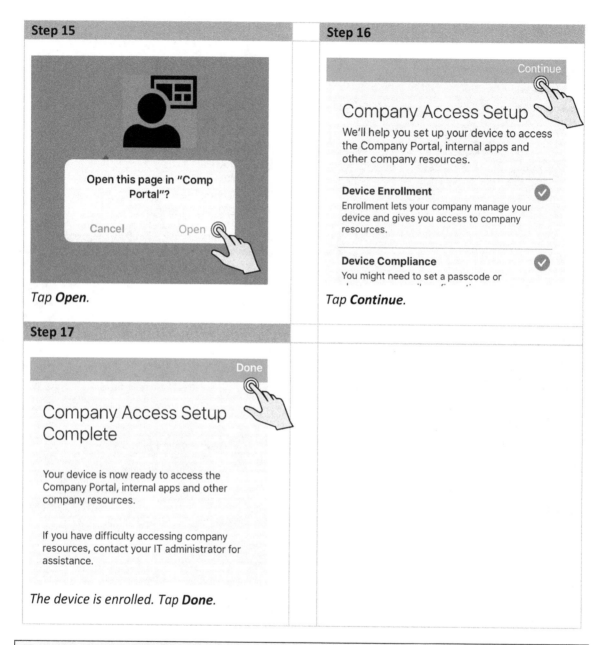

Step 15

Open this page in "Comp Portal"?

Cancel   Open

*Tap **Open**.*

Step 16

Continue

Company Access Setup

We'll help you set up your device to access the Company Portal, internal apps and other company resources.

Device Enrollment ✓

Enrollment lets your company manage your device and gives you access to company resources.

Device Compliance ✓

You might need to set a passcode or

*Tap **Continue**.*

Step 17

Done

Company Access Setup Complete

Your device is now ready to access the Company Portal, internal apps and other company resources.

If you have difficulty accessing company resources, contact your IT administrator for assistance.

*The device is enrolled. Tap **Done**.*

Real World Note: The device is now enrolled. Because the policies are configured and deployed, the device may not be compliant. Be sure to configure the device so it is compliant.

The iOS Architecture

Managing iOS devices works via four components, two of which are controlled by Microsoft and two by Apple. On the iOS device, you have the Apple MDM agent and the Company Portal, and in the cloud, you have Microsoft Intune and Apple Cloud Services. When enrolling iOS devices, the Company Portal plays only a small part in the process (almost like a bootstrap job on a computer). The Company Portal hands off the process to Microsoft Intune and the built-in Apple MDM agent. These two components are responsible for establishing the trust between the device and Microsoft Intune. The Apple MDM agent is used to download policies from Microsoft Intune.

When initiating a remote command on the device, such as remote wipe, retire, passcode reset or remote lock, Microsoft Intune communicates with Apple Cloud Services to initiate the commands. The following processes take place:

1. The administrator initiates a remote action from the console.

2. The remote action request is sent to the Microsoft Intune service in the cloud.

3. Microsoft Intune sends the remote request to Apple Cloud Services.

4. Apple Cloud Services communicates with the local Apple MDM agent on the device.

5. The Apple MDM agent responds to the remote command and does what it's told.

Normal policies and communication between the device and Intune happens with Intune sending a push notification to the Apple MDM agent asking it to check in and download new policies.

Mac OS X

Microsoft Intune also offers management for Mac OS X devices. To use the management options, you need to enroll the devices:

1. On the **Mac OS X** device, go to **http://portal.manage.microsoft.com** in the **Safari** web browser and supply your email address. You are redirected from the Microsoft Intune logon page to the AD FS sign-in page.

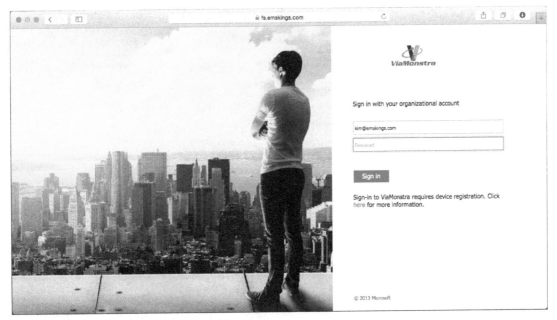

AD FS sign-in page in the Safari web browser.

2. Supply your password and click **Sign in**.

3. Click the notification bar stating **This device is either not enrolled or the Company Portal can't identify it.**

4. On the **Identity or Enroll this device** page, click **Enroll**.

5. On the **Enroll this device** page, click **Install** to install the Management Profile.

6. On the **Install "Management Profile"** page, click **Install**.

Installing the Management Profile.

7. Optionally, supply the password of your administrative local user and click **OK**.

8. Click **Show Profile** to see which profile is going to be installed and then click **Continue**.

9. Click **Install** in the **Are you sure you want to install profile "Management Profile"** dialog box.

10. Close the Preferences and Safari. Then start Safari again to sign back in to the Company Portal website **http://portal.manage.microsoft.com**.

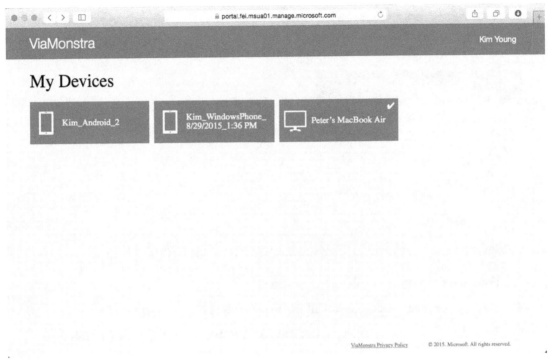

Mac OS X is enrolled.

Troubleshooting

Troubleshooting has long been a very important discipline when working with enterprise client management. Introducing mobility isn't much different, except that your troubleshooting options are somewhat limited. However, there are a few things you have to know when working with the different devices: how to initiate a policy synchronization, evaluate compliance settings, and send log files from the device to the local administrator. In the following examples, we have used fully enrolled devices with applications, policy and compliance rules applied.

Android

Android devices allow you to access log files stored locally on the device, initiate policy synchronizations, and check compliance on the device manually. To initiate policy synchronization manually on the Android device, follow these steps:

1. Sign in to the **Company Portal**.

2. To perform a policy synchronization, from the upper right corner, touch the **Software** button.

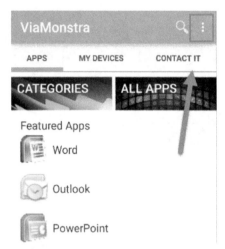

Refreshing security policies on an Android device from the Software button.

3. From the drop-down menu, select **Settings**.

4. From the **Settings** menu, scroll all the way down and click **Sync**.

5. To check device compliance, select **MY DEVICES** and tap **Check Compliance**.

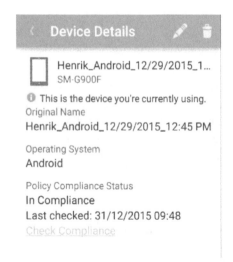

Manually checking the compliance state of the Android device.

There are three useful log files when you work with Android devices:

- **CompanyPortalX.log.** This log file contains a lot of information about the communication between the device and Microsoft Intune, such as policy requests, conditional access states, and authentication.

- **Omadmlog.log**. OMA-DM is an open mobile standard for managing mobile devices. You learn more about it as you read this book. Part of the standard is OMA-URI policy.

Among other things, you can use those policies to apply security settings and Wi-Fi profiles. The log file contains information about detecting and applying those settings.

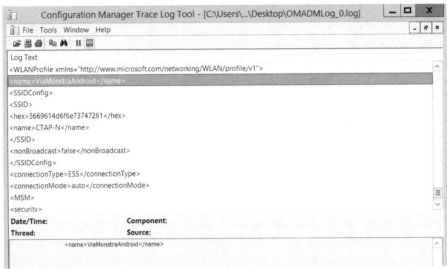

The OMADM log file provides valuable information about Wi-Fi profiles and other OMA-URI policies.

- **com.microsoft.intune.mam.managedAppName.log.** For each managed application, you have a log file with the name of the managed application. The log file is stored in a ZIP file. All you have to do is extract the file to get access to information about the managed application and the policies applied with the application.

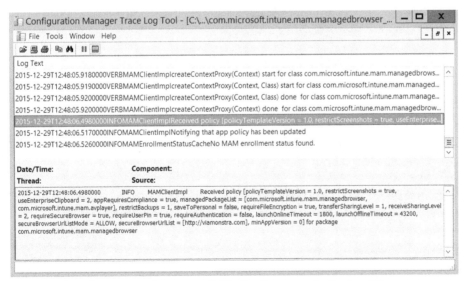

Managed application policies available in clear text in the log file.

You have a couple of options for accessing log files on Android devices. You either can email the files or connect the device to your computer and access them directly.

You can email the log files from the Company Portal's Settings page:

In **Settings**, tap **SEND DATA**. This launches the email application and attaches all the log files to the email message.

To access the log files via a direct connection, follow these steps:

1. Attach the device using a USB cable.

2. Open **<Device>\Phone\Android\data\com.microsoft.windowsintune.companyportal\files** and copy the log files.

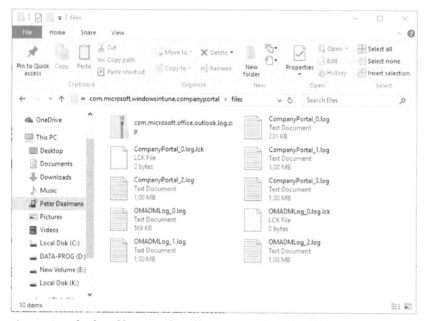

Accessing the log files on a locally connected Android device.

Real World Note: You can enable and disable verbose logging on Android devices from Settings. We highly encourage you to enable verbose while going through all of the exercises in this book.

iOS and Mac OS X

There is a slight difference in how you initiate a compliance check. Mac OS X does not (yet) offer a company portal; instead, you access the portal from a browser.

Compliance Check Mac OS X

1. On the MacBook, open Safari, navigate to **http://portal.manage.microsoft.com**, and sign in.

2. From the list of devices, select the MacBook and click **Check compliance**.

Performing a compliance check on a Mac OS X device.

Additional log information is stored in the system.log file. To access and view the information, follow these steps:

1. Open the **Console** application on the Mac OS X device.

2. From the list of files, select **system.log**.

3. In **Filter**, type **mdmclient**. You are presented with all the Intune information

iOS

Accessing diagnostic information on iOS devices is kind of cool. They have a built-in "shake the device" feature; all you have to do is shake the device to get the log files:

1. Open the **Company Portal** and shake the device. This opens the Diagnostics dialog box.

2. Tap **EMAIL**. The email message contains the companyportal.log file and a screenshot of the company portal.

If you ever need a good laugh, we encourage you to record a movie of yourself while using the "shake" feature to get the diagnostic log files. You'll be surprised how difficult it is to look cool while shaking an iPad!

Real World Note: On iOS devices, you can control the shake gesture and telemetry data from Settings / Comp Portal. Both settings are enabled by default.

You also can access log files using the following option:

1. Tap the user name in the upper right corner and select **About**.

2. From **About**, tap **Send Diagnostic Report**. An email message with the logs is created. It can be sent to the administrator for troubleshooting.

To synchronize policies and check compliance, follow these steps:

1. In the **Company Portal**, from **My Devices**, open the local iOS device.

2. Touch **Sync**. This initiates a compliance check and synchronizes the policies at the same time.

To access additional log files, you first need to connect the iOS device to a Mac computer:

1. Download and install **Xcode** from the **App Store**.

2. Connect the **iOS** device to the **Mac OS X** device.

3. Launch **Xcode** from the **Launchpad**.

4. Click **Window / Devices**.

5. Click the **iPhone**.

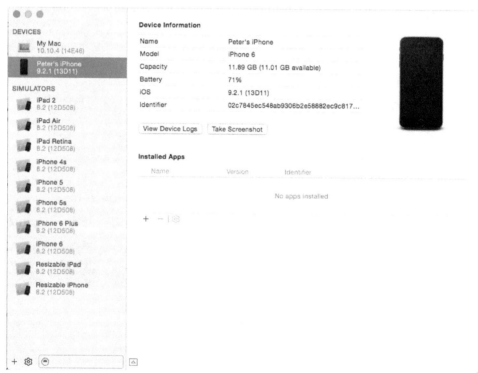

Click the iPhone to access the device logs.

6. Click **View Device Logs** and click **All Logs** to see the logs of processes that have issues.

7. Browse to the app process that is crashing and try to identify the issue. You can copy and paste the log text to a file on the computer, or right-click the process and select Export to export the log file.

Accessing the device logs.

Windows Mobile

For Windows Mobile, there is a specific Intune application, Field Medic, that is used to collect diagnostic data. Field Medic records system events that you can use to troubleshoot Windows Mobile issues. Field Medic uses profiles to define the data to be collected. You configure those profiles from the Advanced menu. You also can author custom profiles. A custom profile is a .wprp XML file as described in this TechNet article: https://msdn.microsoft.com/en-us/library/windows/hardware/hh448223.aspx.

The application also can give you detailed information about the device, such as memory, battery, network, and much more. It would be nice if all that information were part of the default inventory!

To configure and use the Field Medic application, follow these steps:

1. From the **Windows Store**, search for **Field Medic** and install the application.

2. Open the **Field Medic** application, open **Advanced**, and check out the different information you can log.

3. From the main window, click **Start Logging**. Actions from the Company Portal are now collected.

4. To generate some traffic:

    a. Open **Settings / Accounts / Work access / ViaMonstra** and tap **Sync** to generate some traffic.

    b. Open the **Company Portal**, select **MY DEVICES**, and tap **Check compliance**.

5. Back in the **Field Medic** application, tap **Stop Logging**, add a report title, and add the repro steps. The repro steps provide a short explanation of what you did while collecting data. Notice that you can include pictures in the report.

6. Reports are stored locally on the Windows Mobile device. You access the data by connecting the device to your computer and copying the files from **<Device>\Windows phone\Phone\Documents\FieldMedic**. You can open the files in **Windows Performance Analyzer**.

Chapter 7

Managing Devices and Data with Microsoft EMS Standalone

Managing the devices and their data is key when you think of the Microsoft Enterprise Mobility Suite. This chapter describes how to configure conditional access based, not only on identity, but also on the device and the state of the device.

Conditional Access

So, now that Microsoft Intune is configured, you need to configure conditional access for Exchange Online and SharePoint Online. This way devices that do not comply with the compliance policies or that are not enrolled into and secured by Microsoft Intune do not get access to the corporate resources.

With conditional access, you are able to check whether a device is allowed access to Exchange Online, on-premises Exchange, or SharePoint Online based on a compliance policy. If the device is compliant, then the user gets access to the corporate resources.

How Does Conditional Access Work?

The best way to describe conditional access is by looking at the following figure. In this figure, conditional access for Office 365 uses Azure Active Directory and Microsoft Intune to control the access.

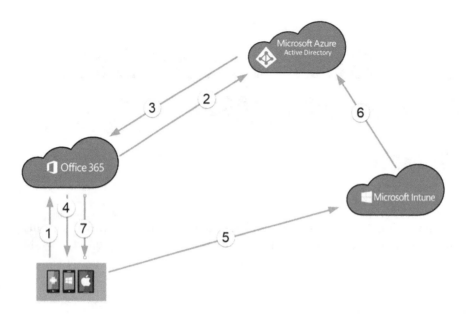

The conditional access for Office 365 process.

1. A user logs on to the mobile device and tries to configure email.

2. Office 365 checks with Azure Active Directory to see whether the device is managed and compliant.

3. Azure Active Directory returns the device state and in this case, sees the device is not yet managed by Microsoft Intune.

4. The device is placed into quarantine, and the user receives a quarantine email message with three steps that the user must walk through to get access to the mail in Office 365.

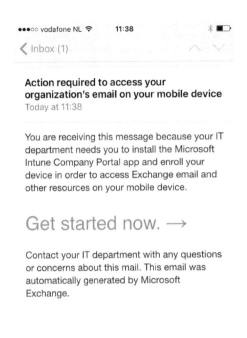

The user needs to enroll the device and check/remediate the compliance.

5. The device is enrolled into Microsoft Intune, and the compliance is remediated.

6. Microsoft Intune sets the device management and compliance status in Azure Active Directory.

7. The user triggers a compliance check, and if the device is compliant, access to email is granted.

When accessing SharePoint via the OneDrive App, the user does not receive an email message. Instead, the user is forced to enroll and make the device compliant before access to the files on SharePoint is granted. The enrollment process is described in Chapter 6.

The device needs to be enrolled and compliant before getting access to SharePoint Online.

Configure Compliance Policy

First, you need to be able to check whether devices are compliant. You do this by creating one or more compliance policies that are deployed to the users:

1. Go to the webpage **http://manage.microsoft.com** and log in with your administrative account.

2. In the **Microsoft Intune console**, go to **Policy and Compliance Policies**.

3. Click **Add** and create the policy with the information provided in the following table:

Setting	ViaMonstra Value	Your Value
Name	Secure Email	
Description		
Require a password to unlock mobile devices	Yes	
Allow simple passwords	No	
Minimum password length	6	
Required password type	Not configured	
Minimum number of character sets	Not configured	
Password quality	At least numeric	
Minutes of inactivity before password is required	15 minutes	

Setting	ViaMonstra Value	Your Value
Password expiration (days)	Not configured	
Remember password history	Not configured	
Prevent reuse of previous passwords	Not configured	
Require encryption on mobile device	Yes	
Email account must be managed by Intune	Not configured	
Select the email profile that must be managed by Intune	Not configured	
Require devices to be reported as healthy	Enabled	
Device must not be jailbroken or rooted	Enabled	
Minimum Windows Version	8.10	
Maximum Windows Version	Not configured	
Minimum Windows Phone or Windows 10 Mobile Version	8.10	
Maximum Windows Phone or Windows 10 Mobile Version	Not configured	
Minimum Android Version	4.4.2	
Maximum Android Version	Not configured	
Minimum iOS Version	7.1	
Maximum iOS Version	Not configured	

4. Click **Save** to store the compliance policy. In the **Deploy Policy: Secure Email** dialog box, click **Yes**.

5. Select **All Users**, click **Add**, and then click **OK** to deploy the compliance policy.

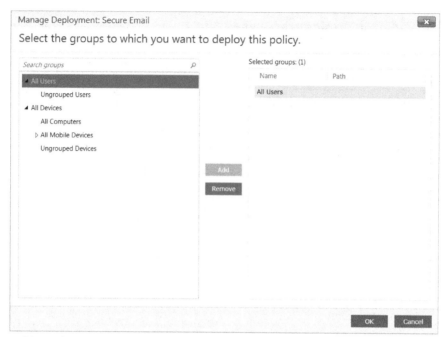

Adding the All Users group to the policy deployment list.

Configure Conditional Access for Exchange Online

1. Go to the webpage **http://manage.microsoft.com** and log in with your administrative account.

2. In the **Microsoft Intune console**, go to **Policy / Conditional Access / Exchange Online Policy**.

3. Select the **Enable conditional access policy** check box.

4. To use conditional access for apps that support modern authentication, select the supported device platforms: **iOS**, **Android**, and **Windows 10 Mobile**.

5. Also select also **Windows devices must meet the following requirements** and select **Devices must be domain joined or compliant**.

6. For Exchange ActiveSync mail apps, select **Require mobile devices to be compliant** and **Block access to email from devices that are not supported by Microsoft Intune**.

7. In the **Targeted Groups** field, click **Modify** and select the group **s**. Click **Add** and then **OK**.

Real World Note: EMS-enabled Users is a user group that is synced from the local Active Directory to the Azure Active Directory. If the group does not exist, create it in the local Active Directory. You also can use the default All Users option.

You can specify Exempted Groups to control who should not be controlled by conditional access. Members in these groups have access to email whether their device is enrolled into Intune or not.

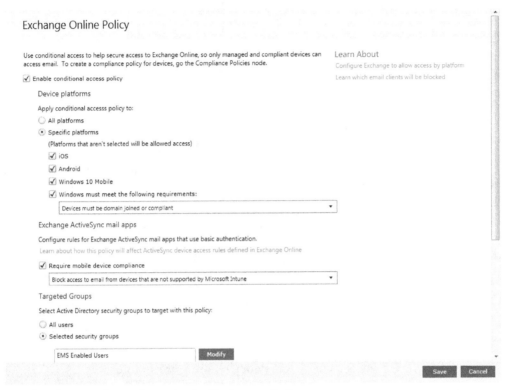

Configuring conditional access for Exchange Online.

8. Click **Save**.

Configure Conditional Access for SharePoint

1. Go to the webpage **http://manage.microsoft.com** and log in with your administrative account.

2. In the **Microsoft Intune console**, select **Policy / Conditional Access** and click **SharePoint Online Policy**.

3. Enable the check box to **Enable conditional access policy for SharePoint Online**.

4. To use conditional access for apps that support modern authentication, you need to select the supported device platforms: **iOS**, **Android**, and **Windows Mobile**.

5. Select also **Windows devices must meet the following requirements** and select **Devices must be domain joined or compliant**.

6. In the **Targeted Groups** field, select **All Users**.

179

Real World Note: By default, you want to block all noncompliant users from access to Exchange Online and SharePoint Online. If you want to do it selectively, do so by using a security group with all of your users who have access to Exchange Online and SharePoint Online. Forgetting to add someone to the group will give the user access without being compliant

You can use Exempted Groups when someone needs quick access to their email without having to enroll their device or check whether the device is compliant or not. ViaMonstra does not allow email access from devices that are not compliant.

7. Click **Save**.

Managing Devices Using Policies

Before you can enroll devices, you need to deploy and configure configuration policies; otherwise, devices will most likely not show as being compliant and users will not have access to their email and documents on SharePoint Online.

Read World Note: Microsoft Intune is enhanced constantly with new features and new policies that can be configured. See the latest policies via this URL: http://ref.ms/IntunePolicies.

Windows Phone Configuration Policy

1. Go to the webpage **http://manage.microsoft.com** and log in with your administrative account.

2. In the **Microsoft Intune console**, select **Policy / Configuration Policies**.

3. Click **Add** and select **Windows / General Configuration (Windows Phone 8.1 and later)**.

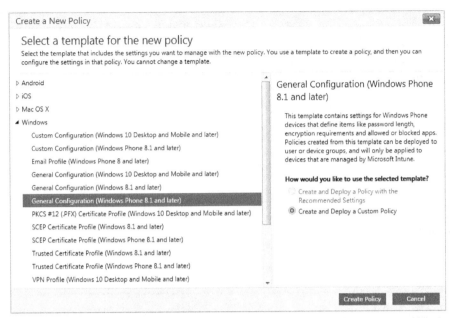

Selecting General Configuration (Windows Phone 8.1 and later).

4. Click **Create Policy** and supply the information listed in the following table:

Setting	ViaMonstra Value	Your Value
General		
Name	MDM Windows Phones	
Description	Policy for all Windows Phones	
Applicability		
Apply all configurations to Windows 10	Yes	
Security		
Require a password to unlock mobile devices	Yes	
Required password type	Numeric	
Minimum number of character sets	Not configured	
Minimum password length	6	
Allow simple passwords	Yes	
Number of repeated sign-in failures to allow before the device is wiped	6	

Setting	ViaMonstra Value	Your Value
Minutes of inactivity before password is required	15 minutes	
Password expiration (days)	Not configured	
Remember password history	Not configured	
Encryption		
Require encryption on mobile device	Yes	
System		
Allow Screen capture	Not configured	
Allow diagnostic data submission	Not configured	
Cloud		
Allow Microsoft account	Not configured	
Email		
Allow custom email accounts	Not configured	
Applications		
Allow web browser	Not configured	
Allow application store	Not configured	
Device Capabilities		
Allow Camera	Not configured	
Allow removable storage	Not configured	
Allow Wi-Fi	Not configured	
Allow Wi-Fi tethering	Enabled	
Allow automatic connection to free Wi-Fi hotspots	Not configured	
Allow Wi-Fi hotspots reporting	Not configured	
Allow geolocation	Not configured	
Allow NFC	Not configured	
Allow Bluetooth	Not configured	
Allow copy and paste	Not configured	
Complaint & Blocked Apps list for Windows Phone		
Manage settings for Windows Phone devices	Not configured	

5.   Click **Save Policy** after configuring the settings as described in the table.

6. In the **Do you want to deploy this policy now?** dialog box, click **Yes**.

7. Select **All Users**, click **Add**, and then click **OK**.

Windows 10 Configuration Policy

1. Go to the webpage **http://manage.microsoft.com** and log in with your administrative account.

2. In the **Microsoft Intune console**, select **Policy / Configuration Policies**.

3. Click **Add** and select **Windows / General Configuration (Windows 10 Desktop and Mobile and later)**.

4. Click **Create Policy** and supply the information listed in the following table:

Setting	ViaMonstra Value	Your Value
General		
Name	MDM Windows 10	
Description	Policy for all Windows 10 devices	
Security		
Require a password to unlock mobile devices	Yes	
Required password type	Numeric	
Minimum number of character sets	Not configured	
Minimum password length	6	
Number of repeated sign-in failures to allow before the device is wiped	6	
Minutes of inactivity before screen turns off	15 minutes	
Password expiration (days)	Not configured	
Remember password history	Not configured	
Allow picture password and pin	Not configured	
Require a password when device returns from idle state	Yes	
Encryption		
Require encryption on mobile device	Yes	
System		

Setting	ViaMonstra Value	Your Value
Allow Screen capture	Not configured	
Allow manual unenrollment	No	
Allow manual root certificate installation	Not configured	
Allow diagnostic data submission	Not configured	
Cloud		
Allow Microsoft account	Not configured	
Allow adding non-Microsoft accounts manually	Not configured	
Allow settings synchronization for Microsoft accounts	Not configured	
Microsoft Edge		
Allow web browser	Not configured	
Allow search suggestions in address bar	Not configured	
Allow sending intranet traffic to Internet Explorer	Not configured	
Allow do not track	Not configured	
Enable SmartScreen	Not configured	
Allow active scripting	Not configured	
Allow pop-ups	Not configured	
Allow cookies	Not configured	
Allow autofill	Not configured	
Allow Password Manager	Not configured	
Allow Enterprise Mode site list location	Not configured	
Apps		
Allow application store	Not configured	
Device Capabilities		
Allow Camera	Not configured	
Allow removable storage	Not configured	
Allow Wi-Fi	Not configured	
Allow internet sharing	Not configured	
Allow manual Wi-Fi configuration	Not configured	

Setting	ViaMonstra Value	Your Value
Allow automatic connection to free Wi-Fi hotspots	Not configured	
Allow geolocation	Not configured	
Allow NFC	Not configured	
Allow Bluetooth	Not configured	
Allow Bluetooth discoverable mode	Not configured	
Allow Bluetooth advertising	Not configured	
Allow phone reset	Not configured	
Features		
Allow copy and paste	Not configured	
Allow voice recording	Not configured	
Allow Cortana	Yes	
Allow action center notifications	Yes	
Updates		
Allow automatic updates	Notify update	
Allow pre-release features	Yes – Settings only	

5.   Click **Save Policy** after configuring the settings as described in the table.

6.   In the **Do you want to deploy this policy now?** dialog box, click **Yes**.

7.   Select **All Users**, click **Add**, and then click **OK**.

Android Configuration Policy

1.   Go to the webpage **http://manage.microsoft.com** and log in with your administrative account.

2.   In the **Microsoft Intune console**, select **Policy / Configuration Policies**.

3.   Click **Add** and select **Android / General Configuration (Android 4 and later, Samsung KNOX Standard 4.0 and later)**.

4.   Click **Create Policy** and supply the information listed in the following table:

Setting up the Android configuration policy.

Setting	ViaMonstra Value	Your Value
General		
Name	MDM Android Devices	
Description	Policy for all Android Devices	
Security		
Require a password to unlock mobile devices	Yes	
Minimum password length	6	
Number of repeated sign-in failures to allow before the device is wiped	6	
Minutes of inactivity before screen turns off	15	
Password expiration (days)	Not configured	
Remember password history		
Password quality	At least numeric	
Allow fingerprint unlock	Not configured	
Allow Smart Lock and other trust agents	No	

Setting	ViaMonstra Value	Your Value
Encryption		
Require encryption on mobile device	Yes	
Require encryption on storage cards	No	
System		
Allow screen capture	Not configured	
Allow diagnostic data submission	Not configured	
Allow factory reset	Not configured	
Cloud		
Allow Google Backup	No	
Allow Google account auto sync	Yes	
Browser		
Allow web browser	Not configured	
Allow autofill	Not configured	
Allow pop-up blocker	Not configured	
Allow cookies	Not configured	
Allow active scripting	Not configured	
Apps		
Allow Google Play Store	Not configured	
Device Capabilities		
Allow Camera	Yes	
Allow removable storage	Yes	
Allow Wi-Fi	Allowed	
Allow Wi-Fi tethering	Enabled	
Allow geolocation	Yes	
Allow NFC	Yes	
Allow Bluetooth	Yes	
Allow Power Off	Not configured	
Allow voice roaming	Not configured	
Allow data roaming	Not configured	

Setting	ViaMonstra Value	Your Value
Allow SMS/MMS messaging	Not configured	
Allow voice assistant	Not configured	
Allow voice dialing	Not configured	
Allow copy and paste	No	
Allow clipboard share between applications	No	
Allow YouTube	Not configured	
Complaint & Noncompliant Apps list for Android		
Manage settings for Android devices	Not configured	
Kiosk		
Select a managed app that will be allowed to run when the devices is in kiosk mode	Not configured	
Allow volume buttons	Not configured	
Allow screen sleep wake button	Not configured	

5. Click **Save Policy** after configuring the settings as described in the table.

6. In the **Do you want to deploy this policy now?** dialog box, click **Yes**.

7. Select **All Users**, click **Add**, and then click **OK**.

iOS Configuration Policy

1. Go to the webpage **http://manage.microsoft.com** and log in with your administrative account.

2. In the **Microsoft Intune console**, select **Policy / Configuration Policies**.

3. Click **Add** and select **iOS / General Configuration (iOS 7.1 and later)**.

4. Click **Create Policy** and supply the information listed in the following table:

Setting	ViaMonstra Value	Your Value
General		
Name	MDM iOS Devices	
Description	Policy for all iOS Devices	

Setting	ViaMonstra Value	Your Value
Security		
Require a password to unlock mobile devices	Yes	
Required password type	Numeric	
Minimum number complex characters required in password	Not configured	
Minimum password length	6	
Allow simple passwords	Yes	
Number of repeated sign-in failures to allow before the device is wiped	6	
Minutes of inactivity before password is required	15 minutes	
Password expiration (days)	Not configured	
Remember password history	Not configured	
Minutes of inactivity before screen turns off	15 minutes	
Allow fingerprint unlock	Yes	
System		
Allow Screenshot	Yes	
Allow control center in lock screen	No	
Allow notification view in lock screen	No	
Allow today view in lock screen	Yes	
Allow Untrusted TLS certificates prompt	Yes	
Allow diagnostic data submission	No	
Allow passbook while locked	No	
Cloud		
Allow backup to iCloud	No	
Allow documents sync to iCloud	No	
Allow Photo Stream sync to iCloud	No	
Require encrypted backup	Not configured	
Applications		
Allow Safari	Not configured	

Setting	ViaMonstra Value	Your Value
Allow autofill	Not configured	
Allow pop-up blocker	Not configured	
Allow cookies	Not configured	
Allow java scripting	Not configured	
Allow fraud warning	Not configured	
Allow application store	Not configured	
Require a password to access application store	Not configured	
Allow in-app purchases	Not configured	
Allow managed document in other unmanaged apps	No	
Allow unmanaged document in other managed apps	Yes	
Allow video conferencing	Not configured	
Allow adult content in media store	Not configured	
Allow adding game center friends	Not configured	
Allow multiplayer gaming	Not configured	
Device Capabilities		
Allow Camera	Not configured	
Allow voice roaming	Not configured	
Allow data roaming	Not configured	
Allow global background fetch while roaming	Not configured	
Allow Siri	Not configured	
Allow Siri while device is locked	Not configured	
Allow voice dialing	Not configured	
Complaint & Noncompliant Apps List for iOS		
Manage settings for iOS devices	Not configured	
Kiosk		
Select a managed app that will be allowed to run when the devices is in kiosk mode	Not configured	
Allow Touch	Not configured	
Allow screen rotation	Not configured	

Setting	ViaMonstra Value	Your Value
Allow volume buttons	Not configured	
Allow ringer switch	Not configured	
Allow screen sleep wake button	Not configured	
Allow auto lock	Not configured	
Enable mono audio	Not configured	
Enable voice over	Not configured	
Enable zoom	Not configured	
Enable invert colors	Not configured	
Enable assistive touch	Not configured	
Enable speech selection	Not configured	
Enrollment		
Allow Activation Lock when the device is in supervised mode	Not Configured	

5. Click **Save Policy** after configuring the settings as described in the table.

6. In the **Do you want to deploy this policy now?** dialog box, click **Yes**.

Click Yes to deploy the configuration policy.

7. Select **All Users**, click **Add**, and then click **OK**.

Mac OS X Configuration Policy

1. Go to the webpage **http://manage.microsoft.com** and log in with your administrative account.

2. In the **Microsoft Intune console**, select **Policy / Configuration Policies**.

3. Click **Add** and select **Mac OS X / General Configuration (Mac OS X 10.9 and later).**

4. Click **Create Policy** and supply the information listed in the following table:

Setting	ViaMonstra Value	Your Value
General		
Name	MDM OS X Devices	
Description	Policy for all OS X Devices	
Security		
Require a password to unlock mobile devices	Yes	
Required password type	Alphanumeric	
Number of complex characters required in password	Not configured	
Minimum password length	6	
Allow simple passwords	No	
Minutes of inactivity before password is required	15 minutes	
Password expiration (days)	Not configured	
Remember password history	Not configured	
Minutes of inactivity before screensaver activates	15 minutes	
Compliant & Noncompliant App List for Mac OS X		
Managed setting for device	Not configured	
Report noncompliance when user install the listed apps	Not configured	
Report noncompliance when users install apps which are not listed	Not configured	
Apps list		

5. Click **Save Policy** after configuring the settings as described in the table.

6. In the **Do you want to deploy this policy now?** dialog box, click **Yes**.

7. Select **All Mobile Devices**, click **Add**, and then click **OK**.

Apple Configurator

Not all settings that Apple allows you to preconfigure or manage are manageable via the templates in Microsoft Intune. With Microsoft Intune, however, you are able to deploy configuration profiles created with the Apple Configurator.

How to Create a Profile with the Apple Configurator

To use the Apple Configurator, you need a Mac OS X computer. Unfortunately, no Windows version of the Apple Configurator is available to create profiles for iOS and Mac OS X devices.

1. Go to the Mac OS X device and start the **Apple Configurator**, which you are able to download from the Apple Store.

2. On the **Prepare** tab, supply the name **EMSKings**.

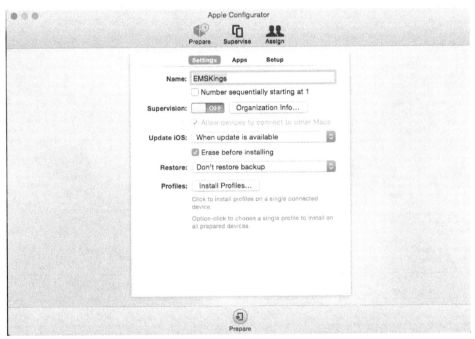

Preparing the configuration profile.

3. Click the **Supervise** tab and click the **plus sign** (+) and choose **Create New Profile**.

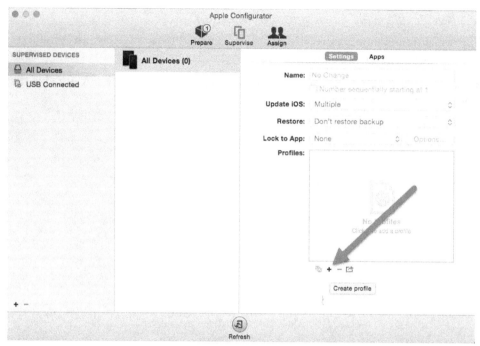

Creating a new profile for iOS devices.

4. Create a profile with the following settings (only the changes are documented):

Settings	ViaMonstra Value	Your Value
General		
Name	EMSKings	
Organization	ViaMonstra	
Description	This profile is created to manage Apple iOS devices that are connecting to the corporate environment.	
Consent Message	Please be patient. ViaMonstra is configuring and securing your device.	
Security - controls when the profile can be removed	With Authorization	
Security - Authorization password	P@ssw0rd	

Settings	ViaMonstra Value	Your Value
Security - Automatically remove profile	Never	
Restrictions		
Allow voice dialing when device is locked	Disabled	
Allow Siri while device is locked	Disabled	
Allow in-app purchase	Disabled	
Require iTunes Store password for all purchases	Enabled	

5. Click **Save** after configuring the changes described in the table.

6. Select the created profile and click the **Export Profile** button to export the XML file (.mobileconfig) that you can import into Microsoft Intune as a Custom Configuration policy.

Exporting the new profile.

7. Click **Save** to store the file on the local computer or a share where you can access it from a computer running the Microsoft Intune console.

Deploy a Custom Profile

Next, you need to create a custom policy that holds the profile created with the Apple Configurator:

1. Go to the webpage **http://manage.microsoft.com** and log in with your administrative account.

2. In the **Microsoft Intune console**, select **Policy / Configuration Policies**.

3. Click **Add** and select **iOS / iOS Custom Policy**.

4. Click **Create Policy** and supply a **Name** and **Description** for the policy.

5. Supply a **Custom configuration profile name** and click **Import**.

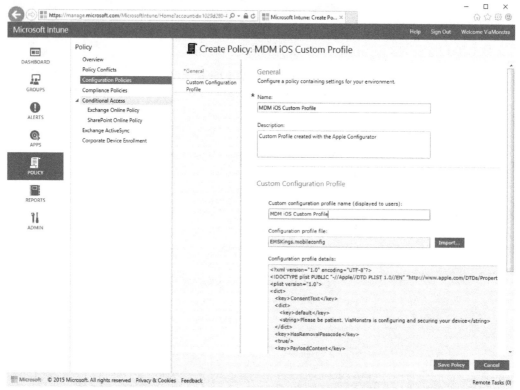

Create the custom profile for iOS devices

6. Locate the newly created **.MOBILECONFIG** file (**EMSKings.mobileconfig**) and click **Open**.

7. Click **Save Policy** and then click **Yes**.

8. Select **All Devices / All Mobile Devices / All Direct Managed Devices** and click **Add**. Click **OK** to deploy the policy.

MDM Profiles

Microsoft Intune allows you to manage and deploy different kinds of profiles and configurations. This section discusses email, VPN, Wi-Fi, and certificate profiles.

Email Profiles

Microsoft Intune allows you to preconfigure the email profile that you can deploy to the different operating systems. Because all of ViaMonstra's email is in Office 365, the email profile must be configured and pushed by Microsoft Intune. When a device is selectively wiped, the managed email profile with its data also is removed.

1. Go to the webpage **http://manage.microsoft.com** and log in with your administrative account.

2. In the **Microsoft Intune console**, select **Policy / Configuration Policies** and click **Add**.

3. Expand **iOS** and click **Email Profile (iOS 7.1 and later)**.

4. Click **Create Policy** and create a Wi-Fi profile with the following settings:

Setting	ViaMonstra Value	Your Value
Exchange ActiveSync		
Name	MailPrf iOS	
Description	Allows access to ViaMonstra email	
Host	outlook.office365.com	
Account Name	ViaMonstra Email	
Username	User Principal Name	
Email address	Primary SMTP Address	
Authentication Method (iOS and Android Only)	Username and Password	
Use S/MIME (iOS and Android Only)	Not selected	
Synchronization Settings		
Number of days of email to synchronize	One Week	
Sync Schedule (Android, Windows Phone and Windows 10 Desktop and Mobile only)	Manual	

Setting	ViaMonstra Value	Your Value
Use SSL	Selected	
Allow messages to be moved to other email accounts (iOS only)	Not selected	
Allow email to be send from third party applications (iOS only)	Not selected	
Synchronize recently used email addresses (iOS only)	Not selected	
Content type to synchronize (Android and Windows Phone, Windows 10 Desktop and Mobile only)	Email (selected) Contacts (selected) Calendar (selected) Tasks (selected) Notes (not selected)	

5.   Click **Save Policy** and then click **Yes** to deploy the policy to the **All Exchange Online Users** group. Click **OK**.

6.   Repeat the steps for the Android email profile: click **Add**, expand **Android**, and click **Email Profile for Samsung KNOX Standard (4.0 and later)**.

7.   Click **Create Policy** and create the email profile with the same settings as in the table but with the name **MailPrf Android**.

8.   Click **Save Policy** and then click **Yes** to deploy the policy to the **All Exchange Online Users** group. Click **OK**.

9.   Repeat the steps for the Windows Phone email profile: click **Add**, expand **Windows**, and click **Email Profile (Windows Phone 8 and later)**.

10. Click **Create Policy** and create the email profile with the same settings as in the table but with the name **MailPrf Windows Phone**.

11. Click **Save Policy** and then click **Yes** to deploy the policy to the **All Exchange Online Users** group. Click **OK**.

12. Repeat the steps for the Windows Phone email profile: click **Add**, expand **Windows**, and click **Email Profile (Windows 10 Desktop and Mobile and later)**.

13. Click **Create Policy** and create the email profile with the same settings as in the table but with the name **MailPrf Windows 10 Desktop and Mobile.**

14. Click **Save Policy** and then click **Yes** to deploy the policy to the **All Exchange Online Users** group. Click **OK**.

Certificate Profiles

To deploy certificates to mobile devices, you need an NDES infrastructure. Appendix E describes how to install and configure NDES for ViaMonstra.

Create a Trusted Certificate Profile

After a successful enrollment, the connector is configured correctly and ready to use. The first thing you need to do is create a Trusted Certificate Profile with the ViaMonstra Root CA certificate. The certificate (corp-DC01-CA.cer) is exported in Appendix E.

1. Go to the webpage **http://manage.microsoft.com** and log in with your administrative account.

2. In the **Microsoft Intune console**, select **Policy / Add Policy**.

3. Expand **iOS**, select **Trusted Certificate Profile (iOS 7.1 and later)**, and click **Create Policy**.

4. Supply a name and description, and then import the **corp-DC01-CA.cer** file.

5. Click **Save Policy**.

Creating the Certificate Authority profile.

6. Click **Yes** in the **Do you want to deploy this policy now?** dialog box.

7. Select **All Users**, click **Add**, and then click **OK**.

Create a SCEP Certificate Profile

After creating a profile for the Root CA certificate, you need to create the SCEP Certificate profile:

1. Go to the webpage **http://manage.microsoft.com** and log in with your administrative account.

2. In the **Microsoft Intune console**, select **Policy / Add Policy**.

3. Expand **iOS**, select **SCEP Certificate Profile (iOS 7.1 and later)**, and click **Create Policy**.

4. Supply the information in the following table:

Setting	Value	Your Value
Name	SCEP-iOS User Certificate	
Description	Cert used for user authentication of app X	
SCEP server URL	https://ndes01.corp.viamonstra. com/certsrv/mscep/mscep.dll	
Subject Alternative Name	User principal name (UPN) - checked	
Certificate validity period	1 Year	
Key usage	Digital Signature – checked	
Key size (bits)	2048	
Extended Key Usage	Secure Email	
Select Root Certificate	CERT-iOS CA Profile	

5. Click **Save Policy**, and in the **Do you want to deploy this policy now?** dialog box, click **Yes**.

6. Select **All Users**, click **Add**, and then click **OK**.

Check the Certificate on the Device, on the CA, and in Microsoft Intune

In this example, an iOS device for user tim@emskings.com is used.

1. In **iOS**, go to **Settings**.

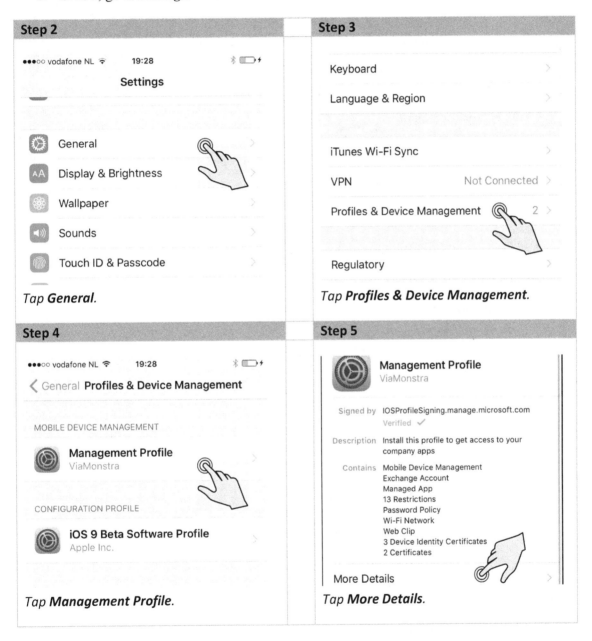

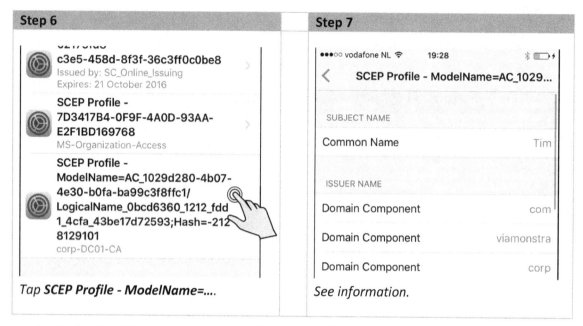

Step 6	Step 7

Step 6

c3e5-458d-8f3f-36c3ff0c0be8
Issued by: SC_Online_Issuing
Expires: 21 October 2016

SCEP Profile -
7D3417B4-0F9F-4A0D-93AA-
E2F1BD169768
MS-Organization-Access

SCEP Profile -
ModelName=AC_1029d280-4b07-
4e30-b0fa-ba99c3f8ffc1/
LogicalName_0bcd6360_1212_fdd
1_4cfa_43be17d72593;Hash=-212
8129101
corp-DC01-CA

*Tap **SCEP Profile - ModelName=…***

Step 7

•••○○ vodafone NL 🤝   19:28   ⚡ ▭ ⚡

‹   SCEP Profile - ModelName=AC_1029…

SUBJECT NAME

Common Name   Tim

ISSUER NAME

Domain Component   com

Domain Component   viamonstra

Domain Component   corp

See information.

2. In the **Certificate Authority**, go to **Issued certificates** and double-click the just issued certificate.

The certificate issued to Tim.

3. In the **Microsoft Intune console**, select **Reports / Certificate Compliance Reports**.

4. Click **View Report** to see all issued certificates for all users and all devices.

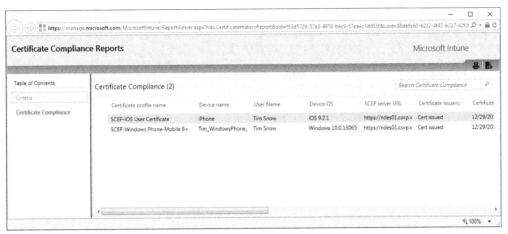

All certificates issued by the local CA in combination with the NDES server.

VPN Profiles

ViaMonstra uses a VPN solution to which mobile devices are able to connect. You can create VPN profiles for every platform supported by Microsoft Intune:

- Android 4 and later

- iOS 7.1 and later

- Mac OS X 10.9 and later

- Windows 10 (Desktop and Mobile) and later

- Windows 8.1

- Windows Phone 8.1

To configure a VPN profile, follow these steps:

1. Go to the webpage **http://manage.microsoft.com** and log in with your administrative account.

2. In the **Microsoft Intune console**, select **Policy / Configuration Policies** and click **Add**.

3. Expand **Android** and click **VPN Profile (Android 4 and later)**. The properties may vary based on the configured connection type and not all connection types are available for every operating system. In this example, an Android device is used.

Setting	ViaMonstra Value	Your Value
Name	VPN Android	
Description	ViaMonstra VPN Profile for Android	
VPN connection name	ViaMonstra VPN	

Setting	ViaMonstra Value	Your Value
Connection type	Cisco AnyConnect	
VPN Server description	ViaMonstra VPN	
Server IP address or FQDN	vpn.viamonstra.com	
Send all network traffic through the VPN Connection	Selected	
Authentication method	Certificates	
Remember the user credentials	Selected	
Select a client certificate for client authentication (certificate only)	Select the cert profile created earlier	
iOS Only: Per App VPN	Selected	
iOS + Mac OS X Only: Automatically detect proxy settings	Not selected	
iOS + Mac OS X Only: Use automatic configuration script	Not selected	
iOS + Mac OS X Only: Use proxy server	Not selected	

4. Click **Save Policy** and then click **Yes** to deploy the policy to the **All Users** group.

5. Repeat steps 2–4 for iOS and Mac OS X.

Wi-Fi Profiles

Personally owned mobile devices are allowed to connect to a VIAGUEST Wi-Fi network that is available in all ViaMonstra offices. Devices that are enrolled into Microsoft Intune must receive a Wi-Fi profile that connects automatically to the VIAGUEST network.

1. Go to the webpage **http://manage.microsoft.com** and log in with your administrative account.

2. In the **Microsoft Intune console**, select **Policy / Configuration Policies** and click **Add**.

3. Expand **Android** and click **Wi-Fi Profile (Android 4 and later)**.

4. Click **Create Policy** and create the Wi-Fi profile with the following settings:

Setting	ViaMonstra Value	Your Value
Name	VIAGUEST_Android	
Description	Allows access to the ViaMonstra Guest Wi-Fi network	
Network Name	VIAGUEST	
SSID	VIAGUEST	
Connect automatically when this network is in range	Selected	
Connect when the network is not broadcasting its name (SSID)	Selected	
Security Type	No authentication	
(Optional) EAP Type	Not configured	
(Optional) Select root certificate for server validation)	Not configured	
(Optional) Authentication	Not configured	
Proxy settings for this Wi-Fi connection (iOS and Mac OS X only)	Not configured	

5. Click **Save Policy** and then click **Yes** to deploy the policy to the **All Users** group.

6. Repeat the steps for the iOS Wi-Fi profile. Click **Add**, expand **iOS**, and click **Wi-Fi Profile (iOS 7.1 and later)**.

7. Click **Create Policy** and create the Wi-Fi profile with the same settings as in the table but with the name **VIAGUEST_iOS**.

8. Click **Save Policy** and then click **Yes** to deploy the policy to the **All Users** group.

9. Do the same for the OS X Wi-Fi profile. Click **Add**, expand **Mac OS X**, and click **Wi-Fi Profile (Mac OS X 10.9 and later)**.

10. Click **Create Policy** and create the Wi-Fi profile with the same settings as in the preceding table but with the name **VIAGUEST_OSX**.

11. Click **Save Policy** and then click **Yes** to deploy the policy to the **All Users** group.

Mobile Applications

Microsoft Intune provides the capability to use the Company Store to provide users with a collection of approved applications. Those "approved" apps can live in the stores or not, and they can be developed by software vendors or your own software development department. Microsoft Intune allows the deployment of any of these. In addition to the native apps that need to be installed, you also can deploy web apps with Microsoft Intune.

Deep-Linked Apps

Deep-linked apps are apps that live in the different app stores like the Windows Phone, Google Play, and Apple App Stores. The IT department can use deep-linked apps to point users to the company's preferred apps. The downside is that the users need to configure an account that has access to the app store. In the examples that follow, you create deep-linked apps for Twitter in Microsoft Intune for all the different mobile platforms.

Android

1. Go to the webpage **http://manage.microsoft.com** and log in with your administrative account.

2. In the **Microsoft Intune console**, select **Apps / Apps** and click **Add App**.

3. Supply your administrator credentials and click **Sign in**.

4. Click **Next**, and for **Select how this software is made available to devices**, select **External Link**.

5. Open a different **Internet Explorer** (or other browser that supports Silverlight) window, and enter **http://ref.ms/androidtwitter**. You are redirected to Twitter in the Google Play store. Select the URL and copy it.

6. Paste the URL in the **Specify the URL** field.

7. Click **Next** and supply the information to describe the software as shown in the following table:

Setting	Value
Publisher	Twitter
Name	Twitter for Android
Description	Twitter app approved by ViaMonstra
Category	Other Apps
Display this as a featured app and highlight it in the company portal	Selected

8. Click **Next**.

9. Review the information about the software that will be added to Microsoft Intune and click **Upload**.

10. Click **Close**.

iOS

1. Go to the webpage http://manage.microsoft.com and log in with your administrative account.

2. In the **Microsoft Intune console**, select **Apps / Apps** and click **Add App**.

3. Supply your administrator credentials and click **Sign in**.

4. Click **Next**, and for **Select how this software is made available to devices**, select **Managed iOS App from the App Store**.

5. Open a different **Internet Explorer** window and enter **http://ref.ms/iostwitter**. You are redirected to Twitter in the Apple App Store. Select the URL and copy it.

6. Paste the URL in the **Specify the URL** field.

7. Click **Next** and supply the information to describe the software as shown in the following table:

Setting	Value
Publisher	Twitter
Name	Twitter for iOS
Description	Twitter app approved by ViaMonstra
Category	Other Apps
Display this as a featured app and highlight it in the company portal	Selected

8. Click **Next**.

9. Leave **Mobile device type** with the default value, or select **iPad** and **iPhone/iPod Touch**. Then click **Next**.

10. Review the information about the software that will be added to Microsoft Intune and click **Upload**.

11. Click **Close**.

Windows Phone and Windows

1. Go to the webpage **http://manage.microsoft.com** and log in with your administrative account.

2. In the **Microsoft Intune console**, select **Apps / Apps** and click **Add App**.

3. Supply your administrator credentials and click **Sign in**.

4. Click **Next**, and for **Select how this software is made available to devices**, select **External Link**.

5. Open a different **Internet Explorer** window and enter **http://ref.ms/wintwitter**. You are redirected to Twitter in the Microsoft Windows Phone Store. Select the URL and copy it.

6. Paste the URL in the **Specify the URL** field.

7. Click **Next** and supply the information to describe the software as shown in the following table:

Setting	Value
Publisher	Twitter
Name	Twitter for Windows Phone
Description	Twitter app approved by ViaMonstra
Category	Other Apps
Display this as a featured app and highlight it in the company portal	Selected

8. Click **Next**.

9. Change **Mobile device type** to **Windows Phone** and click **Next**.

   The reason why Windows 8 or later also is listed is that the app can be installed on both Windows Phone and Windows 8 or later.

10. Review the information about the software that will be added to Microsoft Intune and click **Upload**.

11. Click **Close**. Repeat the steps with the name **Twitter for Windows** and select **Windows 8 or later** as the mobile device type.

Native Apps

Native apps in Intune are called *software installers*. Intune supports deploying and installing software for several different operating system platforms. For ViaMonstra in this book, only the mobile apps are covered.

Installing apps for other platforms must be treated differently and different versions of the apps need to be acquired.

Android App Package

Android is an open source operating system and an open platform, so there is a lot of diversity and numerous of ways apps can be acquired. The apps can normally be acquired from the Google Play store, but also from dozens of websites or developers themselves. In this example, you download

Adobe Acrobat Reader from the Adobe website so you are sure that the file is safe to use and because the app is free and no license requirements are needed.

1. Go to **http://ref.ms/getadobereader** and select **Android** in **Step 1** on the Adobe Acrobat Reader DC website.

2. Select your language in **Step 2** and select the latest version in **Step 3**. Click **Download now** to get the APK file.

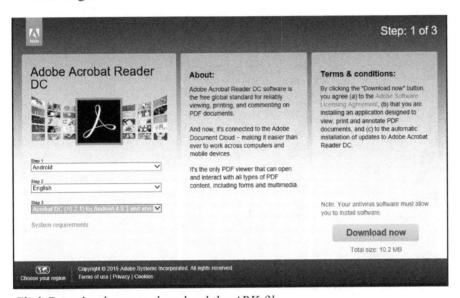

Click Download now to download the APK file.

3. Save the ZIP file and store it on a location where you are able to access it from the Microsoft Intune console. Rename the ZIP file to APK.

4. Go to the webpage **http://manage.microsoft.com** and log in with your administrative account.

5. In the **Microsoft Intune console**, select **Apps** and click **Add Apps** in the task pane.

Signing in to Microsoft Intune.

6. Supply your administrator credentials and click **Sign in**.

7. Click **Next** and for **Select how this software is made available to devices**, select **Software Installer**. Then select **App Package for Android (*.apk file)** and click **Browse**.

8. Select the **APK** file, click **Open**, and then click **Next**.

9. Supply the software description as show in the following table and click **Next**:

Setting	Value
Publisher	Adobe
Name	Adobe Reader for Android
Description	Reader for PDF files
Category	Productivity
Display this as a featured app and highlight it in the company portal	Selected

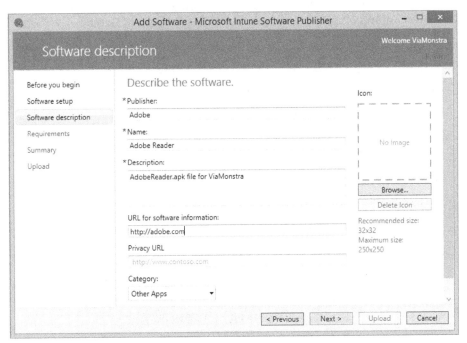

Supplying the information about the app.

10. Select **4.0.3 or later** (the downloaded file supports only 4.0.3 or later) and click **Next**.

11. Review the summary and click **Upload**.

12. Click **Close** after the upload to Microsoft Intune completes successfully.

iOS App Package

Downloading an iOS app package is different. The only safe way is to use iTunes to download the file and copy it from the iTunes folder on the computer.

1. Go to **http://ref.ms/iosadobereader** and click **View in iTunes**. Click **Allow** to let the website open a program on your computer.

2. After iTunes has started, click **Download**. (Depending on your iTunes settings, you may need to sign in first.) After Adobe Acrobat Reader downloads, click **My Apps**. Select **Adobe Acrobat Reader** and right-click the app.

Selecting Show in Windows Explorer.

3. Click **Show in Windows Explorer** and copy the **IPA** file to the desktop.

4. Go to the webpage **http://manage.microsoft.com** and log in with your administrative account.

5. In the **Microsoft Intune console**, select **Apps** and click **Add Apps** in the task pane.

6. Supply your administrator credentials and click **Sign in**.

7. Click **Next**, and for **Select how this software is made available to devices**, select **Software Installer**. Then select **App Package for iOS (*.ipa file)** and click **Browse**.

8. Select the **IPA** file, click **Open**, and then click **Next**.

9. Supply the required information as shown in the following table and click **Next**:

Setting	Value
Publisher	Adobe
Name	Adobe Reader for iOS
Description	Reader for PDF files
Category	Productivity
Display this as a featured app and highlighted it in the company portal	Selected

10. Supply the minimum version of the supported operating system and on which device type the app is supported. Click **Next**.

11. Review the software that is being uploaded to Microsoft Intune and click **Upload**.

12. Click **Close** after the app uploads successfully.

Real World Note: Be aware that you cannot deploy every iOS app like this. The apps may be protected for sideloading or hooked to your Apple ID, which results in a deployment failure.

Web Apps

When you deploy a web app, a shortcut to the web app's URL is placed in the menu or home screen of the device.

1. Go to the webpage **http://manage.microsoft.com** and log in with your administrative account.

2. In the **Microsoft Intune console**, select **Apps** and click **Add Apps** in the task pane.

3. Supply your administrator credentials and click **Sign in**.

4. Click **Next**, and for **Select how this software is made available to devices**, select **External Link**. Then supply the URL that needs to be deployed, for instance **http://emskings.com**, and click **Next**.

5. Supply the information in the table and click **Next**:

Setting	Value
Publisher	ViaMonstra
Name	EMSKings
Description	Link to the corporate EMSKings website
Category	Business
Display this as a featured app and highlighted it in the company portal	Checked

6. After reviewing the external link, click **Upload**.

Deploying the Apps

In the preceding section, you added a lot of applications in Microsoft Intune. Without deploying them to groups of users in Microsoft Intune, nothing actually happens. In the following steps, you see how to deploy the created apps:

1. Go to the webpage **http://manage.microsoft.com** and log in with your administrative account.

2. In the **Microsoft Intune console**, select **Apps / Apps** and select the **Adobe Reader for iOS** application. Click **Manage Deployment**.

3. Select the group **SW_Adobe_Reader_Install** and click **Add**. Click **Next** to configure the deployment action.

4. Select **Required Install** and click **Next**.

5. Click **Finish** on the **VPN Profile** page.

6. Repeat the steps for all the other apps you added with the following deployment settings:

App name	Intune Group	Deployment
Twitter for Android	SW_Preferred_Apps	Available Install
Twitter for iOS	SW_Preferred_Apps	Required Install
Twitter for Windows	SW_Preferred_Apps	Available Install
Twitter for Windows Phone	SW_Preferred_Apps	Available Install
EMSKings	SW_Preferred_Apps	Required Install
Adobe Reader for Android	SW_Adobe_Reader_Install	Available Install
Adobe Reader for Windows	SW_Adobe_Reader_Install	Available Install

App name	Intune Group	Deployment
Adobe Reader for Windows Phone	SW_Adobe_Reader_Install	Available Install

Uninstalling Apps

With Microsoft Intune, you also are able to uninstall an application. Without deploying the Uninstall action to groups of users in Microsoft Intune, nothing actually happens.

1. Go to the webpage **http://manage.microsoft.com** and log in with your administrative account.

2. In the **Microsoft Intune console**, select **Apps / Apps** and select the **Adobe Reader for iOS** application. Click **Manage Deployment**.

3. Select the group **SW_Adobe_Reader_Uninstall** and click **Add**. Click **Next** to configure the deployment action.

4. Select **Uninstall** and click **Next**.

Selecting Uninstall as a deployment action.

5. Click **Finish** on the **VPN Profile** page.

6. Repeat the steps for all the other apps you added, using the following deployment settings:

App name	Intune Group	Deployment Action
Adobe Reader for Android	SW_Adobe_Reader_Uninstall	Uninstall

Managed Apps

Microsoft Intune is able to secure applications with mobile application management (MAM) policies. "Managed apps" can be deep-linked apps but also custom LOB apps that support the Microsoft Intune SDK.

Configure MAM Policies

ViaMonstra wants to use the Office suite that is provided via Google Play and the Apple App Store.

1. Go to the webpage **http://manage.microsoft.com** and log in with your administrative account.

2. In the **Microsoft Intune console**, select **Policy / Configuration Policies** and click **Add**.

3. Expand **Software** and click **Mobile Application Management Policy (iOS 7.1 and later)**.

4. Select **Create a Custom Policy** and click **Create Policy**.

5. Configure the mobile application policy as shown in the following table:

Setting	ViaMonstra Value	Your Value
Name	MAM iOS Office	
Description		
Restrict web content to display in the Managed Browser	Yes	
Prevent iTunes and iCloud backups	Yes	
Allow app to transfer data to other apps	Policy Managed Apps	
Allow app to receive data from other apps	Any App	
Prevent "Save As"	Yes	
Restrict cut, copy, paste with other apps	Policy Managed Apps with Paste In	
Require simple PIN for access	Yes	
Number of attempts before PIN reset	5	
Require corporate credentials for access	No	

Setting	ViaMonstra Value	Your Value
Require device compliance with corporate policy for access	Yes	
Recheck the access requirements after (minutes)	Timeout: 30 Offline grace period: 720	
Encrypt app data	When device is locked	

6. Click **Save Policy** to store the new MAM policy.

You need to configure the same kind of MAM policy for Android.

1. In the **Microsoft Intune console**, select **Policy / Configuration Policies** and click **Add**.

2. Expand **Software** and click **Mobile Application Management Policy (Android 4 and later)**.

3. Select **Create a Custom Policy** and click **Create Policy**.

4. Configure the mobile application policy as shown in the following table:

Setting	ViaMonstra Value	Your Value
Name	MAM Android Office	
Description		
Restrict web content to display in the Managed Browser	Yes	
Prevent Android backups	Yes	
Allow app to transfer data to other apps	Policy Managed Apps	
Allow app to receive data from other apps	Any App	
Prevent "Save As"	Yes	
Restrict cut, copy, paste with other apps	Policy Managed Apps with Paste In	
Require simple PIN for access	Yes	
Number of attempts before PIN reset	5	
Require corporate credentials for access	No	

216

Setting	ViaMonstra Value	Your Value
Require device compliance with corporate policy for access	Yes	
Recheck the access requirements after (minutes)	Timeout: 30 Offline grace period: 720	
Encrypt app data	Yes	
Block screen capture	Yes	

5. Click **Save Policy** to store the new MAM policy.

You cannot deploy mobile application management policies to users or devices directly; they need to be associated to the deployment of an application that is enabled for Intune MAM support.

Deploy Microsoft Office

One of the key usability components of the Enterprise Mobility Suite is the collection of very rich Microsoft Office apps that fully integrate with Office 365 and Microsoft Intune. All the apps are manageable via the application policies as described in preceding sections.

The table provides the Office app URLs that you use in the following guide:

App	Android URL	iOS URL
Microsoft Excel	http://ref.ms/androidexcel	http://ref.ms/iosexcel
Microsoft Office Hub	http://ref.ms/androidofficehub	
Microsoft OneDrive	http://ref.ms/androidonedrive	http://ref.ms/iosonedrive
Microsoft OneNote		http://ref.ms/iosonenote
Microsoft Outlook	http://ref.ms/androidoutlook	http://ref.ms/iosoutlook
Microsoft PowerPoint	http://ref.ms/androidpowerpoint	http://ref.ms/iospowerpoint
Microsoft Word	http://ref.ms/androidword	http://ref.ms/iosword

To deploy the Office apps, use the following steps:

1. Go to the webpage **http://manage.microsoft.com** and log in with your administrative account.

2. In the **Microsoft Intune console**, select **Apps / Apps** and click **Add App**.

3. Supply your administrator credentials and click **Sign in**.

4. Click **Next**, and for **Select how this software is made available to devices**, select **Managed iOS App from the App Store**.

5. Open a different **Internet Explorer** window and enter **http://ref.ms/iosword**. You are redirected to Microsoft Word in the Apple App Store. Select the URL and copy it.

6. Paste the URL in the **Specify the URL** field and click **Next**.

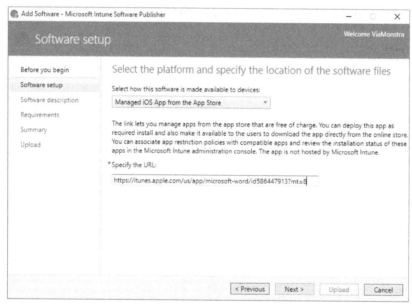

Adding the URL to an iOS app in the App Store.

7. Supply the information to describe the software as shown in the following table:

Setting	Value
Publisher	Microsoft
Name	Word
Description	Managed Microsoft Word app for ViaMonstra
Category	Productivity
Display this as a featured app and highlight it in the company portal	Selected

8. Click **Next**.

9. Leave the **Mobile device type** with the default value (**Any**), or select **iPad** and **iPhone/iPod Touch**. Then click **Next**.

10. Review the information about the software that will be added to Microsoft Intune and click **Upload**. Then click **Close**.

11. Repeat the steps for all other Microsoft Office for iOS apps.

Adding Microsoft Word for Android devices is slightly different:

1. In the **Microsoft Intune console**, select **Apps / Apps** and click **Add App**.

2. Supply your administrator credentials and click **Sign in**.

3. Click **Next**, and for **Select how this software is made available to devices**, select **External Links**.

4. Open a different **Internet Explorer** window and enter **http://ref.ms/androidword**. You are redirected to Microsoft Word in the Google Play store. Select the URL and copy it.

5. Paste the URL in the **Specify the URL** field and click **Next**.

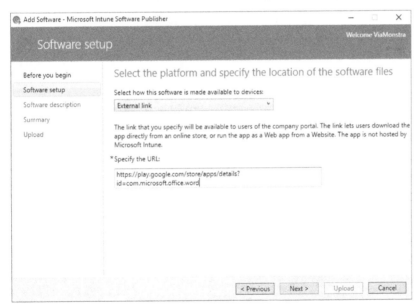

Pasting the URL to the app in the Google Play store.

6. Supply the information to describe the software as shown in the following table:

Setting	Value
Publisher	Microsoft
Name	Word

Setting	Value
Description	Managed Microsoft Word app for ViaMonstra
Category	Productivity
Display this as a featured app and highlight it in the company portal	Selected

7. Click **Next**.

8. Review the information about the software that will be added to Microsoft Intune and click **Upload**. Then click **Close**.

9. Repeat the steps for all other Microsoft Office for Android apps.

After adding the Microsoft Office apps, you need to make the apps available for users. You can do this by deploying the apps to one of the Intune groups that you created earlier:

1. Go to the webpage **http://manage.microsoft.com** and log in with your administrative account.

2. In the **Microsoft Intune console**, select **Apps / Apps** and select the **Word** application. Click **Manage Deployment**.

3. Select the group **SW_Office_Install** and click **Add**. Click **Next** to configure the deployment action.

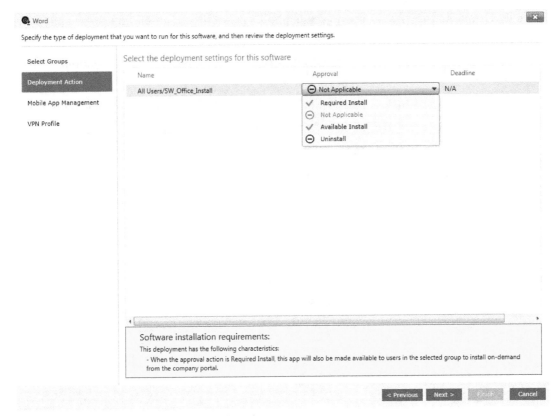

Selecting how the application is deployed.

4. Select **Available Install** and click **Next**.

5. On the **Mobile App Management** page, select **MAM iOS Office** and click **Next**.

6. Click **Finish** on the **VPN Profile** page.

Real World Note: The Office apps are huge (about 1.2 GB), so you do not want to deploy them as a required install. Instruct the users to install the apps when they need to access the company resources in a safe way.

Mobile App Configuration Policies

Applications for iOS devices can be preconfigured while deploying them from the App Store or when deploying a LOB app. An app in the App Store doesn't necessarily have to be an app that supports the Intune SDK. Apps do not need to support the ability to preconfigure certain settings.

Real World Note: Currently not many (free) applications are available in the App Store that support app configuration. See a complete list here: **http://ref.ms/mamlist**.

For the PoC, ViaMonstra uses a free app called Foldr to test the capability to use the app configuration policies.

1. Go to the webpage **http://manage.microsoft.com** and log in with your administrative account.

2. In the **Microsoft Intune console**, select **Policy / Configuration Policies** and click **Add**.

3. Expand **Software** and click **Mobile App Configuration Policy (iOS 7.1 and later)**.

4. Select **Create a Custom Policy** and click **Create Policy**.

5. Supply a name (**MCFG Foldr**) and paste the XML snippet in the configuration area.

```
<dict>

    <key>appMode</key>

    <integer>1</integer>

    <key>serverURL</key>

    <string>foldr.emskings.com</string>

    <key>requirePIN</key>

    <false />

    <key>requirePassword</key>

    <false />

    <key>requireSecurityOnWake</key>

    <false />

</dict>
```

6. Click **Validate** and **Save**.

Now that you have configured the mobile app configuration policy, you need to add the Foldr app to Microsoft Intune. You can find the Foldr app here: http://ref.ms/foldr. After adding the Foldr app, you need to deploy the app:

1. Go to the webpage **http://manage.microsoft.com** and log in with your administrative account.

2. In the **Microsoft Intune console**, select **Apps / Apps** and select the **Foldr** application you want to deploy. Click **Manage Deployment**.

3. Select the group **SW_Preferred_Apps** and click **Add**. Click **Next** to configure the deployment action.

4. Select **Available Install** and click **Next**. Then click **Next** on the **VPN Profile** page.

5. On the **Mobile App Configuration** page, select the just created policy and click **Finish**.

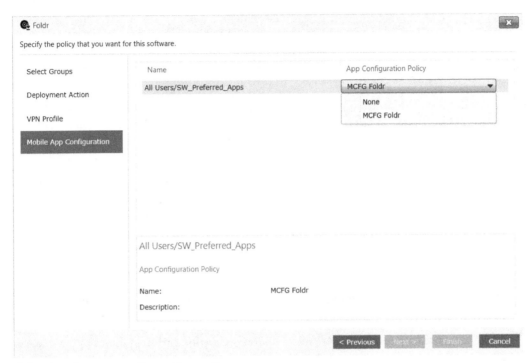

Selecting the app configuration policy.

Managed Viewers

For Android devices, Microsoft created three document viewers that you can manage via the application policies. The managed viewers can be used to view attachments that come with email messages, for instance, when using the managed Outlook app, or when using any other managed app. You can deploy the viewers the same way as deploying the Microsoft Office productivity apps.

The following table includes the viewer URLs used to deploy them.

App	Android URL
Microsoft Intune AV Player	http://ref.ms/androidavplayer
Microsoft Intune Image Viewer	http://ref.ms/androidimageviewer
Microsoft Intune PDF Viewer	http://ref.ms/androidpdfviewer

Setting Up Managed Browser Policies

Microsoft created Internet browsers that you can manage via the managed browser policies. With those policies, you are able to allow or disallow certain websites that can be accessed. Scenarios for using managed browsers can be one of the following:

- **Kiosk devices.** When using an iPad in a kiosk mode, for instance, you are able to configure the managed browser to be the only browser that is allowed to run. With managed browser policies, you are able to configure only one or more sites that can be accessed and nothing else or a list of websites that can explicitly not be accessed.

- **(Internal) corporate website access.** Links in managed documents can be for corporate (internal) websites that contain sensitive information. That information must not be copied to Twitter, for instance, or an unmanaged app that can leak data to the competition. If used for internal corporate websites, you need to publish the internal corporate websites securely.

Use the following steps to set up a managed browser policy:

1. Go to the webpage **http://manage.microsoft.com** and log in with your administrative account.

2. In the **Microsoft Intune console**, select **Policy / Configuration Policies** and click **Add**.

3. Expand **Software** and click **Managed Browser Policy (iOS 7.1 and later)**.

4. Select **Create a Custom Policy** and click **Create Policy**.

5. Configure the managed browser policy as follows:

Setting	ViaMonstra Value	Your Value
Name	MAM iOS Managed Browser	
Description		
Allow the managed browser to open only the URLs listed below	Selected	
Block the managed browser from opening the URLs listed below	Not selected	
URLs	http://emskings.com/* http://viamonstra.com/*	

6. Click **Save Policy** to store the new managed browser policy.

A managed browser policy also needs to be created for Android:

1. In the **Microsoft Intune console**, select **Policy / Configuration Policies** and click **Add**.

2. Expand **Software** and click **Managed Browser Policy (Android 4 and later)**.

3. Select **Create a Custom Policy** and click **Create Policy**.

4. Configure the managed browser policy as follows:

Setting	ViaMonstra Value	Your Value
Name	MAM Android Managed Browser	
Description		
Allow the managed browser to open only the URLs listed below	Selected	
Block the managed browser from opening the URLs listed below	Not selected	
URLs	http://emskings.com/* http://viamonstra.com/*	

5. Click **Save Policy** to store the new managed browser policy.

Deploy Managed Browser

As with mobile application management policies, managed browser policies cannot be deployed to users or devices directly; they need to be associated to the deployment of a managed browser application that is enabled for Intune MAM support.

The Managed Browser app is a deep linked app in the Apple Store and Google Play store and can be added the same way as described earlier using the URLs in the following table.

App	Android URL	iOS URL
Microsoft Intune Managed Browser	http://ref.ms/androidmanagedbrowser	http://ref.ms/iosmanagedbrowser

After adding the Managed Browser apps, you need to deploy the apps:

1. Go to the webpage **http://manage.microsoft.com** and log in with your administrative account.

2. In the **Microsoft Intune console**, select **Apps / Apps** and select the **Intune Managed Browser** application. Click **Manage Deployment**.

3. Select the group **SW_Managed_Viewers_Install** and click **Add**. Click **Next** to configure the deployment action.

4. Select **Available Install** and click **Next**.

5. On the **Mobile App Management** page, select a special policy or just **MAM Android Office**, and then click **Next**.

6. In the **Managed Browser Policy** drop-down list, select **MAM Android Managed Browser**.

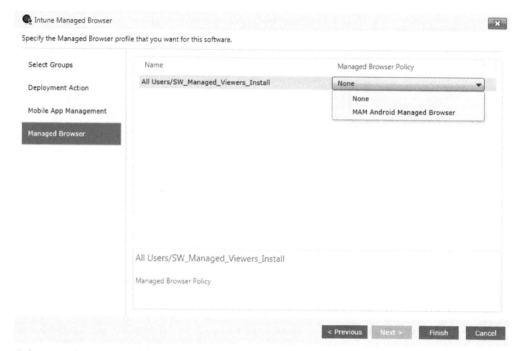

Selecting the managed browser policy.

7. Click **Finish** on the **Managed Browser** page.

8. Repeat the steps for the iOS Managed Browser.

Two managed browsers are now available with the application management policies and managed browser policies configured.

Wrap Your Own LOB (Notepad) App

ViaMonstra has a line-of-business app that was developed internally for the company. The data within the app needs to be controlled by mobile application management policies from Microsoft Intune. There are two ways of allowing Microsoft Intune to control the application. One is by integrating the Intune Software Developer Kit (SDK) into the Android or iOS application, and the second option is to wrap the application with the Intune App Wrapper. ViaMonstra prefers to wrap the application so that no redevelopment of the application is necessary.

ViaMonstra uses only LOB apps for iOS devices. Not every iOS application can be wrapped by the Intune App wrapper, however, because it cannot be encrypted, be unsigned, or have extended file attributes.

Before you can wrap any app for iOS, the following requirements must be met:

- An Apple Developer Account (https://developer.apple.com/)
- Access to a Mac OS X 10.8.5 or later with Xcode installed
- A provisioning profile
- An enterprise distribution certificate
- A device based on iOS 7.01 or later
- A developed iOS LOB application

When you have taken care of these requirements, you can wrap the iOS app as follows:

1. Download the **Microsoft Intune App Wrapping Tool** from **http://ref.ms/iosappwrap** to your Mac OS X system:

    a. Select the language and click **Download**.

    b. On the next page, select the DMG that needs to be downloaded and click **Next**.

2. Search for the right file in the right language, click the **<language>.DMG** link to download it (e.g. **English (US).dmg**), and click **Agree**.

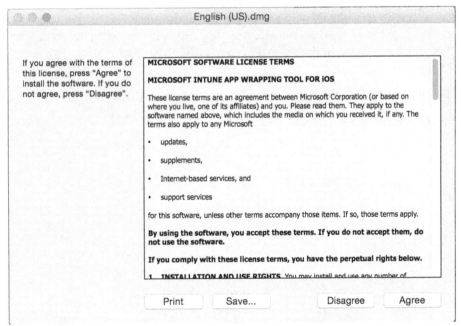

Click Agree to extract the Microsoft Intune App Wrapper Tool.

3. After the installer is mounted and shown, select the folder **IntuneMAMPackager** and copy (**Command + C**) and paste (**Command + V**) it to, for instance, the desktop.

4. Open a bash terminal session on the Mac OS X device and create the following command line:

```
./IntuneMAMPackager/Contents/MacOS/IntuneMAMPackager -i
./Notepad/Notepad-tobewapped.ipa -p ./Notepad/
Provisioning_Profile.mobileprovision -o ./Notepad/Notepad-
wrapped.ipa -c CEDE193A623DEC5B98D3E31A3E8B2641A1C86893
```

Keep in mind the following:

- o   -i is the source IPA file.

- o   -p is the provisioning file downloaded from the Apple developers site.

- o   -o is the wrapped IPA file.

- o   -c is the SHA1 hash of the signing (distribution) certificate.

5. After successfully wrapping the application, add the wrapped version to Microsoft Intune as described earlier in this chapter where you added the Adobe Reader apps. The only difference is that now mobile application management policies also can be added to deployment.

MAM Support for Office on Non-Managed Devices

ViaMonstra works often with consultants who do not want to enroll their device into Microsoft Intune but still require access to internal documents way. Microsoft Intune offers together with the Office Apps for iOS and Android the ability to manage the Office apps and prevent data leakage without needing to enroll the device.

1. Go to https**://portal.Azure.com** and log in with the administrative credentials.

2. Click **Browse**, search for **Intune**, and click the star next to it to add Intune to the portal menu.

Adding Intune to the menu.

3. Click **Intune** and then click **Policy** in the **APP CONFIGURATION** section of the settings.

4. Click **Add Policy,** and for **Policy name**, type **ViaMonstra MAM for iOS**.

5. Click **Choose Apps**, select the Office apps that need to be managed, as shown in the following figure, and click **Select**.

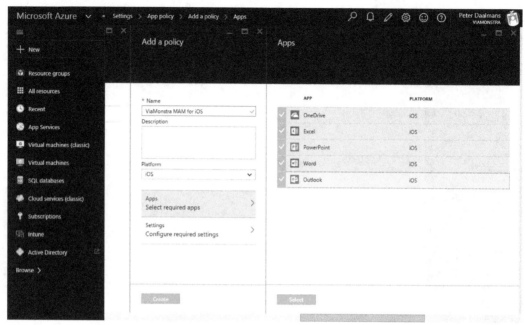

Selecting the Office apps that need to be managed.

6. Click **Configure required settings** and configure the settings as in the following table:

Setting	ViaMonstra Value	Your Value
Prevent iTunes and iCloud backups	Yes	
Allow app to transfer data to other apps	Policy Managed Apps	
Allow app to receive data from other apps	Any App	
Prevent "Save As"	Yes	
Restrict cut, copy, paste with other apps	Policy Managed Apps with Paste In	
Require simple PIN for access	Yes	
Number of attempts before PIN reset	5	
Allow fingerprint instead of PIN (iOS 8+)	Yes	
Require corporate credentials for access	No	

Setting	ViaMonstra Value	Your Value
Block managed apps from running on jailbroken or rooted devices	Yes	
Recheck the access requirements after (minutes)	Timeout : 30 Offline grace period: 720	
Offline interval (days) before app data is wiped	90	

7. Click **OK** and **Create**.

8. Click the newly created MAM policy and select **User groups**.

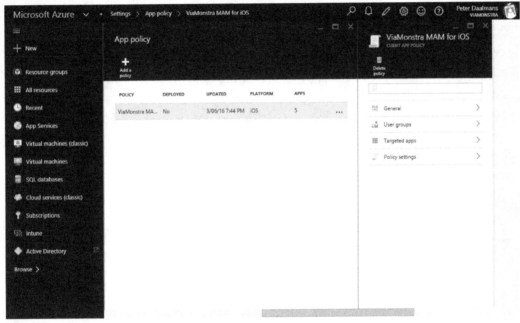

Select User groups.

9. Click **Add user group** and search for the **SW_Office_Install** group, for example, that is created to enable external users to use the Office apps to access ViaMonstra documents without being enrolled in Microsoft Intune.

10. Select the group and click **Select**.

11. On each tab, click the × to close the tabs. Then create the same policy to support Office apps on Android devices.

Real World Note: Microsoft and third-party vendors are investing to make their apps Intune-aware, and they implement the Intune SDK in their applications so that the app can be managed via Intune application management policies. You can find a complete list of managed applications at http://ref.ms/mamlist.

Mobile Device Inventory

With Microsoft Intune, you are limited as to what information can be inventoried. What is inventoried cannot be extended as it can be in ConfigMgr. There are two ways to gather information about the devices that are connected with and managed by Microsoft Intune. One way is to browse to the device from which you need information; the other way is discussed in the "Reporting" section later in this chapter.

The information that can be gathered about the mobile device and the installed apps differs across platforms. For instance, Android and iOS do not allow the same information about the device to be gathered.

The browse method for gathering information is described in the following procedure:

1. Go to the webpage **http://manage.microsoft.com** and log in with your administrative account.

2. In the **Microsoft Intune console**, select **Groups / All Devices**, select a user's mobile phone, and click **View Properties**.

3. In the **General** tab, click **Hardware**.

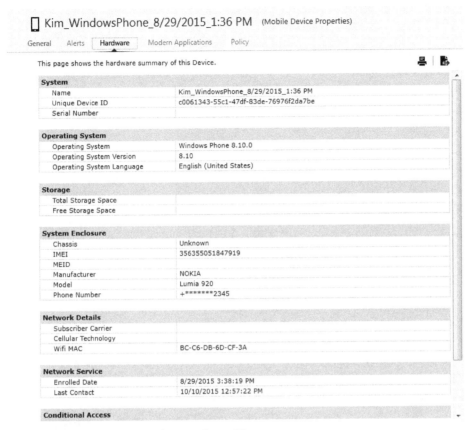

The hardware inventory of a Windows Phone.

By default, only the software installed via the Microsoft Intune Company Portal is inventoried. This is due to privacy regulations because Microsoft Intune or the administrator currently cannot make a distinction between what a private device or company-owned device is. For Mac OS X devices, all software also is inventoried.

When enabling the whitelisting or blacklisting apps on a mobile device via the Complaint & Noncompliant Apps list in the General Configuration policies for the platforms, all applications are inventoried. This way a device can be marked noncompliant if an app is installed that can compromise corporate security.

Getting the Right PLIST Values

When deploying native Apple iOS applications, you need an IPA file and a preference (PLIST) file. A properly developed application comes with a PLIST file. If not, however, follow the instructions that follow to configure the PLIST file.

First, you need a PLIST file that is set up well and has the right format. You can use the following PLIST example, but if you have only an IPA file and no PLIST file, how do you get the information needed to replace the [INSERT XXXX HERE] strings?

```xml
<?xml version="1.0" encoding="UTF-8"?>

<!DOCTYPE plist PUBLIC "-//Apple//DTD PLIST 1.0//EN"
"http://www.apple.com/DTDs/PropertyList-1.0.dtd">

<plist version="1.0">

<dict>

 <key>items</key>

   <array>

     <dict>

       <key>assets</key>

        <array>

          <dict>

            <key>kind</key>

            <string>software-package</string>

            <key>url</key>

            <string>[INSERT URL HERE]</string>

          </dict>

        </array>

       <key>metadata</key>

       <dict>

          <key>bundle-identifier</key>

          <string>[INSERT BUNDLE ID HERE]</string>

          <key>bundle-version</key>

          <string>[INSERT VERSION HERE]</string>

          <key>kind</key>
```

```
            <string>software</string>

            <key>title</key>

            <string>[INSERT APP TITLE HERE]</string>

        </dict>

      </dict>

    </array>

  </dict>

</plist>
```

You can find the right values for the PLIST file in the IPA. You need to extract the IPA file, which you can do on a Mac OS X computer, as in this guide, or on a Windows device with 7Zip.

1. On a Mac OS X computer, open the **Finder** and browse to the **IPA** file; select it and click **Open With / Archive Utility (10.XX)**.

2. If a warning appears indicating that the developer is not identified or trusted, click **Open** (if you know the source of the app).

3. Open the **Payload** folder and select the application in this folder. Click the gear and select **Show Package Contents**.

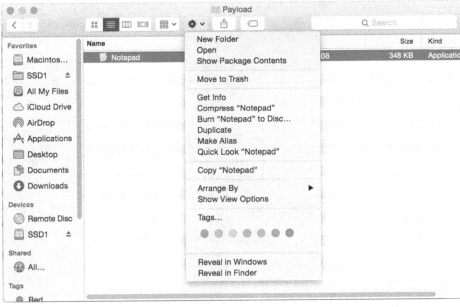

Selecting Show Package Contents.

235

4. Select the **Info.plist** or other .plist file in the root of the package content, and use the spacebar to see the content of the PLIST file in readable format so you can identify the needed values.

Identifying the needed PLIST values.

Real World Note: The PLIST file also is used to detect whether the application is already installed. Failure to create the correct PLIST file causes the application to fail the detection and, as a result, prompt the user for a reinstallation.

Reporting

EMS consists of different products that ViaMonstra uses. This section explains the reporting options.

Microsoft Intune

Microsoft Intune has a couple of reports available that you can use to report information about device compliance and information gathered during an inventory. Currently, Microsoft Intune does not support extending the reporting functionality by adding reports or information to the existing reports.

Microsoft Intune has the following reports available when enabling and configuring Mobile Device Management support for iOS, Windows 10 Mobile, Windows Phone 8.x, Android, and Mac OS X.

Report	Description
Mobile device inventory reports	Information about the mobile devices that are managed, filtered on OS or by whether a device is jailbroken or rooted
Terms and conditions reports	Information about which users have accepted the terms and conditions (and which version) and which users who did not (yet) accept them
Noncompliant app reports	All the noncompliant apps that are inventoried
Certificate compliance reports	When using NDES, all certificates that have been issued

Report	Description
Device history reports	Information about a device's different states: the device retire, wipe and delete actions and who initiated those actions
Mac OS X hardware report	All inventoried hardware information about the enrolled Mac OS X devices
Mac OS X software report	All inventoried software items on the enrolled Mac OS X devices
Health Attestation reports	The health of Windows 10 (mobile) devices

You can access the reports in Microsoft Intune from the Microsoft Intune console:

1. Go to the webpage **http://manage.microsoft.com** and log in with your administrative account.

2. In the **Microsoft Intune console**, select **Reports / Mobile Device Inventory Reports** and click **Include only the following**. Then select **Windows Phone**, **iPhone**, and **Android** and click **Save As**.

3. Give a name for the report (e.g. All Mobile Devices of ViaMonstra) and click **OK** to safe the settings for the report for future use.

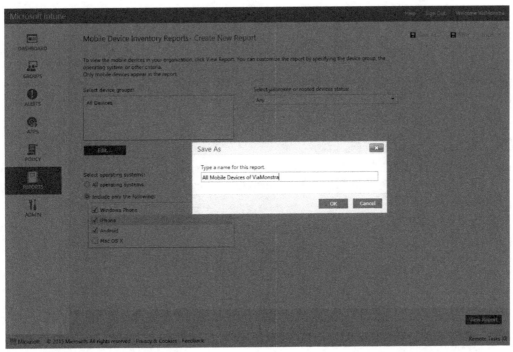

Saving the report for future use.

4. Click **View Report** to view the report.

In the report view, you can print or export the results using the buttons in the upper right corner.

Name	Operating System	Manufacturer	Model	Management Ch
Henrik_iPhone	iOS		iPhone7C2	Managed by Excl
kenny_Android	Android		Outlook for iOS and .	Managed by Excl
kenny_Android_8/18/2015_6:08 AM	Android 5.0.0	samsung	SM-G900F	Managed by Mic
kenny_WindowsPhone_8/25/2015_.	Windows 10.0.13003	NOKIA	Lumia 925	Managed by Mic
Kim_Android_2	Android		Outlook	Managed by Excl
Kim_WindowsPhone_8/29/2015_1:3	Windows Phone 8.10.0	NOKIA	Lumia 920	Managed by Mic

A standard mobile device inventory report.

When accessing the Mobile Device Inventory report in the Reports node the next time, you can load the old report settings by using the Load option in the upper right of the window.

Protecting Devices

Personal or company-owned devices that access corporate resources may have sensitive data on them. For this reason, you need to be able to control the devices not only via MDM or compliance policies but also via remote actions.

Microsoft Intune currently supports four different actions that you can use to protect or control the devices.

- Remote lock devices
- Remote reset passcode
- Retire devices
- Wipe devices

Remote Lock Devices

Devices that have a looser control over idle time and screen lock policies may be accessible if a device is left unattended. In such a case, a user is able to call the Intune administrator and ask him or her to lock the device remotely.

1. Go to the webpage **http://manage.microsoft.com** and log in with your administrative account.

2. In the **Microsoft Intune console**, select **Groups / All Mobile Devices** and click **Devices** to display all mobile devices that are managed by Microsoft Intune.

3. Select the device, expand **Remote Tasks**, and click **Remote Lock**.

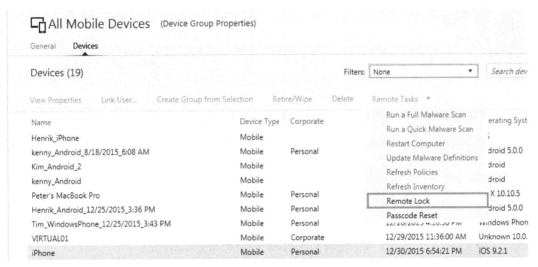

Remote locking a device.

4. Click **Yes** in the **Are you sure you want to lock <mobile device>?** message box.

5. Go to the **Remote Tasks** in the lower right corner to see the status of the remote lock.

Remote Task Status.

6. Click **Close** to close the **Remote Task Status** window.

Not every device responds in the same way to the remote lock task. The following table shows you how different devices respond.

Platform	Responds
Android	The device is locked without any warning.
iOS	The device is locked without any warning.
Windows Phone 8.x	The device is locked with the message "Your company has locked your device. You can use your PIN to unlock it."
Windows 10 Mobile	The device is locked without any warning.

Remote Reset Passcode

Policies, such as requiring a passcode change every 40 days or after being on holiday, may cause users forget their passcode. A policy that wipes the device after six wrong passcodes may cause some irritating calls to the service desk. For this reason, the Intune administrator is able to reset the passcode of the devices.

1. Go to the webpage **http://manage.microsoft.com** and log in with your administrative account.

2. In the **Microsoft Intune console**, select **Groups / All Mobile Devices** and click **Devices** to display all mobile devices that are managed by Microsoft Intune.

3. Select the device, expand **Remote Tasks**, and click **Passcode Reset**.

4. Go to the **Remote Tasks** in the lower right corner to see the status of the passcode reset.

Depending on the platform, the new passcode is listed in the information pane of the device.

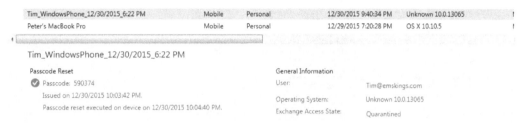

The new passcode is listed in the details of the mobile device.

Like the remote lock, not every device responds in the same way. The following table shows you how different devices respond.

Platform	Responds
Android	The passcode is reset to a very strong passcode of 16 characters.
iOS	The passcode of the device is removed. The user needs to configure a new passcode.
Windows Phone 8.x	Device is locked stating "Your company has reset your password. Contact your company's support person to learn the password."
Windows 10 Mobile	Device is locked stating "Your company has reset your PIN. Contact your company's support person to learn the PIN."

Retire and Wipe Devices

When a device is stolen or sold, a complete factory default of the device is often the solution for removing all company and personal data on the mobile device. You can initiate this action remotely:

1. Go to the webpage **http://manage.microsoft.com** and log in with your administrative account.

2. In the **Microsoft Intune console**, select **Groups / All Mobile Devices** and click **Devices** to display all mobile devices that Microsoft Intune manages.

3. Select the device and click **Retire/Wipe**.

4. If the device really needs to return to the factory default, choose **Full wipe the device and return it to factory default settings**. On all devices, the behavior is the same.

Wiping the device.

5. In the **Microsoft Intune console**, the device is removed automatically and the remote wipe is initiated.

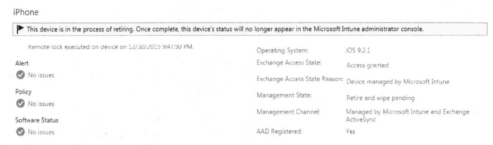

The device is being retired.

Wipe Company Content

Luckily, Microsoft Intune also supports something called *selective wipe of company data*. So, when an employee leaves ViaMonstra, you do not have to wipe the device completely. You are able to remove only company-related data.

1. Go to the webpage **http://manage.microsoft.com** and log in with your administrative account.

2. In the **Microsoft Intune console**, select **Groups / All Mobile Devices** and click **Devices** to display all mobile devices that are managed by Microsoft Intune.

3. Select the device and click **Retire/Wipe**.

4. To remove only company-related data, choose **Selectively wipe the device**.

Depending on the platform, selective wipe is implemented in different ways (mostly due to operating system restrictions).

Data Type	iOS	Android	Android Knox	Windows Phone/Mobile
Company apps and its data installed by Intune	Apps are uninstalled. Company app data is removed. App data from Microsoft apps that use MAM is removed. The app is not removed.	n/a	n/a	Apps are uninstalled. Company app data is removed.
Web links	Removed	Removed	Removed	n/a
Unmanaged Google Play apps	n/a	Untouched	Untouched	n/a
Unmanaged line of business apps	Removed	Untouched	Apps are uninstalled. No data outside the app is removed.	n/a
Managed Google Play apps	n/a	App data is removed. App is not removed. Data protected by MAM encryption outside the app (e.g. SD card) remain encrypted, but are not removed.	App data is removed. App is not removed. Data protected by MAM encryption outside the app (e.g. SD card) remain encrypted, but are not removed.	n/a

Data Type	iOS	Android	Android Knox	Windows Phone/Mobile
Managed line of business apps	Removed	App data is removed. App is not removed. Data protected by MAM encryption outside the app (e.g. SD card) remain encrypted, but are not removed.	App data is removed. App is not removed. Data protected by MAM encryption outside the app (e.g. SD card) remain encrypted, but are not removed.	n/a
Settings	Settings are not enforced anymore; users can change settings again.			
Wi-Fi and VPN profile settings	Removed	Removed	Removed	n/a
Certificate profiles	Certificates are removed and revoked.	Certificates are removed and not revoked.	Certificates are removed and revoked.	n/a
Management agent	Management is removed.			
Email	Provisioned email profile and data are removed.	Email in the Microsoft Outlook app is removed.	Provisioned email profile and data are removed.	Provisioned email profile and data are removed.
AAD record	AAD record is removed.			

Chapter 8

Managing Devices and Data with Microsoft EMS Hybrid

Managing mobile devices using Configuration Manager is almost like inviting an old friend for dinner: not many surprises, but just a good time in pleasant company. Management of mobile devices is almost identical as managing normal desktop computers in the sense that you are working with security policies and inventory data, deploying applications, and providing access to company resources. As you start the endeavor, you will realize that some settings configured for traditional device management also apply to your mobile devices.

Collections

A collection in ConfigMgr is the target for any user or device policy that you are deploying in the environment. You can populate collections with users or devices directly or by applying dynamic queries. Collections also are used as a foundation for role-based administration and often used as a limitation when running reports. For that matter, designing collections is an important task, and one that must be planned by all participants in the enterprise client management group. ViaMonstra is planning the mobile device collections list in the following table.

Collection	Type	Purpose
All mobile devices	Device	Top-level collection for all mobile device management
All <OS> devices	Device	One collection for each operating system (e.g. Android, iOS, and Windows). These collections are intended to be used as limitations when running reports.
All noncompliant devices	Device	Tracks devices that do not comply with the company compliance policies
All personal devices	Device	Contains all devices that are personally owned
All corporate devices	Device	Contains all devices that are owned by ViaMonstra

Collection	Type	Purpose
All jailbroken devices	Device	Contains all devices that are either rooted or jailbroken
All non-compliant users	User	Lists all users who own one or more non-compliant devices
All sales users	User	Contains all users in the sales department. Users in sales have access to confidential data, customer lists, et.al.
All executive users	User	Contains all "executive" users. Executive users are treated a bit differently. Some of the policies are not enforced but deployed to monitor only.
All jailbroken users	User	Lists all users who are the primary owner of any jailbroken or rooted device

Create the Collections

To create the collections, you use the PowerShell ISE and ConfigMgr cmdlets.

1. Log on to **CM01** as **VIAMONSTRA\Administrator**.

2. Press **Windows logo key + Q** and type **powershell**; then from the list of applications, right-click **Windows PowerShell ISE** and click **Run As Administrator**.

3. From the **View** menu, select **Show Script Pane**.

4. In the script pane, type the following PowerShell code (the script can be downloaded along with the other script examples in this book):

```
#Import SCCM Module

Import-Module
$env:SMS_ADMIN_UI_PATH.Replace("\bin\i386","\bin
\configurationmanager.psd1")

$SiteCode = Get-PSDrive -PSProvider CMSITE

Set-Location "$($SiteCode.Name):\"

#Create Collection Folders

New-Item -Path .\DeviceCollection -Name 'Mobile Devices'
```

```
New-Item -Path .\DeviceCollection -Name 'Software'

New-Item -Path .\DeviceCollection -Name 'Compliance
Settings'

New-Item -Path .\UserCollection -Name 'Software'

New-Item -Path .\UserCollection -Name 'Compliance Settings'

#Schedules for MDM collections

$Schedule = New-CMSchedule -RecurCount 1 -RecurInterval Days

#Create MDM collections

#Android

$Collection1 = New-CMDeviceCollection -
LimitingCollectionName "All Mobile Devices" -Name "All
Android Devices" -Comment All -RefreshType Both
-RefreshSchedule $Schedule

Add-CMDeviceCollectionQueryMembershipRule -CollectionName
"All Android Devices" -QueryExpression 'select
SMS_R_SYSTEM.ResourceID,SMS_R_SYSTEM.ResourceType,SMS_R_SYST
EM.Name,SMS_R_SYSTEM.SMSUniqueIdentifier,SMS_R_SYSTEM.Resour
ceDomainORWorkgroup,SMS_R_SYSTEM.Client from SMS_R_System
where SMS_R_System.OperatingSystemNameandVersion like
"%Android%"'-RuleName Android

#IOS

$Collection2 = New-CMDeviceCollection -
LimitingCollectionName "All Mobile Devices" -Name "All iOS
Devices" -Comment All -RefreshType Both -RefreshSchedule
$Schedule

Add-CMDeviceCollectionQueryMembershipRule -CollectionName
"All iOS Devices" -QueryExpression 'select
SMS_R_SYSTEM.ResourceID,SMS_R_SYSTEM.ResourceType,SMS_R_SYST
EM.Name,SMS_R_SYSTEM.SMSUniqueIdentifier,SMS_R_SYSTEM.Resour
ceDomainORWorkgroup,SMS_R_SYSTEM.Client from SMS_R_System
where SMS_R_System.OperatingSystemNameandVersion like
"%iOS%"'-RuleName iOS

#Windows Phone

$Collection3 = New-CMDeviceCollection -
LimitingCollectionName "All Mobile Devices" -Name "All
Windows Phones" -Comment All -RefreshType Both
-RefreshSchedule $Schedule
```

```
Add-CMDeviceCollectionQueryMembershipRule -CollectionName
"All Windows Phones" -QueryExpression 'select
SMS_R_SYSTEM.ResourceID,SMS_R_SYSTEM.ResourceType,SMS_R_SYST
EM.Name,SMS_R_SYSTEM.SMSUniqueIdentifier,SMS_R_SYSTEM.Resour
ceDomainORWorkgroup,SMS_R_SYSTEM.Client from SMS_R_System
where SMS_R_System.OperatingSystemNameandVersion like
"%Windows Phone%"' -RuleName WP

#Jailbroken collection

$Collection4 = New-CMDeviceCollection
-LimitingCollectionName "All Mobile Devices" -Name "All
Jailbroken" -Comment All -RefreshType Both -RefreshSchedule
$Schedule

Add-CMDeviceCollectionQueryMembershipRule -CollectionName
"All Jailbroken" -QueryExpression 'select
SMS_R_SYSTEM.ResourceID,SMS_R_SYSTEM.ResourceType,SMS_R_SYST
EM.Name,SMS_R_SYSTEM.SMSUniqueIdentifier,SMS_R_SYSTEM.Resour
ceDomainORWorkgroup,SMS_R_SYSTEM.Client from SMS_R_System
inner join SMS_G_System_DEVICE_COMPUTERSYSTEM on
SMS_G_System_DEVICE_COMPUTERSYSTEM.ResourceId =
SMS_R_System.ResourceId where
SMS_G_System_DEVICE_COMPUTERSYSTEM.Jailbroken = 1' -RuleName
Jailbroken

#Company owned collection

$Collection5 = New-CMDeviceCollection -
LimitingCollectionName "All Mobile Devices" -Name "All
Company Owned" -Comment All -RefreshType Both -
RefreshSchedule $Schedule

Add-CMDeviceCollectionQueryMembershipRule -CollectionName
"All Company Owned" -QueryExpression 'select
SMS_R_SYSTEM.ResourceID,SMS_R_SYSTEM.ResourceType,SMS_R_SYST
EM.Name,SMS_R_SYSTEM.SMSUniqueIdentifier,SMS_R_SYSTEM.Resour
ceDomainORWorkgroup,SMS_R_SYSTEM.Client from SMS_R_System
where SMS_R_System.DeviceOwner = 1'-RuleName Company

#Personally owned collection

$Collection6 = New-CMDeviceCollection
-LimitingCollectionName "All Mobile Devices" -Name "All
Personal Owned" -Comment All -RefreshType Both
-RefreshSchedule $Schedule

Add-CMDeviceCollectionQueryMembershipRule -CollectionName
"All Personal Owned" -QueryExpression 'select
SMS_R_SYSTEM.ResourceID,SMS_R_SYSTEM.ResourceType,SMS_R_SYST
```

```
EM.Name,SMS_R_SYSTEM.SMSUniqueIdentifier,SMS_R_SYSTEM.Resour
ceDomainORWorkgroup,SMS_R_SYSTEM.Client from SMS_R_System
where SMS_R_System.DeviceOwner = 2' -RuleName Personal

#user collections

$Collection7 = New-CMUserCollection -LimitingCollectionName
"All Users" -Name "All Jailbroksen Users" -Comment "Users
who have a rooted or jailbroken device" -RefreshType Both
-RefreshSchedule $Schedule

$Collection8 = New-CMUserCollection -LimitingCollectionName
"All Users" -Name "All Sales Users" -Comment "Users who
belong to sales" -RefreshType Both -RefreshSchedule
$Schedule

$Collection9 = New-CMUserCollection -LimitingCollectionName
"All Users" -Name "All Executiv Users" -Comment "Users who
belong to Management" -RefreshType Both -RefreshSchedule
$Schedule

Move-CMObject -FolderPath '.\DeviceCollection\Mobile
Devices' -InputObject $Collection1

Move-CMObject -FolderPath '.\DeviceCollection\Mobile
Devices' -InputObject $Collection2

Move-CMObject -FolderPath '.\DeviceCollection\Mobile
Devices' -InputObject $Collection3

Move-CMObject -FolderPath '.\DeviceCollection\Mobile
Devices' -InputObject $Collection4

Move-CMObject -FolderPath '.\DeviceCollection\Mobile
Devices' -InputObject $Collection5

Move-CMObject -FolderPath '.\DeviceCollection\Mobile
Devices' -InputObject $Collection6

Move-CMObject -FolderPath '.\DeviceCollection\Mobile
Devices' -InputObject $Collection7
```

Device Ownership

Device ownership indicates whether a device is owned personally or by the company. Corporate devices allow more management options, like full inventory of *all* applications (unlike personally owned devices where you can gather information only about applications installed *through the company portal*).

Many organizations have different security policies applied to a device depending on device ownership. By default, all devices are enrolled as personal devices. In ViaMonstra, most devices are corporate owned, so you have to change device ownership right after enrolling the device. To change device ownership, you can use a custom PowerShell script provided with this book. The script finds all personally owned devices in the collection specified in $CollectionName, changes the device ownership, and writes the output to an HTML file.

1. Log on to **CM01** as **VIAMONSTRA\Administrator**.

2. Press **Windows logo key + Q** and type **powershell**; from the list of applications, right-click **Windows PowerShell ISE** and click **Run as administrator**.

3. From the **View** menu, select **Show Script Pane**.

4. In the script pane, type the following PowerShell code (the script can be downloaded along with the other script examples in this book):

```
#Create a HTML report with all person enrolled devices,
change the device ownership

$CollectionName = 'All Personal Owned'

$Policy = 'Company' #This value can be Company or Personal

$ReportLocation = "C:\Setup"

$DeviceReport = @()

Import-Module
$env:SMS_ADMIN_UI_PATH.Replace("\bin\i386","\bin
\configurationmanager.psd1")

$SiteCode = Get-PSDrive -PSProvider CMSITE

Set-Location "$($SiteCode.Name):\"

Function Write-Log

{


    PARAM(

        [String]$Message,

        [String]$Path =
"$env:windir\TEMP\CTDeviceOwner.log",

        [int]$severity,

        [string]$component,

        [Switch]$NoScreen

        )

        $TimeZoneBias = Get-WmiObject -Query "Select Bias
from Win32_TimeZone"

        $Date = Get-Date -Format "HH:mm:ss.fff"
```

```
            $Date2 = Get-Date -Format "MM-dd-yyyy"

            $Type = 1


"<![LOG[$Message]LOG]!><time=$([char]34)$date+$($TimeZoneBia
s.bias)$([char]34) date=$([char]34)$date2$([char]34)
component=$([char]34)$component$([char]34)
context=$([char]34)$([char]34)
type=$([char]34)$severity$([char]34)
thread=$([char]34)$([char]34) file=$([char]34)$([char]34)>"|
Out-File -FilePath $Path -Append -NoClobber -Encoding
default
  }
Write-Log -Message "Starting to change Device Owner - $(Get
-Date)" -severity 1 -component 'START'

Write-Log -Message "Site Code: $($SiteCode.Name)" -severity
1 -component 'START'

$Devices = Get-CMDevice -CollectionName $CollectionName

Write-Log -Message "Total Devices in $CollectionName :
$($Devices.Count)" -severity 1 -component 'Device Query'


foreach($Device in $Devices){
    Write-Log -Message "Currently working on device:
$($Device.Name)" -severity 1 -component 'Process'

    If($Device.DeviceOwner -eq 1){
        Write-Log -Message "Current device owner: Company"
-severity 1 -component 'Process'

    }
    Else{
        Write-Log -Message "Current device owner: Personal"
-severity 1 -component 'Process'

    }
    Write-Log -Message "Changing Device owner to $Policy"
-severity 1 -component 'Process'

    Set-CMDeviceOwnership -DeviceId $Device.ResourceID
-OwnershipType $Policy

}
```

251

```
Write-Log -Message "Building final report" -severity 1
-component 'Process'

$Devices = Get-CMDevice -CollectionName $CollectionName

foreach($Device in $Devices){

    Switch($Device.DeviceOwner){

        1 {$DeviceOwner = 'Company'; Break}

        2 {$DeviceOwner = 'Personal'; Break}

    }

    #Build the Object

    $Props = {

            [Ordered]@{

                        Name = $Device.Name

                        ResourceID = $Device.ResourceID

                        DeviceOwner = $DeviceOwner

                        DeviceOS = $Device.DeviceOS

            }

    }

    #Save the Object

    $DeviceReport += New-Object PSObject -Property (&$Props)

}

$CurrentDate = Get-Date

#HTML style

$TableStyle = @"

    <style>

    TABLE {border-width: 1px;border-style: solid;border
-color: black;border-collapse: collapse;}

    TH {border-width: 1px;padding: 3px;border-style:
solid;border-color: black;background-color: #6495ED;}

    TD {border-width: 1px;padding: 3px;border-style:
solid;border-color: black;}

    </style>

"@
```

```
Try{

    $DeviceReport | ConvertTo-Html -Head $TableStyle
-Body "<h2>Configuration Manager Device Ownership report
- $CurrentDate</h2>" -ErrorAction STOP | Out-File
"$ReportLocation\DeviceOwners.html" -Force

    }

Catch{

    Write-Log -Message $_.Exception.Message -severity 3
-component 'Build Report'

    }
```

The output of the report will look like the following example.

Documenting all personally owned devices.

To change the device ownership manually, right-click any device and select **Change Ownership**.

Real World Note: Remember that you always can add or remove columns in the ConfigMgr console. One of the extra columns is DeviceOwner.

Mobile Device Inventory

Windows computers with a full desktop or server operating system are configured with a management layer called Windows Management Instrumentation (WMI) from which you can pull a lot of hardware, software, and configuration information about the device. Mobile devices do not have the same rich management layer, not that it's a huge issue because you often are interested only in knowing the OS version, IMEI code, and serial number. To view an inventory from any device, follow these steps:

1. Open the **ConfigMgr console**, and in **the Assets and Compliance** workspace, navigate to **Overview / Device Collections / Mobile Devices**.

2. In the **Mobile Devices** folder, open the **All Personally Owned** collection.

3. Right-click any of the devices, and then click **Start / Resource Explorer**.

4. Expand **Hardware / Mobile Device Computer System** and right-click the result and select **Properties**.

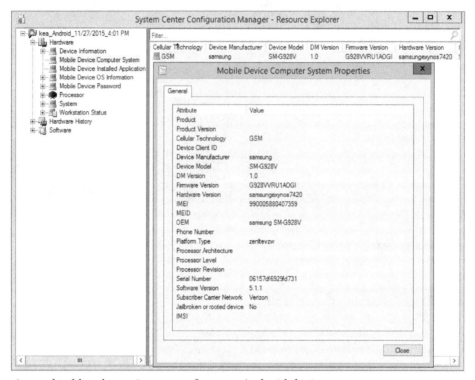

A standard hardware inventory from an Android device.

Extending a Custom Hardware Inventory

Windows Phone 8.1/10 Mobile devices support extending hardware information. The process is somewhat similar to extending hardware inventory information on a "normal" Windows computer. You extend hardware information by creating a custom MOF file as in the following example. The MOF file, which also allows you to inventory the device name, IMEI number and phone number, is then imported into ConfigMgr. After extending the hardware inventory, Windows 10 Mobile applies the information added by the MOF file and returns the requested data to ConfigMgr.

```
#pragma namespace ("\\\\.\\root\\cimv2")

instance of __Namespace

{

    Name = "SMS" ;
```

```
};

#pragma namespace ("\\\\.\\root\\cimv2\\SMS")

instance of __Namespace

{

    Name = "INV_TEMP" ;

};

#pragma namespace ("\\\\.\\root\\cimv2\\SMS\\INV_TEMP")

class SMS_Class_Template

{

};

[ SMS_Report (TRUE),

  SMS_Group_Name ("Device_CUSTOMINFO"),

  SMS_Class_ID ("MICROSOFT|DEVICE_CUSTOMINFO|1.0"),

  Namespace ("Reserved"),

  SMS_DEVICE_URI ("") ]

class Device_CUSTOMINFO : SMS_Class_Template

{

    [SMS_Report (TRUE),
SMS_DEVICE_URI("WM:./DevDetail/Ext/Microsoft/DeviceName")]

    String    DeviceName;

    [SMS_Report (TRUE),
SMS_DEVICE_URI("WM:./Vendor/MSFT/DeviceInstanceService/IMEI")]

    String    IMEI;
```

```
[SMS_Report (TRUE),
SMS_DEVICE_URI("WM:./Vendor/MSFT/DeviceInstanceService/PhoneNumbe
r")]

    String     PhoneNumber;

};
```

In the following example, you extend the hardware inventory information on Windows 10 Mobile devices with the custom MOF file:

1. Open the **ConfigMgr console**, and in the **Administration** workspace, navigate to **Overview / Site Configuration / Client Settings** and open the **Default Client Settings** properties.

2. In the **Hardware Inventory** pane, click **Set Classes / Import** and browse to the **C:\Setup\Inventory\DeviceName and IMEI and Phone Number.MOF** file.

3. Click **Open / Import**. Notice that the new class is listed at the top.

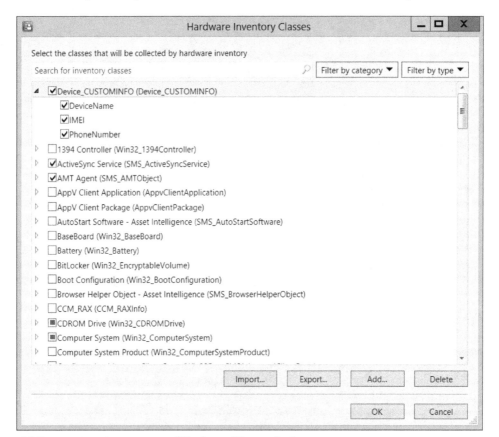

Adding custom inventory to Windows Phone devices.

4. Click **OK** twice.

Windows Phone devices automatically download the configuration changes during the next policy synchronization. Note that even if you include a phone number in the MOF file, that information will be not be gathered because some operating system do not allow you to gather data that is considered private.

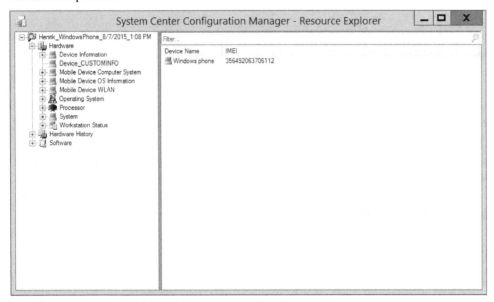

Hardware inventory after enabling custom hardware classes.

Working with Jailbroken and Rooted Devices

Working with a jailbroken or rooted device is like taking care of someone else's kids. On the outside, you think you know what you are dealing with, but the truth is that you have no idea and the little human can contain all sorts of reactions that you didn't dream of. The same can be said about a device that has been tampered with. On the outside, it looks like a normal operating system, but you have no idea what the device is capable of doing. Users are full admins of their phones and can bypass protections by the OS vendor, the phone vendor, or any settings you try to enforce.

It is crucial to any organization to be able not only to detect rooted/jailbroken devices, but also to identify their primary owners. ViaMonstra trusts its employees, but is not naïve. The approach is to discover jailbroken/rooted devices, inform the users, and lockdown all devices belonging to those users. The intent is to have users step forward and ask for help. The solution has a couple of steps:

1. Identify devices using a standard collection

2. Identify the users by adding a custom query

3. Apply a custom security policy

The collection to detect jailbroken/rooted devices was created using the PowerShell script earlier in this chapter. If you have a closer look at the query, you'll notice that the query is looking in the Mobile Device Computer System class for the Jailbroken or rooted devices attribute. A value of 1 means that the device is jailbroken or rooted.

```
select
SMS_R_SYSTEM.ResourceID,SMS_R_SYSTEM.ResourceType,SMS_R_SYSTEM.Na
me,SMS_R_SYSTEM.SMSUniqueIdentifier,SMS_R_SYSTEM.ResourceDomainOR
Workgroup,SMS_R_SYSTEM.Client from SMS_R_System inner join
SMS_G_System_DEVICE_COMPUTERSYSTEM on
SMS_G_System_DEVICE_COMPUTERSYSTEM.ResourceId =
SMS_R_System.ResourceId where
SMS_G_System_DEVICE_COMPUTERSYSTEM.Jailbroken = 1
```

The second part of the solution is a custom PowerShell script that detects all devices in a specific collection, finds all the primary users, and adds them as direct rules to a custom user collection. You do not need a jailbroken or rooted device to test the script. All you have to do is add a device to the collection named All Jailbroken Devices and run the script.

```
$DebugPreference = "continue"

#import the ConfigMgr Module

Import-Module -Name "$(split-path
$Env:SMS_ADMIN_UI_PATH)\ConfigurationManager.psd1"

$CMSite = (Get-PSDrive -PSProvider "CMSite").Name

cd ($CMSite + ":")

$Devices = Get-CMDevice -CollectionName "All Jailbroken"

Foreach ($device in $devices)

    {

    #Find primary user

    $Query = "SELECT SMS_R_User.UniqueUserName,
SMS_R_User.ResourceID FROM SMS_R_System

    JOIN SMS_UserMachineRelationship ON
SMS_R_System.Name=SMS_UserMachineRelationship.MachineResourceName
```

```
      JOIN SMS_R_User ON
SMS_UserMachineRelationship.UniqueUserName=SMS_R_User.UniqueUserN
ame

      WHERE SMS_R_System.ResourceID = '$($Device.ResourceID)'"

    $user =  Get-CimInstance -Query $Query -Namespace
"ROOT/SMS/site_$CMSite"

    if ($user.Count -eq 0) {

    Write-debug "No primary user(s) found for $($device.Name)"

      continue

    }

    #Check & Add user

    if(!(Get-CMUser -CollectionName "All Jailbroken Users" -Name
"*$($User.UniqueUserName)*"))

    {

      Write-Debug "Adding user $($User.UniqueUserName)"

      Add-CMUserCollectionDirectMembershipRule -CollectionName
"All Jailbroken Users" -ResourceID $User.ResourceID

    }

    else

    {

    Write-Debug "Already member user $($User.UniqueUserName)"

    }

  }
```

After adding the users, all you have to do is deploy a very restrictive set of policies to the specified user collection. You can find more information about how to do this later in this chapter in the "Configure Compliance Policies" section.

Reports

ConfigMgr ships with more than 400 reports, hosted in SQL Reporting Services. Before running reports, you need to install and configure the Reporting Service Point site system role as described in Chapter 2. When accessing the reporting servicing point, you find a dedicated Device Management folder containing not only Intune-managed devices, but also the old legacy ConfigMgr mobile devices. For that reason, some of the reports will be empty unless you are managing Nokia Symbian and Windows Phone 6.X devices. To access the reports, follow these steps:

1. Open **Internet Explorer**, browse to **http://cm01/reports**, and open the **ConfigMgr_PS1** folder.

2. Open the **Device Management** folder and run the **All mobile device clients** report.

This report gives you valuable information about the activity of your devices, like heartbeat information and latest hardware inventory date. Other reports that are worth looking at are

- Count of mobile devices by operating system

- Mobile devices that are jailbroken or rooted

- The number of devices enrolled per user in Microsoft Intune

Conditional Access

As described in Chapter 7, conditional access is one of the most important features when it comes to managing mobile devices. The idea at ViaMonstra is to implement conditional access for all mobile devices users; however, as with many other new services, you need to test how it works in the organization first. For that reason, you will not include members of the Executive Users security group.

Configure Access to Exchange Online

Configuring conditional access to Exchange Online is initiated from ConfigMgr, but essentially the feature is configured in Microsoft Intune. The following example blocks access to Exchange Online for all users with noncompliant devices, except users in the on-premises Executive Users AD group.

1. Log on to **CM01** and open the **ConfigMgr console**.

2. Navigate to **Assets and Compliance/ Compliance Settings/ Conditional Access/ Exchange Online** and click **Configure conditional access policy in the Intune console**.

3. When prompted, sign in with the **admin@mdmhybrid.onmicrosoft.com** account.

4. In the **Microsoft Intune console**, select **Enable conditional access policy**.

5. For **Device platforms**, select **All platforms**.

6. For **Require mobile device compliance**, select **Block access to email from devices that are not supported by Microsoft Intune**.

7. For **Targeted Groups**, click **Modify**, select the **EMS Enabled Users** group, click **Add**, and then click **OK**.

8. On the **Exempt Groups**, click **Modify,** select the **Executive Users** group, click **Add**, and then click **OK**.

Configuring Exchange Online conditional access.

9. Click **Save**. Users are now being blocked from accessing mail without first enrolling the device into Intune.

Compliance Policies and Email Profiles

Compliance policies are a little like configuration items except that they do not require a baseline. They work with conditional access and are used to define whether the device will be granted access to company resources like email and the SharePoint site.

Real World Note: In the event of a conflict between compliance policies and security baselines, a compliance policy always takes precedence.

Configure an Email Profile

Access to corporate email might still be the single most important company resource for most users. In fact, many of the projects we have done were driven by organizations wanting to secure access to corporate mailboxes. Before you can create a compliance policy, you first need to have a valid email profile. Follow these steps:

1. In the **Assets and Compliance** workspace, select **Compliance Settings / Company Resource Access / Email profiles** and click **Create Exchange Active Sync Profile** on the ribbon.

2. On the **General** page, in **Name**, type **Exchange Online**, and click **Next**.

3. On the **Exchange ActiveSync** page, configure these settings and click **Next**:

    a. Exchange ActiveSync host: **outlook.office365.com**

    b. Account name: **ViaMonstra**

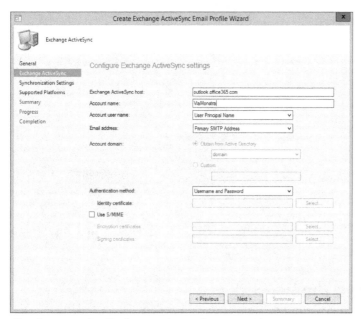

Configuring the Exchange ActiveSync settings.

4. On the **Synchronization Settings** page, configure these settings and click **Next**:

    a. Number of days of email to synchronize: **2 weeks**

    b. Allow email to be sent from third-party applications: **Enabled**

    c. Content type to synchronize: **Select all**

Configuring the synchronization settings.

5. On the **Supported Platforms** page, select all the platforms and finish the wizard.

6. Select the just created **Exchange Online** email profile and click **Deploy** on the ribbon.

7. In the **Deploy Exchange ActiveSync Email Profile** window, click **Browse**, select **All Intune Users**, and click **OK**.

Configure Compliance Policies

A compliance policy is in essence what Microsoft Enterprise Mobility Suite is all about. It is about protecting data, and a key aspect in protecting data is demanding that devices follow certain rules. ViaMonstra requires that all devices are encrypted and use a six-digit pin code to unlock the screen. Noncompliant devices are not allowed access to corporate email.

1. In the **Assets and Compliance** workspace, select **Compliance Settings / Compliance Policies** and click **Create Compliance Policy** on the ribbon.

2. On the **General** page, in **Name**, type **ViaMonstra Users**, and click **Next**.

3. On the **Supported Platforms** page, select **Android**, **iPhone**, **iPad**, **Windows Phone**, **Mac OS X**, and **Windows 10\All Windows 10 Mobile and higher** and then click **Next**.

4. On the **Rules** page, click **New** and complete the following steps:

   a. In **Condition**, select **Email profile must be managed by Intune**.

   b. In **Profile**, select **Exchange Online**, click **OK**, and finish the wizard.

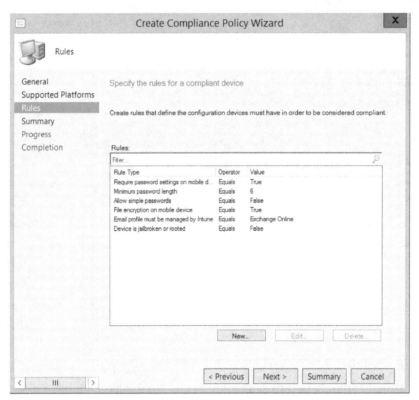

Configuring compliance policy to control access to corporate email.

5. In **Compliance policies**, select **ViaMonstra Users** and click **Deploy** on the ribbon.

6. In **Collection**, click **Browse**, select the **All Intune Users** collection, and click **OK** twice.

> **Real World Note**: Requiring encryption on a device is where the fun begins when working with multiple platforms. On the Android devices, you receive a message saying the device does not comply to the security policies, as it's not encrypted by default. The Intune Company Portal is not able to force encryption, but it's smart enough to guide the user through the process.

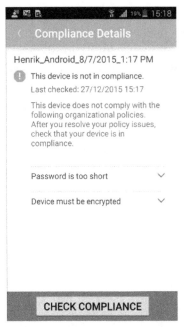

A noncompliant device.

Configure Conditional Access to Exchange On-Premises

The main difference between Exchange on-premises and Exchange Online is the need for installing a connector when working with a non-online solution. Prior to installing the connector, you need to ensure you have an Exchange Connector account with permissions to run these PowerShell cmdlets:

- Get-ActiveSyncOrganizationSettings, Set-ActiveSyncOrganizationSettings
- Get-CasMailbox, Set-CasMailbox
- Get-ActiveSyncMailboxPolicy, Set-ActiveSyncMailboxPolicy, New-ActiveSyncMailboxPolicy, Remove-ActiveSyncMailboxPolicy
- Get-ActiveSyncDeviceAccessRule, Set-ActiveSyncDeviceAccessRule, New-ActiveSyncDeviceAccessRule, Remove-ActiveSyncDeviceAccessRule
- Get-ActiveSyncDeviceStatistics
- Get-ActiveSyncDevice
- Get-ExchangeServer
- Get-ActiveSyncDeviceClass
- Get-Recipient
- Clear-ActiveSyncDevice, Remove-ActiveSyncDevice
- Set-ADServerSettings
- Get-Command

Installing the Exchange Connector also synchronizes information about all Exchange ActiveSync-registered devices. In some scenarios, you may want to compare the number of Intune-managed devices with the number of Exchange ActiveSync devices. To create the connector, follow these steps. (The example requires that you have an existing on-premise Exchange Server named EX01 and a user account with the required permissions.)

1. In the **Administration** workspace, select **Hierarchy Configuration / Exchange Server Connectors**, and click **Add Exchange Server** on the ribbon.

2. On the **General** page, select **On-premises Exchange Server**; in **Server address (URL)**, type **http://ex01.corp.viamonstra.com/powershell**; and click **Next**.

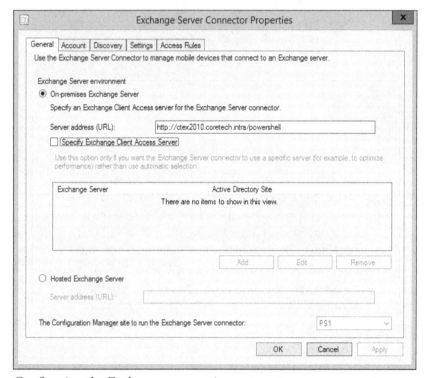

Configuring the Exchange on-premises connector.

3. On the **Account** page, configure these settings accounts and click **Next**:

    a. Exchange Server Connection Account: **VIAMONSTRA\CM_EX**

    b. Conditional Access Email Notification Account: **security@viamonstra.com**

4. On the **Discovery** page, leave the default settings and click **Next**.

5. On the **Settings** page, leave the default settings and click **Next**.

6. On the **Summary** page, read the summary and click **Next**.

7. On the **Completion** page, click **Close**.

After you create the connector, the next step is to configure access to on-premises Exchange. As with Exchange Online, you can configure a group to target and a group of exempted users. Unlike with Exchange Online, the users are selected based on collection membership. For that reason, you should have a collection with all Intune users and a collection with exempted users.

1. Open the **ConfigMgr console**, navigate to **Assets and Compliance / Compliance Settings / Conditional Access / On-Premises Exchange**, and click **Configure conditional access policy in the Intune console**. (Yes, we know the text is wrong, but that is what ConfigMgr current branch is saying at the time of writing.)

2. On the **General** page, configure the following setting and click **Next**:

    Domain Name: **Viamonstra.com**

3. On the **Targeted Collections** page, configure this setting and click **Next**:

    Targeted collections: Click **Add**, select **All Intune Users**, and click **OK**.

4. On the **Exempted Collections** page, configure this setting and click **Next**:

    Targeted collections: Click **Add**, select **All Management Users**, and click **OK**.

5. On the **End User Notification** page, leave the default settings and click **Next**.

6. On the **Summary** page, read the summary and click **Next**.

7. On the **Completion** page, click **Close**.

Real World Note: Working with on-premises Exchange is a different experience compared to Exchange Online. It might take several hours before the conditional access policies are applied. That can lead to a lot of useless troubleshooting when trying to figure out why the policies are not being applied.

Certificates

ConfigMgr has support for deploying various certificates profiles, like trusted CA certificates, Simple Certificate Enrollment Protocol (SCEP) certificates, and MIME certificates. ViaMonstra needs a solution for deploying a certificate to domain and non-domain joined Windows 10 devices so the devices can install modern-style applications.

Appendix E explains how you configure all the prerequisites for NDES.

The following steps explain how you can deploy a certificate associated with a modern-style Windows application. The steps require that you have copied the ViaMonstra LOB application to \\cm01\sccm_sources$\Software\Viamonstra.

1. On **CM01**, log on as **VIAMONSTRA\Administrator** and open the **ConfigMgr console**.

2. In **Assets and Compliance Library**, navigate to **Compliance Settings / Company Resource Access / Certificate Profiles**.

3. Click **Create Certificate Profile** on the ribbon.

4. On the **General** page, configure these settings and click **Next**:

    a. Name: **ViaMonstra LOB**

    b. Description: **ViaMonstra LOB self-signed certificate**

    c. Trusted CA-certificate: **Enabled**

5. On the **Trusted CA Certificate** page, configure these settings and click **Next**:

    a. Certificate file: **\\cm01\sccm_sources$\Software\ViaMonstra LOB\AppPackages\ViaMonstra LOB II_1.0.0.0_AnyCPU_Test\ViaMonstra LOB II_1.0.0.0_AnyCPU.cer**

    b. Destination store: **Computer certificate store – Root**

6. On the **Supported platforms** page, expand **Windows 10**, select **Windows 10 (64-bit)**, and click **Next**.

7. On the **Summary** page, click **Next**.

8. On the **Completion** page, click **Close**.

After you deploy the certificate to a Windows 10 device, it is added to the Trusted Root certificate store.

Wi-Fi

Wi-Fi profiles come in several flavors, those that require user-based certificates (and an NDES server to deploy the certificates) and those that have a pre-shared secret. We have seen and configured both. The pre-shared secret Wi-Fi profiles are a little tricky because they are not created or deployed using the Wi-Fi feature. Instead, you first create an XML file with all the information and then import the XML file into a configuration item.

In ViaMonstra, the wireless settings are configured like this:

*   SSID: ViaMonstra

*   Pre-shared secret: Ynwa2005

*   Encryption: WPA2

Windows Phone

There is no option in the ConfigMgr UI for configuring a pre-shared secret when deploying Wi-Fi profiles to Windows Phones. Instead, you have to export an existing configuration from a Windows 10 device or create a custom XML file as in the following example. To create and deploy the Wi-Fi profile, follow these steps (which require that you have downloaded the book example files to C:\Setup on CM01):

1. On **CM01**, log on as **VIAMONSTRA\Administrator** and open the **ConfigMgr console**.

2. In **Assets and Compliance Library**, navigate to **Compliance Settings / Company Resource Access / Wi-Fi Profiles**.

3. Click **Create Certificate Profile** on the ribbon.

4. On the **General** page, configure these settings and click **Next**:

    a. Name: **WPViaMonstra**

    b. Enable: **Import an existing Wi-Fi profile from a file**

5. On the **Import Wi-Fi Profile** page, click **Add**, select **\\CM01\C$\Setup\WiFi\WP10.xml**, click **Open**, and click **Next**.

6. On the **Supported Platforms** page, expand **Windows 10**, select **All Windows 10 Mobile and higher**, and click **Next**.

7. On the **Summary** page, click **Next**.

8. On the **Completion** page, click **Close**.

9. To deploy the profile, select **WPViaMonstra** and click **Deploy** on the ribbon.

10. From the **Deploy Wi-Fi Profile** dialog box, in **Collection**, click **Browse**, select the **All Intune Users** collection, and click **OK** twice.

The following is the example file used to configure the Windows mobile Wi-Fi profile:

```xml
<?xml version="1.0"?>

<WLANProfile
xmlns="http://www.microsoft.com/networking/WLAN/profile/v1">

  <name>ViaMonstra</name>

  <SSIDConfig>

    <SSID>

      <hex>6D69746E6574</hex>

      <name>ViaMonstra</name>

    </SSID>

  </SSIDConfig>

  <connectionType>ESS</connectionType>

  <connectionMode>Automatic</connectionMode>

  <MSM>
```

```
    <security>

      <authEncryption>

        <authentication>WPA2PSK</authentication>

        <encryption>AES</encryption>

        <useOneX>false</useOneX>

      </authEncryption>

      <sharedKey>

        <keyType>passPhrase</keyType>

        <protected>false</protected>

        <keyMaterial>Ynwa2005</keyMaterial>

      </sharedKey>

    </security>

  </MSM>

</WLANProfile>
```

An easy way to create the Wi-Fi profile's XML file is to create the profile on a Windows 10 computer and then export the profile. To do that, use these steps:

1. To list all the Wi-Fi profiles on the computer, launch **PowerShell** as administrator, type **netsh wlan show profiles**, and make a note of the Wi-Fi profile name.

2. Next, type **netsh wlan export profile name=ViaMonstraWIFI key=clear folder=c:\temp**, where ViaMonstraWIFI is the name of your Wi-Fi profile. This creates the XML file in C:\temp.

Wi-Fi for Android

To create the Wi-Fi examples, start by creating a XML file for Android devices:

1. Launch a web browser and open **http://johnathonb.com/2015/05/intune-android-pre-shared-key-generator**.

2. Enter the following information into the XML generator and click **Create file**:

    a. sSSID: **ViaMonstra**

270

      b. Pass phrase: **Ynwa2005**

      c. Encryption: **AES**

3. Copy the content of the file and paste into an empty XML file.

4. In the XML file, change **<name>"SSID"</name>** to **<name> ViaMonstraAndroid </name>** and save the XML file as **C:\Setup\WiFi\Android.xml** on **CM01**. The following example shows what the file looks like:

```xml
<?xml version="1.0"?>

<WLANProfile
xmlns="http://www.microsoft.com/networking/WLAN/profile/v1">

  <name>ViaMonstraAndroid</name>

    <SSIDConfig>

      <SSID>

        <hex>5669614d6f6e73747261</hex>

        <name>ViaMonstra</name>

      </SSID>

      <nonBroadcast>false</nonBroadcast>

    </SSIDConfig>

    <connectionType>ESS</connectionType>

    <connectionMode>auto</connectionMode>

    <MSM>

      <security>

        <authEncryption>

        <authentication>WPA2PSK</authentication>

        <encryption>AES</encryption>

        <useOneX>false</useOneX>
```

```
        </authEncryption>

        <sharedKey>

            <keyType>passPhrase</keyType>

            <protected>true</protected>

            <keyMaterial>Ynwa2005</keyMaterial>

        </sharedKey>

    </security>

  </MSM>

</WLANProfile>
```

5. Open the **ConfigMgr console**, and in the **Assets and Compliance** workspace, select **Compliance Settings / Configuration Items** and click **Create Configuration Item** on the ribbon.

6. On the **General** page, configure these settings and click **Next**:

    a. Name: **ViaMonstraAndroid**

    b. Settings for devices managed without the Configuration Manager client: **Android and Samsung KNOX**

7. On the **Supported Platforms** page, click **Next**.

8. On the **Mobile Device Settings** page, enable **Configure additional settings that are not in the default settings group** and click **Next**.

9. On the **Additional Settings** page, click **Add** and click **Create**.

10. Configure the **Create Setting** dialog box with these settings and click **OK**:

    a. Name: **ViaMonstraAndroid**

    b. Setting type: **OMA URI**

    c. Data type: **XML**

    d. OME-URI: **./Vendor/MSFT/WiFi/Profile/ViaMonstraAndroid/Settings**

Configuring the Android Wi-Fi profile using OMA-URI.

11. In the **Browse Settings** dialog box, select **ViaMonstraAndroid** from the list and click **Select**.

12. In the **Create Rule** dialog box, paste the XML code from the Android PSK Generator tool, click **OK**, and then click **Close**.

13. On the **Additional Settings** page, click **Next**.

14. On the **Platform Applicability** page, click **Next**.

15. On the **Completion** page, click **Close**.

iOS and Mac OS X

For Apple iOS, you need to get a hold of a Mac OS X computer and install the Apple configurator as described in the Chapter 7. The XML file is stored as a *.mobileconfig file. You create the Wi-Fi profile as a configuration item just like the Android profile. After creating the file, copy it to C:\Setup\WiFi on CM01 and follow the instructions in these steps to create the Wi-Fi profile:

1. Open the **ConfigMgr console**, and in the **Assets and Compliance** workspace, select **Compliance Settings / Configuration Items** and click **Create Configuration Item** on the ribbon.

2. On the **General** page, configure these settings and click **Next**:

   a. Name: **ViaMonstraiOS**

   b. Settings for devices managed without the Configuration Manager client: **iOS and Mac OS X**

3. On the **Supported Platforms** page, click **Next**.

4. On the **Device Settings** page, select **iOS and Mac OS X Custom Profile** and click **Next**.

5. On the **iOS and Mac OS X Custom Profile** page, configure these settings and click **Next**:

   a. Custom configuration profile name: **ViaMonstra**

   b. Configuration profile details: **\\cm01\d$\setup\viamonstra.mobileconfig**

6. On the **Additional Settings** page, click **Next**.

7. On the **Platform Applicability** page, click **Next**.

8. On the **Completion** page, click **Close**.

Deploy the Wi-Fi Profiles

The Wi-Fi profiles are grouped in a baseline and deployed. You can choose to create one baseline for each platform or group both configuration items in the same baseline.

1. In the **Assets and Compliance** workspace, select **Compliance Settings / Configuration Baselines** and click **Create Configuration Baseline** on the ribbon.

2. Configure these settings and click **OK**:

   a. Name: **Wi-Fi profiles**

   b. Configuration data: Click **Add / Configuration Items** and select the Wi-Fi configuration items you created for Android and Apple iOS/Mac OS X.

3. Select the **Wi-Fi profiles** baseline, and click **Deploy** on the ribbon.

4. In the **Deploy Configuration Baselines** window, configure these settings and click **OK**:

   a. Remediate noncompliant rules when supported: **Enabled**

   b. Collection: **All Intune Users**.

VPN

With the VPN management feature, you can create and deploy VPN profiles to the following devices:

- Windows RT 8.1

- Windows 8.1

- Windows 10

- Windows Phone

- iOS

- Android

- Mac OS X

ViaMonstra has a Microsoft VPN connection, and to access data via the ViaMonstra LOB application you deployed in Chapter 7, a VPN tunnel must be open.

Create VPN Profiles

1. Log on to **CM01** as **VIAMONSTRA\Administrator** and open the **ConfigMgr console**.

2. In the **Assets and Compliance** workspace, select **Compliance Settings / Company Resource / VPN Profiles**.

3. From the ribbon, click **Create VPN Profile**.

4. On the **General** page, configure these settings and click **Next**:

   a. Name: **ViaMonstra VPN**

   b. Specify the type of VPN profile you want to create: **VPN for any supported operating system**.

5. On the **Connection** page, configure these settings and click **Next**:

   a. Connection type: **Microsoft Automatic**

   b. Server list: Click **Add**; in **Friendly name**, type **ViaMonstra**; in **IP address or FQDN**, type **vpn.viamonstra.com**; and then click **OK**.

   c. Connection specific DNS suffix: **corp.viamonstra.com**

6. On the **Authentication Method** page, ensure **Microsoft EAP-TTLS** is selected and click **Next**.

7. On the **Proxy Settings** page, click **Next**.

8. On the **Automatic VPN** page, click **Enable VPN on-demand**, configure this setting, and click **Next**:

   Click **Add**; in **DNS suffix**, type **corp.viamonstra.com**; in **Action**, select **Establish if needed**; in **DNS Server Addresses**, type **192.168.1.200**; and then click **OK**.

9. On the **Supported Platforms** page, click **Select all** and click **Next**.

10. On the **Summary** page, click **Next**

11. On the **Completion** page, click **Close**.

12. Select the **ViaMonstra VPN** profile and click **Deploy** on the ribbon.

13. In **Collection**, click **Browse**; select **All Intune Users** and click **OK** twice.

The VPN profile will be applied during the next device policy refresh.

Configuration Items

With configuration items, you configure settings such as application settings, security settings, kiosk mode, and many more. The list of settings than can be applied differs per device and is growing monthly. From reading this book, you should already by familiar with custom compliance settings as you used them to configure Wi-Fi profiles. Later in this chapter, you also learn how to configure application policies. For an updated list of all policies, check this TechNet article: http://ref.ms/mobconfigmgr.

Before creating and policies, you need should stop and plan what you are going to apply. Most organizations focus on configuration settings like encryption and pin code, but those settings were already configured as compliance policies earlier in this book. In ViaMonstra, when designing device security, you first look to see whether you can apply the setting as a compliance policy. If not, you configure the setting as a general security policy. Most settings are deployed to users in the organizations; however, some settings such as "force encryption" are targeted to devices.

OMA-URI Policies

OMA-URI (Open Mobile Alliance Uniform Resource Identifier) allows you to create configuration items that are not visible in the ConfigMgr console.

In this example, you create a setting that disables Action Center notifications when the device is locked on Windows Phone devices:

1. In the **Assets and Compliance** workspace, select **Compliance Settings / Configuration Items** and click **Create Configuration Item** on the ribbon.

2. On the **General** page, configure these settings and click **Next**:

    a. Name: **WP DisableActionCenterNotifications**

    b. Settings for devices managed without the Configuration Manager client: **Windows 8.1 and Windows 10**

3. On the **Supported Platforms** page, click **Next**.

4. On the **Device Settings** page, select **Configure additional settings that are not in the default setting group** and click **Next**.

5. On the **Additional Settings** page, click **Add** and then click **Create**.

6. On the **General** page, configure these settings and click **OK**:

    a. Name: **DisableAllowAction**

    b. Setting type: **OMA URI**

    c. Data type: **Integer**

    d. OMA-URI: **./Vendor/MSFT/PolicyManager/My/AboveLock/AllowActionCenterNotificat ions**

7. Back in the **Browse Settings** window, select the newly create **DisableAllowAction** and click **Select**.

8. In **Browse Settings**, scroll down to the setting **Windows Phone - AboveLock/AllowActionCenterNotifications** and select it.

9. Click **Select** and in the **Create Rule** dialog box, next to **for the following values**, configure the value to **0** (0 means the setting is applied). Then click **OK**.

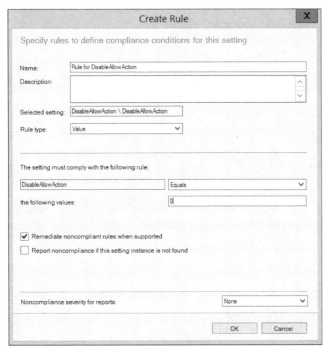

Configuring custom OMA-URI settings.

10. Back in the **Browse Settings** dialog box, click **Close**.

11. On the **Additional Settings** page, click **Next**.

12. On the **Platform Applicability** page, click **Next**.

13. On the **Summary** page, click **Next**.

14. On the **Completion** page, click **Next**.

Read World Note: You also can manage Windows 10 via OMA-URI settings. For an up-to-date list, see this page: http://ref.ms/win10uri.

Kiosk Mode

As described in Chapter 6, you can use the Apple configurator to configure iOS kiosk mode. In kiosk mode, the device can often launch only a single application with a limited set of settings. In ViaMonstra, employees use iOS devices in meeting facilities to project PowerPoint decks. For iOS, you can configure and control managed applications as described in the following steps:

1. In the **Assets and Compliance** workspace, select **Compliance Settings / Configuration Items** and click **Create Configuration Item** on the ribbon.

2. On the **General** page, configure these settings and click **Next**:

    a. Name: **iOS Kiosk**

    b. Settings for devices managed without the Configuration Manager client: **iOS and Mac OS X**

3. On the **Supported Platforms** page, click **Next**.

4. On the **Device Settings** page, select **Kiosk Mode (iOS)** and click **Next**.

5. On the **Configure Kiosk Mode Settings for iOS Devices** page, configure these settings and click **Next**:

    a. Store App: Click **Get ID**, type **https://itunes.apple.com/us/app/microsoft-powerpoint/id586449534?mt=8**, and click **Get ID**. This is the URL to Microsoft PowerPoint.

    b. Touch: **Enabled**

    c. Screen rotation: **Enabled**

6. On the **Platform Applicability** page, click **Next**.

7. On the **Summary** page, click **Close**.

8. On the **Completion** page, click **Close**.

Kiosk settings are unlike most other settings not deployed to a user. Instead, you should create a collection of kiosk devices and target the baseline to that specific collection.

Application Management

With ConfigMgr, software can be created either as packages or applications. When working with mobile devices, all content has to be created as applications. Applications are much more intelligent than packages and allow you, as the administrator, to gain more control over what happens. Applications also are much more user-centric compared to packages. With the correct requirement rules, you control whether and which deployment type is installed to a device. Before creating the applications, you need to understand the basics.

How Applications Are Installed

You can install applications via the Company Portal, Software Center, or the Application Catalog website point. The interface depends on the device you are using and the purpose of the application deployment. It is essential that you know when to use the different options. When deploying an application, the deployment can be either required or available (optional):

- A *required* deployment is a deployment that is installed based on either an event or a schedule. The logged on user might have the option to install the application prior to the scheduled deadline.

- An *available*, or optional, deployment requires user interaction and must be started by a logged on user.

The Application

To understand applications, you first need to learn the high-level overview. An application is not an IPA package, nor is it an .exe file. Instead, an application represents all possible deployment types for a specific software package. For example, Adobe Reader is one application containing multiple deployment types like APK, IPA, and .exe. These different deployment types are all child objects to the same application, but only one of the deployment types is installed on a device. Which one is installed depends on the requirement rules and order of the deployment types.

The following table describes the pages you complete when creating your application using the Create Application Wizard.

Application Tab	Description
Application Properties	The first information you have to worry about when creating a new application. The properties should all follow the same naming standard and that way make it easier for the administrators to work with the application in the ConfigMgr console.
Application Catalog	The end-user metadata. The values in the Application Catalog are used by end users when searching for applications or viewing additional information about the application.
References	Information about links between this application and other applications. On this page, you can see whether the application is superseded by another application and whether other applications have dependencies on this application.

Application Tab	Description
Distribution Settings	Information about the distribution settings of the package, such as how the content is distributed to distribution points that are configured for prestaged content only. Here you also find the setting "Distribute the content for this package to preferred distribution points." With this feature enabled, content is distributed automatically to a distribution point when requested by a user or device.
Deployment Type	A list of the associated deployment types and their priorities. Keep in mind that only one of the deployment types is installed on the device. The first deployment type matching all the requirements is installed, and the remaining deployment types are not applied.
Content Locations	A list of the distribution point(s) and distribution point group(s) where the content can be located. You select each distribution point(s) or group(s) and redistribute the package, remove the package from distribution points, and validate the package. The package validation verifies that all the files used by the package are present in the content library and that all HASH values are correct.
Supersedence	Used to create a supersedence relationship between this application and the application you want to supersede.
Security	Security information for the application.

Real World Note: Applications are presented to users with the application name and an icon. Icons are not created automatically; instead, you have to find the icon and add the object as part of the end-user metadata on the Application Catalog tab. Although icons are not required, we strongly encourage you to locate and apply icons to the application properties. A good resource is http://www.iconarchive.com.

The Deployment Type

An application can have multiple deployment types; each deployment type is often unique to a single platform.

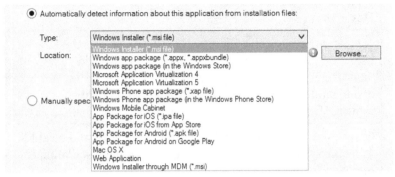

List of the available deployment types in ConfigMgr current branch.

The following table gives you an overview of the available choices.

	Windows 8.1/10	Windows Phone 8.1/10	Apple iOS	Android	Mac OS X
Deeplink	Yes	Yes	Yes	Yes	No
In-house application, or sideloading	*.appx	*.xap	*.ipa	*.apk	*.MPKG *.PKG *.APP *.DMG

The following table describes the tabs in the Deployment Type properties. The tabs and settings depend on the selected deployment type.

Deployment Type Tab	Description
General	Deployment type properties like name, technology, comments, and language.
Content	Source location and information about Microsoft BranchCache support (which allows clients to share content with other clients on the same subnet). Allowing clients to use a fallback source location for content enables them to use another distribution point as a fallback source for the package in the event that the local distribution point is unavailable. On the Content tab, you also can configure whether the client is able to download the package from a slow connection. A "slow connection" is not based on a real time evaluation, but rather on a setting configured in the boundary group.
Programs	Allows you to specify the install and uninstall program.

Deployment Type Tab	Description
Detection Method	Needed for every deployment type. The client uses the detection method to determine whether that specific deployment type is already present on the device. You can create multiple detection methods like MSI product code, registry, file based, or a custom script.
User Experience	Can be used to configure whether the end user should be able to interact with the installation and whether the installation is intended for a user or device.
Requirements	Also known as *global conditions*. Requirements are evaluated in real-time before the application is downloaded and installed. You can create device, user, and custom requirement rules based on registry values, WMI queries, and much more.
Return Codes	Allows you to specify the return code that the specific deployment type returns in the event of a successful installation, restart required, or failure. (We have a dream that one day all software developers start reading the same book and come to a mutual agreement on which return codes to use.)
Dependencies	List of other deployment types that this deployment type depends on. One example is that a virtual App-V application depends on the App-V client being installed on the device.
Publishing	Only available for App-V deployment types and defines the icons that are published when "installing" this deployment type. (We have "installing" in quotation marks because you are not installing a virtual application like a traditional application.)

The Deployment

The settings you can configure for a deployment depend on how and to whom you target the deployment. As mentioned earlier, a deployment can be targeted to a user or device collection, and it can be either available or mandatory (have a deadline for the installation). This table describes the pages you use to configure your deployment.

Deployment Tab	Description
General	Deployment information like software used, collection, and optional comments.
Content	List of the distribution point(s) and distribution point group(s) where the content is available.

Deployment Tab	Description
Deployment Settings	Information about the deployment action, Install or Uninstall; the purpose of the deployment, Available or Required; and the setting to control whether administrator approval is required in order to install the application. If the deployment has a deadline, you also can configure ConfigMgr to send a wakeup package prior to running the deployment. This setting requires that Wake On LAN has been configured.
Scheduling	Defines the application availability time. If not specified, the application becomes available as soon as possible. If the deployment is required, you also have the option to configure the installation deadline. When specifying the installation deadline, you have the option to configure whether the time is based on client local time or UTC.
User Experience	Defines how the deployment interacts with the logged on user. If the deployment is required, you have the option to hide all notifications completely, as well as not displaying anything in the Software Center. For available deployments, you can specify the level of notifications shown, but the deployment is always visible in the Software Center. This is also the page where you can choose to ignore maintenance windows for the deployment. By ignoring maintenance windows, you allow the application to be installed outside of any defined maintenance window.
Alerts	Allows you to set alerts for your deployment. The alerts depend on the deployment purpose. For required deployments, you can specify when alerts are created (that is, created in the ConfigMgr console) for failed and missing deployments. If you have OpsMgr 2012 installed, the deployment also can stop the OpsMgr agent. Note that this does not place the OpsMgr 2012 client in real maintenance mode, so you might generate alerts in the OpsMgr console with this feature.

Deployment Options for Mobile Devices

Mobile device deployment options are controlled by the device ownership. The following table describes the available options and deployment behavior.

Scenario	Windows 10	Windows Phone 8/10	iOS	Android
Available Install deployed to users	Yes	Yes	Yes	Yes
Required Install deployed to users and devices	Company owned: Automatically installed Personally owned: N/A	N/A	Company owned: User is prompted to accept the installation. Personally owned: N/A	Company owned: User is prompted to accept the installation. Personally owned: NA/
Remote Uninstall deployed to users and devices	Automatically uninstalled	N/A	Yes	User is prompted to accept the uninstall.

Requirement Rules

Requirement rules are used to determine which deployment type will be downloaded and installed on the device. Requirement rules for mobile devices are often very easy to create, as you most likely just want to distinguish between the different operating systems. When working with traditional PC management, requirement rules have a tendency to become more complex.

Deploy Store Applications

Store applications also are referred to as deep-link applications. These applications do not have content stored locally on the site server. For that reason, the only objects you have to create are the application, the deployment type(s), and deployment. In the following example, you use PowerShell to create the Twitter and Spotify applications with three deployment types. Spotify has an available deployment to all Intune users and Twitter is deployed as a required application. For this example, we downloaded a Twitter icon file and placed it in C:\Setup\Twitter and a Spotify one to C:\Setup\Spotify.

1. On **CM01**, launch **PowerShell ISE** as administrator and run the following script:

```
#Import ConfigMgr module

Import-Module
$env:SMS_ADMIN_UI_PATH.Replace("\bin\i386","\bin
\configurationmanager.psd1")

$SiteCode = Get-PSDrive -PSProvider CMSITE

Set-Location "$($SiteCode.Name):\"

#Create the Twitter Application

New-CMApplication -Name "Twitter"

#iOS deployment type

Add-CMDeploymentType -ApplicationName "Twitter"
-AutoIdentifyFromInstallationFile -IosDeepLinkInstaller
-DeploymentTypeName "Twitter iOS" -InstallationFileLocation
"https://itunes.apple.com/us/app/twitter/id333903271?mt=8"
-ForceForUnknownPublisher $True

# Windows Phone deployment type

Add-CMDeploymentType -ApplicationName "Twitter"
-AutoIdentifyFromInstallationFile
-WinPhone8DeeplinkInstaller -DeploymentTypeName "Twitter WP"
-InstallationFileLocation "https://www.microsoft.com/en-
us/store/apps/twitter/9wzdncrfj140"
-ForceForUnknownPublisher $True

# Goggle Play deployment type

Add-CMDeploymentType -ApplicationName "Twitter"
-AutoIdentifyFromInstallationFile -AndroidDeepLinkInstaller
-DeploymentTypeName "Twitter Google Play"
-InstallationFileLocation
"https://play.google.com/store/apps/details?id=com.twitter.a
ndroid" -ForceForUnknownPublisher $True

#Create the Spotify application
```

```
New-CMApplication -Name "Spotify"

#To create an iOS deployment type

Add-CMDeploymentType -ApplicationName "Spotify"
-AutoIdentifyFromInstallationFile -IosDeepLinkInstaller
-DeploymentTypeName "Spotify iOS" -InstallationFileLocation
"https://itunes.apple.com/en/app/spotify-
music/id324684580?mt=8" -ForceForUnknownPublisher $True

#To create a Windows Phone deployment type

Add-CMDeploymentType -ApplicationName "Spotify"
-AutoIdentifyFromInstallationFile
-WinPhone8DeeplinkInstaller -DeploymentTypeName "Spotify WP"
-InstallationFileLocation "http://www.windowsphone.com/en-
us/store/app/spotify/10f2995d-1f82-4203-b7fa-46ddbd07a6e6"
-ForceForUnknownPublisher $True

# To create a Goggle Play deployment type

Add-CMDeploymentType -ApplicationName "Spotify"
-AutoIdentifyFromInstallationFile -AndroidDeepLinkInstaller
-DeploymentTypeName "Spotify Google Play"
-InstallationFileLocation
"https://play.google.com/store/apps/details?id=com.spotify.m
usic&hl=en" -ForceForUnknownPublisher $True

#Creating the deployment to All Intune Users

Start-CMApplicationDeployment -Name "Twitter"
-CollectionName "All Intune Users" -DeployAction Install
-DeployPurpose Required -AppRequiresApproval $False
-SendWakeUpPacket $True -UseMeteredNetwork $False

Start-CMApplicationDeployment -Name "Spotify"
-CollectionName "All Intune Users" -DeployAction Install
-DeployPurpose Available -AppRequiresApproval $False
-SendWakeUpPacket $True -UseMeteredNetwork $False
```

2. To modify the application and the iOS deployment type, follow these steps:

    a. In the **Software Library** workspace, select **Application Management /
        Applications**.

    b. Select the **Spotify** application and click the **Deployment Types** tab.

    c. Select the **Spotify iOS** deployment type, and on the ribbon, click **Properties**.

     d. On the **Requirements** tab, click **Add**, configure this requirement rule with the following settings, and click **OK** twice:

- Category: **Device**.

- Condition: **Operating System**

- Value: **iPhone All IOS iPhone or iPod touch devices, All iOS9 iPad devices**

3. In the **Software Library** workspace, select **Application Management / Applications**.

4. Select the **Twitter** application, and on the ribbon, click **Properties**.

5. Select the **Application Catalog** tab, fill out the metadata, and enable **Display this as a featured app and highlight it in the company portal**.

6. In **Icon**, click **Browse** and select the Spotify icon from **C:\Setup\Icons**.

7. In **User categories**, click **Edit / Create**, and type **Entertainment** as a new category name.

8. Click **OK** twice.

Notice that the application install experience is different on the devices. Your iOS device prompts you before installing the required application. Android users are taken to the Google Play store. The Windows Phone installs it silently.

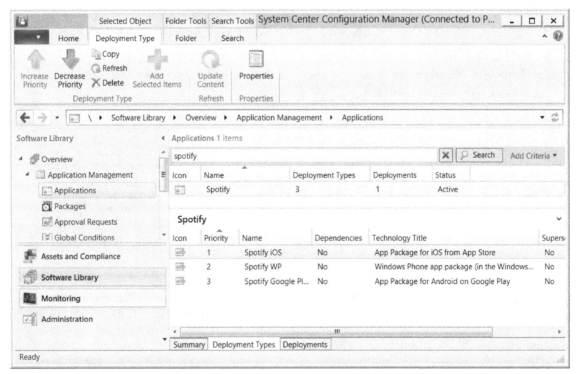

Application with multiple deployment types.

Working with Managed Applications

The managed applications you create with Microsoft Intune are no different from those you create with ConfigMgr. The idea is the same: you create the application and combine the deployment with a managed application policy. In the following example, you use a custom PowerShell script to create all the available managed applications:

1. On **CM01**, launch **PowerShell ISE** as administrator.

2. Run the **C:\Setup\Scripts\CreateManagedApps.ps1** script. The script creates the Office managed applications and deployment types but not any deployments.

Create Managed Application Policies

Application policies have one single purpose: *to protect data*—protect data from being forwarded to the wrong persons and from being accessed if the device falls into the wrong hands. The number of application policies will depend on the use cases you have in your organization. A common scenario is to prevent data from being copied between a managed and non-managed application or to allow access only to certain web sites.

Application policies are integrated with the deployment of an application. For that matter, you need to have several collections and deployments for the same application. ViaMonstra already has an All Sales Users collection that will be used as the target collection. Collections can be populated using dynamic query rules or by adding direct rules. A direct rule is static and does not change until you remove the rule. To add users to the All Sales Users collection using a direct rule, follow these steps:

1. In the **Assets and Compliance** workspace, select **User Collections** and click **Properties** on the ribbon.

2. Select the **Membership Rules** tab and click **Add Rule / Direct Rule**. This launches the Create Direct Membership Rule Wizard.

3. Complete the wizard:

    a. On the **Welcome** page, click **Next**.

    b. On the **Search for Resources** page, in **Value**, type **%** (this is the wildcard and can be used only in a small lab environment like this) and click **Next**.

    c. From the list of users, select **Kim Youno**, **Mia King**, and **Henrik Fahlen**, and then click **Next**.

    d. On the **Summary** page, click **Next**.

    e. On the **Completion** page, click **OK** twice.

With the applications and collections, the next step in the process is to create the managed policies and deployments. Follow these steps to create two general managed policies for iOS and Android and two managed browser policies for Android and iOS:

1. In the **Software Library** workspace, select **Application Management / Application Management Policies** and click **Create Application Management Policy** on the ribbon. This launches the Create Application Management Policy Wizard.

2. Complete the wizard:

    a. On the **General** page, type **Locked down iOS Browser** and click **Next**.

    b. On the **Policy Type** page, select **iOS** as the **Platform** and **Managed Browser** as the **Policy Type**. Then click **Next**.

    c. On the **Managed Browser** page, select **Allow the managed browser to open only the URLs listed below**.

    d. Type **http://viamonstra.com**, click **Add**, and then click **Next**.

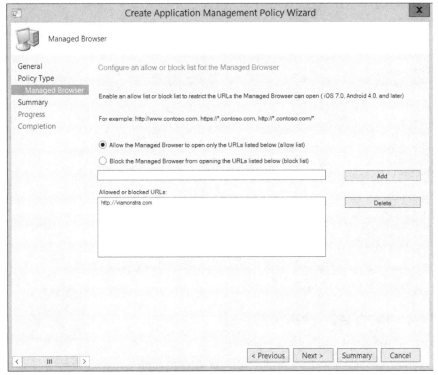

Creating the managed browser application policy.

    e. On the **Summary** page, click **Next**.

    f. On the **Completion** page, click **Close**.

    g. Repeat the steps to create a **Locked down Android Browser** policy.

3. In the **Software Library** workspace, select **Application Management / Application Management Policies** and click **Create Application Management Policy** on the ribbon. This again launches the Create Application Management Policy Wizard.

4. Complete the wizard:

    a. On the **General** page, type **Sales iOS** and click **Next**.

    b. On the **Policy Type** page, select **iOS** as the **Platform** and **General** as the **Policy Type**. Then click **Next**.

    c. On the **iOS Policy** page, leave the default settings and click **Next**.

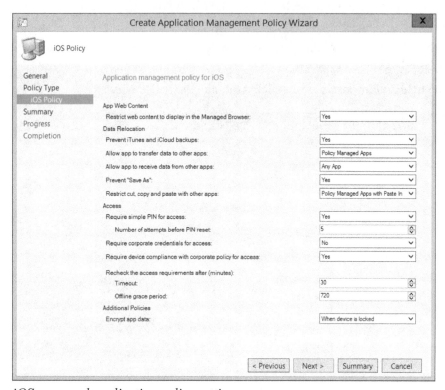

iOS managed application policy settings.

    d. On the **Summary** page, click **Next**.

    e. On the **Completion** page, click **Close**.

    f. Repeat the steps to create a general **Sales Android** policy.

Deploy Managed Applications

If you are wondering whether the application you created is a managed application, then all you have to do is create a deployment. Only managed applications have the Application Management page in the Deploy Software Wizard.

1. In the **Software Library** workspace, select **Application Management / Applications**, select the **Intune Browser** application, and click **Deploy** on the ribbon.

2. On the **General** page, configure this setting and click **Next**:

   Collection: Click **Browse**, select the **All Intune Users** collection, and click **OK**.

3. Click **Next** six times to see the **Application Management** page and then click **Next** again. Notice that each deployment type is already associated with a managed browser policy.

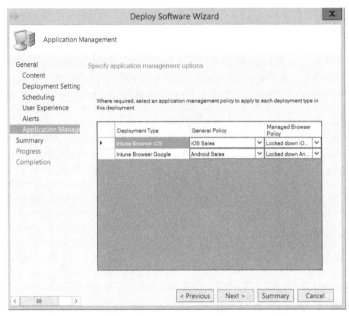

Linking the application policy with a deployment.

4. On the **Summary** page, click **Next**.

5. On the **Completion** page, click **Close**.

To create available deployments and assign a general managed policy, follow these steps:

1. In the **Software Library** workspace, select **Application Management / Applications**, select the **Word** application, and click **Deploy** on the ribbon.

2. On the **General** page, configure this setting and click **Next**:

   Collection: Click **Browse**, select the **All Intune Users** collection, and click **OK**.

3. Click **Next** six times to see the **Application Management** page and then click **Next** again. Notice that each deployment type is already associated with a managed browser policy.

4. On the **Summary** page, click **Next**.

5. On the **Completion** page, click **Close**.

As you noticed, the application policies are applied automatically when you create the deployment. You also can use PowerShell to create the deployments as you learned with Twitter and Spotify. Simply use the Start.CMApplicationDeployment cmdlet as illustrated here:

```
Start-CMApplicationDeployment -Name "AV Player" -CollectionName
"All Intune Users" -DeployAction Install -DeployPurpose Available
-AppRequiresApproval $False -SendWakeUpPacket $True
-UseMeteredNetwork $False
```

Although not mentioned in the preceding, we highly recommend that you spend time filling out the Application Catalog metadata. Always include a custom category and icon as the bare minimum. The downloads for this book include several icons you can use.

Sideloading Applications

Sideloading is the term used when you possess the application files and distribute the application like any other in-house line of business application.

Sideload an Application for Android and iOS

As described earlier in this book, ViaMonstra wants to deploy Adobe Reader to Android and iOS devices. To deploy the required application, gather the files as described earlier in the book for the Microsoft Intune standalone scenario. Copy the gathered AdobeReader.apk and Adobe Acrobat 15.2.1.ipa files to E:\Sources\Software\Adobe Reader\ on CM01.

On **CM01**, launch **PowerShell ISE** as administrator and open the **C:\Setup\Scripts\CreateManagedApps.ps1** script. The script, included here, creates the Adobe Reader applications, distributes the content, and creates the required deployment.

```
#Create the Adobe Reader Application

#Import ConfigMgr module

Import-Module
$env:SMS_ADMIN_UI_PATH.Replace("\bin\i386","\bin
\configurationmanager.psd1")

$SiteCode = Get-PSDrive -PSProvider CMSITE

Set-Location "$($SiteCode.Name):\"

New-CMApplication -Name "Adobe Reader" -Manufacturer "Adobe"
-SoftwareVersion "15"

Add-CMDeploymentType -ApplicationName "Adobe Reader"
-AutoIdentifyFromInstallationFile -IosInstaller
-DeploymentTypeName "Adobe Reader IPA" -ContentLocation
"\\cm01\sccm_sources$\Software\Adobe\Adobe Acrobat
15.2.1.ipa" -ForceForUnknownPublisher $True
```

```
Add-CMDeploymentType -ApplicationName "Adobe Reader"
-AutoIdentifyFromInstallationFile -AndroidInstaller
-DeploymentTypeName "Adobe Reader APK" -ContentLocation
\\cm01\sccm_sources$\Software\Adobe\AdobeReader.apk
-ForceForUnknownPublisher $True

#Distribute the content to Intune distribution point

Start-CMContentDistribution -ApplicationName "Adobe Reader"
-DistributionPointName "manage.microsoft.com"

#Create the deployment

Start-CMApplicationDeployment -Name "Adobe Reader"
-CollectionName "All Intune Users" -DeployAction Install
-DeployPurpose Required -AppRequiresApproval $False
-SendWakeUpPacket $True -UseMeteredNetwork $False
```

Sideloading Windows 10 Applications

ViaMonstra has developed a very important in-house application that must be available to users on all Windows 10 Enterprise devices. Before deploying the application, you first need to create a group policy that enables sideloading and install the certificate on all devices. For these steps, we assume you have downloaded the book sample files, which contain the ViaMonstra modern-style application, and copied it to E:\Sources\Software\ViaMonstra on CM01.

Create the Group Policy

1. On **DC01**, log on as **VIAMONSTRA\Administrator**, and open the **Group Policy Management console**.

2. Expand **Forest: corp.viamonstra.com**.

3. Expand **Domains**.

4. Right-click the **corp.viamonstra.com** domain and select **Create a GPO in this domain, and Link it here**.

5. Create a new Group Policy object called **Allow sideloading application** and click **OK**.

6. Right-click **Allow sideloading application GPO** and select **Edit**.

7. Expand **Computer Configuration / Policies / Administrative Templates / Windows Components**, and select **App Package Deployment**.

8. Double-click **Allow All trusted apps to install**, select **Enabled**, and click **OK**.

9. Close the **Group Policy Management console**.

Create the Application in ConfigMgr

1. In the **Software Library**, navigate to **Application Management / Applications / Optional User**.

2. On the ribbon, click **Create Application**.

3. On the **General** page, select these settings and click **Next**:

   a. Type: **Windows app package (*.appx, *.appxbundle)**

   b. Location: **\\cm01\sccm_sources$\Software\ViaMonstra\ViaMonstra LOB II_1.0.0.0_AnyCPU.appx**

4. On the **Import Information** page, read the imported information and click **Next**.

5. On the **General Information** page, click **Select** and create a **ViaMonstra LOB** category. Click **OK** twice and finish the wizard.

6. Deploy the app via the following **PowerShell** command:

```
Start-CMContentDistribution -ApplicationName "ViaMonstra LOB
II" -DistributionPointName "cm01.corp.viamonstra.com"
```

Configure VPN Support for Modern-style Applications

You can configure a modern-style application like the ViaMonstra LOB application to establish a VPN tunnel automatically when you launch the application.

1. In the **Software Library** workspace, select **Application Management / Applications / Optional User**.

2. Select the ViaMonstra LOB application and click **Deployment Types**.

3. Select the deployment type and click **Properties** on the ribbon.

4.   Enable **Use an automatic VPN connection if configured** and click **OK**.

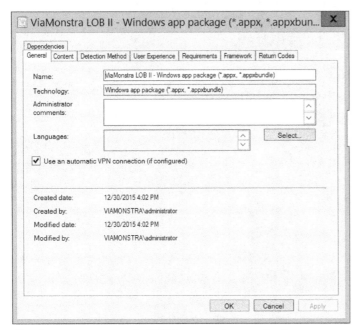

Configuring automatic VPN connection on deployment types.

Tracking and Blocking Applications

When working with Android and iOS, you can create compliance items that can track whether users have noncompliant and/or compliant applications installed. The feature does not block users from running the applications, but it allows the organization to trace compliance. In Windows Phone, you are able to block certain applications.

Compliant and Noncompliant Applications

1.   In the **Assets and Compliance** workspace, select **Compliance Settings / Configuration Items** and click **Create Configuration Item** on the ribbon.

2.   On the **General** page, configure these settings and click **Next**:

     a.   Name: **Noncompliant Apple applications**

     b.   Settings for devices managed without the Configuration Manager client: **iOS and Mac OS X**

3.   On the **Supported Platforms** page, click **Next**.

4. On the **Device Settings** page, select **Compliant and Noncompliant Apps (iOS)** and click **Next**.

Selecting device settings.

5. On the **iOS App Compliance** page, click **Import**, import the **C:\Setup\Compliance \BadiOSApps.csv** file, and click **Next**.

6. On the **Platform Applicability** page, click **Next**.

7. On the **Summary** page, click **Next**.

8. On the **Completion** page, click **Close**.

There also is a BadAndroidApps.csv file that you can import if you want to test the same settings for Android.

Create the Baseline

ConfigMgr does not support deploying individual configuration items. Instead, you can group one or more configuration items into baselines and deploy the baseline as described here:

1. In the **Assets and Compliance** workspace, select **Compliance Settings / Configuration Baselines** and click **Create Configuration Baseline** on the ribbon.

2. Configure these settings and click **OK**:

    a. Name: **Noncompliant MDM applications**

    b. Configuration data: Click **Add / Configuration Items** and select the noncompliant MDM apps Configuration Item that you created in the previous steps.

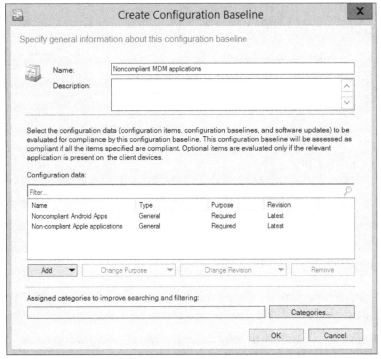

Tracking noncompliant applications using a baseline.

3. Select the **Noncompliant MDM applications** baseline and click **Deploy** on the ribbon.

4. In **Collection**, click **Browse** and select the **All Intune Users** collection.

5. Click **OK** to finish the deployment.

Track Noncompliant Applications

You can use either the built-in reports or the monitoring workspace in the ConfigMgr console to track compliance. When testing, one important thing is patience, as this takes some time. There are a lot of moving parts in this scenario, devices must download policies, and the baseline has to evaluate and upload the results to Intune. After that, Intune has to communicate with ConfigMgr, add the evaluation data to the database, and present the data.

1. To view compliance data in the built-in reports, from **Internet Explorer**, launch **http://cm01/reports** and open the **ConfigMgr_PS1** folder.

2. From the **Compliance and Settings Management** folder, run the report **Summary of Users who have Noncompliant Apps**; in **Device Collection**, select **All Mobile Devices**; and view the report.

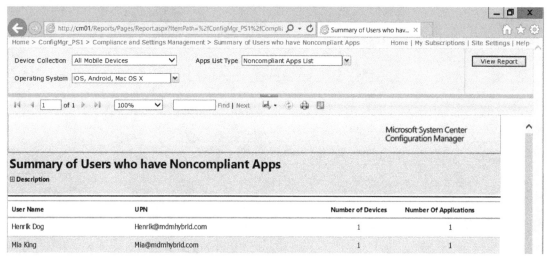

Viewing users with a noncompliant application.

Another very useful report is "List of noncompliant Apps and Devices for a specified user." That report also lists the noncompliant applications installed on the devices.

1. To view compliance data in the **ConfigMgr console**, in the **Monitoring** workspace, navigate to **Deployments**.

2. Select the **Noncompliant MDM Applications** deployment. If no data are shown, click **Run Summarization** on the ribbon and press **F5** for a screen refresh.

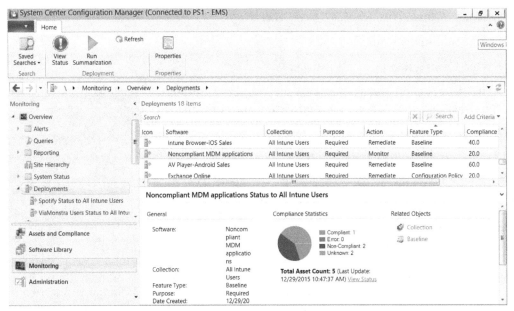

Viewing compliance status in the ConfigMgr console.

You always can drill into the deployment status by clicking View Status. This can be very useful when you want to learn about who is compliant and noncompliant. In the detailed views, you can find information about which applications are noncompliant and on which devices they are detected.

Block Applications in Windows Phone

You can block access to the Windows Store in a variety of ways. You can configure a configuration item to allow only certain applications to be installed, or all applications except the ones you explicitly specify. You also can create a custom OMA-URI configuration item to block a specific application from being installed.

1. In the **Assets and Compliance** workspace, select **Compliance Settings / Configuration Items** and click **Create Configuration Item** on the ribbon.

2. On the **General** page, configure these settings and click **Next**:

    a. Name: **Block Windows Phone applications**

    b. Settings for devices managed without the Configuration Manager client:
        Windows 8.1 and Windows 10

3. On the **Supported Platforms** page, expand **Windows 10**, ensure **All Windows 10 Mobile and higher** is selected, and click **Next**.

4. On the **Device Settings** page, select **Allowed and Blocked Apps list**, and click **Next**.

5. On the **Windows Phone App Compliance** page, click **Import**, import the **C:\Setup\Compliance\BlockWPApps.csv** file, and click **Next**.

6. On the **Platform Applicability** page, click **Next**.

7. On the **Summary** page, click **Next**.

8. On the **Completion** page, click **Close**

9. In the **Assets and Compliance** workspace, select **Compliance Settings / Configuration Baselines** and click **Create Configuration Baseline** on the ribbon.

10. Configure these settings and click **OK**:

   a. Name: **Blocked Applications**

   b. Configuration data: Click **Add / Configuration Items** and select the **Block Windows Phone applications** configuration item.

11. Select the **Blocked Applications** baseline and click **Deploy** on the ribbon.

12. In **Collection**, click **Browse** and select the **All Intune Users** collection.

If the application is already installed on the device, the policy prevents the application from launching. You will notice when reading the csv file, that it includes a link to the application in the Microsoft store. To create additional configuration items, simply find the application in the Microsoft store and copy the link.

Protecting Devices

Occasionally a user forgets a device in the taxi, airport, hotel, and so forth. Of course, it will never happen to you or me, but to our colleagues! With Intune and ConfigMgr, you can wipe a device remotely, the company portion of the device, remote lock the device, and reset the passcode remotely. All of these actions also are referred to as remote actions, which we discussed previously in Chapter 7 while looking at the EMS standalone solution.

Like some of the other features, you will quickly discover that devices behave differently and testing only one device is not sufficient. One example is the remote passcode; iOS and Windows devices are super easy to deal with, whereas Android (at the time of writing this book) gives you a very long temporary passcode that can be hard to memorize.

All remote actions are triggered from devices or device collections in the Assets and Compliance workspace. It's just a matter of finding the device, right-clicking, and selecting the action as explained in the following sections.

Remote Lock Devices

The remote lock devices action locks the device in case the user has left it unlocked. To test this feature, log in to a device and leave the device unlocked.

1. Log on to **CM01** as **VIAMONSTRA\Administrator** and open the **ConfigMgr console**.

2. In the **Assets and Compliance** workspace, select **Devices / All Mobile Devices** and right-click the Android device.

3. Select **Remote Device Actions / Remote Lock**. In the warning window, click **Yes**.

4. Right-click the Android device and select **Remote Device Actions / View Remote Lock State**. Note that it might take some time for the device state to change.

Real World Note: The remote actions do not follow the normal policy synchronization rule. Instead, the devices are "poked," and they then download the policies as soon as possible. In our tests, the average remote action time has been about 32 seconds.

Remote Reset Passcode Devices

1. In the Assets and Compliance workspace, select Devices / All Mobile Devices and right-click the Windows Phone device.

2. Select **Remote Device Actions / Reset Passcode**. In the warning window, click **Yes**.

3. A new passcode is generated. To view the passcode, right-click the device and select **Remote Device Actions / View Passcode**.

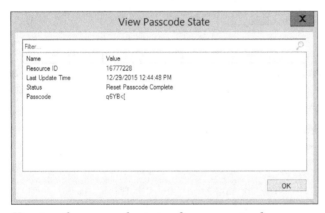

Viewing the passcode state after a remote change.

4. On the device, the end user also receives a message indicating that the passcode has been changed and he/she has to contact support to get the new passcode.

Rain Man Test: Reset the passcode on any Android device, look at the new passcode for 10 seconds, and unlock the device using the new passcode.

Retiring and Wiping Devices

One of the most basic features in any mobile device management system is the ability to retire a device by removing the management profile and completely wipe a device and restore it to factory default. ConfigMgr supports both actions from the devices or device collections, in the Assets and Compliance workspace.

Wipe Company Content

1. Log on to **CM01** as **VIAMONSTRA\Administrator** and open the **ConfigMgr console**.

2. In the **Assets and Compliance** workspace, select **Devices / All Mobile Devices**.

3. Right-click the iOS device and select **Retire/Wipe**.

4. Ensure that **Wipe company content and retire the mobile device from Configuration Manager** is selected and click **OK**.

Initiating a company wipe of a specific device.

5. In the warning text, you get information about what will be removed from the device and when. Notice that wiping company content takes place after the next policy download. Click **Yes** to confirm your action.

   Users receive information on their devices saying that the device is no longer managed. Sideloaded applications, security requirements, and access to company resources like email also are removed as part of the retirement.

6. You can monitor the process from the built-in reports. From your reporting services point, open the **Device Management** folder and run the **Pending wipe request for mobile devices** report.

Factory Reset Devices

Factory resetting a device is something done at ViaMonstra when the device is changing owner or is lost. The user can log in to the Company Portal on another device and perform the reset, or as the administrator, you can reset the device from the ConfigMgr console.

1. Log on to **CM01** as **VIAMONSTRA\Administrator** and open the **ConfigMgr console**.

2. In the **Assets and Compliance** workspace, select **Devices / All Mobile Devices**.

3. Right-click the iOS device and select **Retire/Wipe**. Ensure **Wipe the mobile device and retire the mobile device from Configuration Manager** is selected and click **OK**.

4. In the warning text, you get information about what will be removed from the device and when. Notice that wiping company content takes place after the next policy download. Click **Yes** to confirm your action.

Warning about completely wiping a device.

We have tested the remote wipe on all three devices. All of them received the wipe instructions within 60 seconds. The Android device started by erasing the SD card, and after that, it performed a factory reset.

Chapter 9

Azure Rights Management

In the layered data protection approach of Microsoft, Azure Rights Management (Azure RMS) is used to protect the data itself. In other words, a Microsoft Word or PDF document can be protected in a way that a user can have access to it, but only read it for a certain number of days. Also, the document cannot be forwarded, printed, or copied. Azure RMS is a very powerful service that enables ViaMonstra to protect business critical data.

Real World Note: Implementing Azure RMS throughout a company can be a multiple-month project that can affect the business. Therefore, you need to speak with the business owners and stakeholders to be able to classify data throughout the company so that you are able to protect all of the data. The envisioning phase is the most important phase of an Azure RMS project.

Enabling Azure RMS

Enabling Azure RMS is not a particularly difficult process, and you can do it in two places: via the Office 365 admin center and via the Azure Management Portal. Because Azure RMS is part of the Azure Active Directory Premium feature, all management is done via the Azure Management Portal.

1.   Go to **https://manage.windowsAzure.com** and sign in with the admin account (**admin@emskings.com**).

2.   In the management console, select **Active Directory** and click **Rights Management**.

3.   Select the directory that is available, click **Activate**, and the click **Yes** to activate Rights Management for the Active Directory.

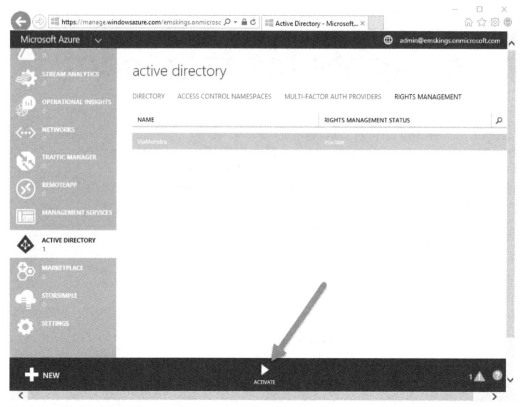

Activate Rights Management for Azure AD ViaMonstra.

If you want to use PowerShell to activate Azure RMS, you can use the following command. Before you can use the Azure RMS cmdlets, however, you need to download and install the Azure AD Rights Management Administration Tool. You can download the Azure AD RMS Admin Tool here: http://ref.ms/Azurermstool.

Open **PowerShell ISE** as administrator, type the following lines, and press **F5** to run the script. When prompted, log in as the global Azure administrator.

```
#Establish the connection to Azure RMS

Connect-AAdrmService

# Enable Azure RMS

Enable-Aadrm

Get-Aadrm
```

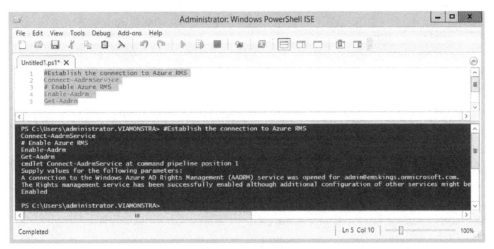

Azure RMS enabled via PowerShell.

Real World Note: You can configure parts of Azure RMS in the Office 365 admin center, but for more advanced configuration, you are redirected to the Azure Management Portal.

Configuring Azure RMS

Azure RMS does not need much configuration work. For ViaMonstra, you need to configure a couple of custom templates.

1. Go to **https://manage.windowsAzure.com** and sign in with the admin account (e.g. admin@emskings.com).

2. In the management console, select **Active Directory** and click **Rights Management**.

3. Click **ViaMonstra** and **Create a new rights policy template**, supply the information as shown in the following table for the first template and click the check mark to complete its creation. Repeat this for the other two templates.

Language	Name	Description
English – United States	ViaMonstra – View for everybody	Content is viewable for everybody.
English – United States	ViaMonstra – Restricted for 2016	Content expires after 12/31/2016.
English – United States	ViaMonstra – Expires after 7 days	Content expires seven days after the content is protected.

4. Click **Manage your rights policy templates** and click the first template you created in step 3 of this procedure.

viamonstra

TEMPLATES

NAME	DESCRIPTION	DATE MODIFIED	STATUS	
ViaMonstra - Confidential	This content is proprietary information int...	6/27/2015 10:46:00 PM	Published	
ViaMonstra - Confidential View Only	This content is proprietary information int...	6/27/2015 10:46:00 PM	Published	
ViaMonstra – Expires after 7 days	Content expires after 7 days after the cont...	11/29/2015 2:26:00 PM	Archived	
ViaMonstra – Restricted for 2016	Content expires after 12/31/2016	11/29/2015 2:26:00 PM	Archived	
ViaMonstra – View for everybody	Content is viewable for everybody	11/29/2015 2:27:00 PM	Archived	

Created Azure RMS templates.

5. Click **Get started** just below **Configure rights for users and groups** to select the users and groups that need access to the templates.

6. Select **Show Users** and click the check mark to view all available groups. Select the user that needs to be added, and click the plus sign (+) next to the user. Click **Next** to configure the permissions.

7. Click **Custom** and select the permissions as shown in the following table:

Name	Users / Group	Permissions
ViaMonstra – View for everybody	Kenny Tree Kim Young	Viewer
ViaMonstra – Restricted for 2016	Henrik Fahlen Tim Snow	Co-Author
ViaMonstra – Expires after 7 days	Peter Blue Mia King	Viewer

8. Click **Complete** and repeat the steps for all other templates that need to be configured.

9. When finished, click the templates again and go to the **Configure** tab and configure the templates with the following settings:

Name	Content Expiration	Offline Access
ViaMonstra – View for everybody	Content never expires	Content is always available.
ViaMonstra – Restricted for 2016	Content expiration date: 2016-12-31	Number of days the content is available without an Internet connection: **7**
ViaMonstra – Expires after 7 days	After the content is protected, content expires after the specified number of days: **7**	Content is available only with an Internet connection

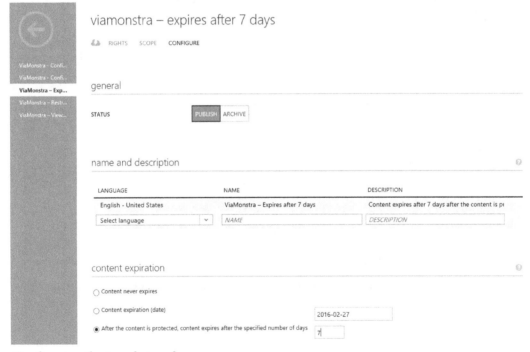

Configuring the template values.

10. Click **Publish** and then click **Save** to publish the custom template to the users.

Integrating Azure RMS with Office 365

Now that you have configured the policy templates, the next step is integrating Azure RMS with Office 365 so that ViaMonstra is able to use Azure RMS together with SharePoint Online and Exchange Online.

Integrate with SharePoint Online

Integrating with SharePoint Online allows documents to stay unprotected until they are downloaded from the SharePoint sites. This way, users are able to search documents because they are not protected. Downloaded documents are protected based on the configured policy in SharePoint Online.

1. Log in to **http://portal.office.com**, go to **Admin**, and click **SharePoint**.

2. In the **SharePoint Admin Center**, click **Settings**.

3. On the **Settings** screen, an **Information Rights Management** section is listed. Select the option **Use the IRM service specified in your configuration** and click **Refresh IRM Settings**.

Click Refresh IRM Settings.

4. Go to the end of the page and click **OK**.

5. To enable a SharePoint site for Azure RMS, go to the SharePoint Site (**https://emskings.sharepointonline.com**) and **Documents**, or any other Document Library.

6. On the ribbon, click **Library / Library Settings**.

7. Click **Information Rights Management** in the **Permissions and Management** section.

8. Enable the option **Restrict permissions on this library on download** and click **Show options**.

Configuring the IRM settings for the Document Library.

9. Configure the library with the following settings:

Setting	Value
Policy Name	View for 90 days
Policy Description	Protect all docs from being printed and expire after 90 days
Do not allow users to upload documents that do not support IRM	Selected
Stop restricting access to the library at	Not Selected
Prevent opening documents in the browser for this Document Library	Selected
Allow viewers to print	Not Selected

Setting	Value
Allow viewers to run script and screen reader to function on downloaded documents	Not Selected
Allow viewers to write on a copy of the downloaded document	Not Selected
After download, document access rights will expire after these number of days (1-365)	Selected (90 days)
Users must verify their credentials using this interval (days)	Selected (30 days)
Allow group protection	Not Selected

10. Click **OK**.

> **Real World Note**: Azure RMS supports every file type to be protected. Normally, all documents from Microsoft Office, figures, text files, and PDFs are supported. For a complete list of supported file types, see http://ref.ms/rmslist.

Integrate with Exchange Online

Not only do documents need to be protected from leaks to people who are not allowed to see the information in those documents, but email also can be a source for data leakage. Azure RMS also integrates with Exchange Online.

You enable Azure RMS in Exchange Online via PowerShell. Execute the following script to enable the features. Use your Global Admin account to configure the service.

```
$UserCredential = Get-Credential

$Session = New-PSSession -ConfigurationName Microsoft.Exchange
-ConnectionUri https://outlook.office365.com/powershell-liveid/
-Credential $UserCredential -Authentication Basic
-AllowRedirection

Import-PSSession $Session

Set-IRMConfiguration -RMSOnlineKeySharingLocation "https://sp-
rms.na.aadrm.com/TenantManagement/ServicePartner.svc"

Import-RMSTrustedPublishingDomain -RMSOnline -name "RMS Online"

Set-IRMConfiguration -InternalLicensingEnabled $true
```

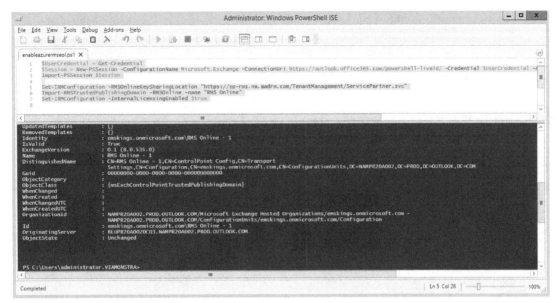

Enabling Azure RMS in Exchange Online.

Integrating Services on Premises with Azure RMS Connector

ViaMonstra does not have all file services moved to Office 365. Some highly classified documents also are located on local file servers. With the Azure RMS connector, you are able to integrate the Azure RMS service with on-premises services like Exchange, SharePoint, and file services.

Before you start and configure the Azure RMS connector with Windows Server FCI, a couple prerequisites needs to be in place.

Each file server where the File Resource Manager with file classification infrastructure will run need the following things to be in place:

- The File Server Resource Manager role is installed on the server with the File Services role.

- The local folder that contains files to protect with rights management are inventoried and identified.

- The RMS Protection tool, including the prerequisites for the tool and for Azure RMS, is installed.

- The server has Internet access.

- The configuration of Azure RMS is finished.

You can install and configure the Azure RMS connector using the following steps. After the connector is installed and configured, it acts as a relay between the on-premises servers and the Azure RMS cloud service.

1. Go to the Azure RMS connector download page **http://ref.ms/Azurermscon/** and click **Download**.

2. Select **all files (GenConnectorConfig.ps1, RMSConnectorAdminToolSetup_x86.exe and RMSConnectorSetup.exe)** and click **Next**.

3. Start the installation by running **RMSConnectorSetup.exe**.

4. Select **Install Microsoft Rights Management connector on this computer** and click **Next**.

5. Click **I accept the terms in the License Agreement** and click **Next**.

6. Supply the **Global Admin** credentials and click **Next**.

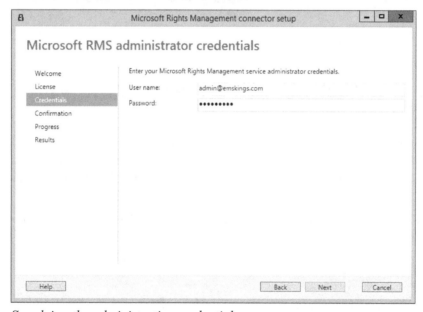

Supplying the administrative credentials.

7. Click **Install**.

8. Click **Finish** to start the Microsoft RMS connector administration tool so that servers can be authorized.

Configure FCI Server

The Azure RMS connector is able to use a File Classification Infrastructure (FCI) server. The FCI is a File Services role that you can add on a Windows Server 2012 R2 server.

1. In the **Microsoft RMS connector** administration tool, click **Add** to add an **FCI (File Classification Infrastructure) Server**.

2. For **Role**, select **FCI Server**; click **Browse**, and select the file server you want to add.

Browsing to the file server.

3. Click **OK** to add the server

4. Click **Close** to close the **Microsoft RMS connector** administration tool.

5. The next step in configuring Azure RMS support for FCI is to start the downloaded cmdlet (**GenConnectorConfig.ps1**). Open **PowerShell ISE** and start the following command on the File Server (FS01) with the File Services Resource Manager service installed:

```
.\GenConnectorConfig.ps1 -ConnectorUri
http://rms01.corp.viamonstra.com -SetFCI2012
```

The GenConnectorConfig script configures the File Server Resource Manager to use the Azure RMS templates while configuring file management tasks.

6. Restart the **File Server Resource Manager** service via the **services.msc**.

Create Classification Properties, Classification Rules, and File Management Tasks

Now that the components are all configured, classification properties, classification rules, and file management tasks need to be created for the shares to be protected. For ViaMonstra, it is important that only its employees can view documents in a folder located on FS01.

1. Open the **File Server Resource Manager** on the **File Server (FS01)**.

2. Click **Classification Properties** and then click **Create Local Property**.

3. Create the local classification property with the following values:

Property	Value
Name	Classified View Only
Description	
Property Type	Yes/No
Value	Yes/No

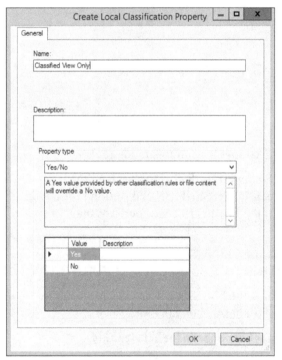

Creating the local classification property.

4. Click **OK** to create the new local classification property.

5. Click **Classification Rules**, and then click **Create Classification Rule** in the **Actions** pane and create the rule with the following values:

Property	Value
General	
Name	Classified View Only Rule
Description	
Scope	
Include all folders that store the following kinds of data	Group Files (selected) User Files (selected)
The following folders are included in this scope	E:\FileShares\ClassifiedViewOnly
Classification	
Classification method	Folder Classifier
Property (name)	Classified View Only
Property (value)	Yes

6. Click **OK** to create the rule.

7. Click **File Management Task**, and then click **Create File Management Task** in the **Actions Pane** and create a file management task with the following values:

Property	Value
General	
Name	Apply Azure RMS Classified View Only
Description	
Scope	
Include all folders that store the following kinds of data	Group Files (selected) User Files (selected)
The following folders are included in this scope	E:\FileShares\ClassifiedViewOnly
Action	
Type	RMS Encryption
Select a template	ViaMonstra – Confidential View Only

Property	Value
Notification	Leave default
Report	Leave default
Condition	Add / Classified View Only Value = Yes
Schedule	Weekly (selected) Sunday (selected) Run continuously on new files (enabled)

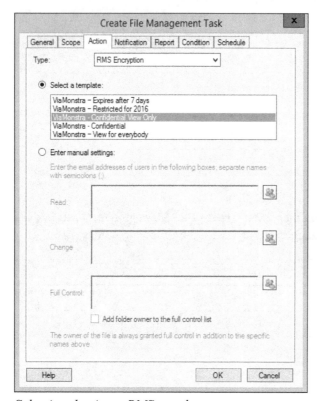

Selecting the Azure RMS templates.

8. After configuring the file management task, click **OK**.

How Does a Document Get Protected?

Based on the policies, the created documents are protected automatically because the option "Run continuously on new files" is selected in the file management task. When a file is saved to the share, it is protected automatically.

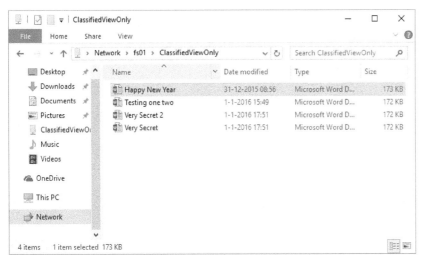

Files in the protected share.

When one of the Word documents in the share is opened, a notification is shown that the document is protected: VIAMONSTRA – CONFIDENTIAL VIEW ONLY. Click View Permissions to see the actual permissions on the file.

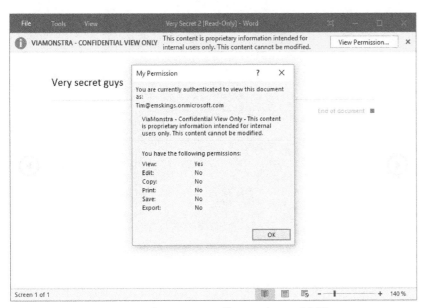

Documents are protected automatically via Azure RMS.

Appendix A

Using the Hydration Kit to Build the PoC Environment

As you learned in Chapter 1, hydration is the concept of using a deployment solution, like MDT, to do a fully automated build of an entire lab, or proof-of-concept environment. If you want to see for yourself how we set up this environment, check out the http://stealingwithpride.com website for a video that shows you the hydration process.

> **Note:** This appendix is here to help you quickly spin up a lab environment that matches up with all the guides we use in this book. The virtual machines you deploy are not configured for production deployment, but will work great in your lab. If you are interested in how to build a ConfigMgr server for production use, we recommend getting the book *System Center 2012 R2 Configuration Manager - Mastering the Fundamentals*, 3rd Edition, by Kent Agerlund. Check this link: http://deploymentartist.com/Books.aspx.

Here are the detailed steps for installing and configuring the hydration kit provided in the book sample files. This hydration kit allows you to build the same environment that is used for this book in a virtual environment. We recommend using Hyper-V in Windows Server 2012 R2 as your virtual platform, but we have tested the hydration kit on the following virtual platforms:

- Hyper-V in Windows 10 and Windows Server 2012 R2
- VMware Workstation 12

The Base Servers
Using the hydration kit, you build the following list of servers.

New York Site Servers (192.168.1.0/24)
- **DC01.** Domain Controller, DNS, PKI, and DHCP
- **GW01.** Virtual Router (optional server used for Internet access)
- **ADFS01.** Member Server, and SQL Server 2012 SP1 Express
- **WAP01.** Standalone Server.

- **NDES01**. Member Server

- **CM01.** SQL Server 2014 SP1 and ConfigMgr

Internet Access

Some of the guides in this book require you to have Internet access on the virtual machines. To help you achieve that and still have the virtual machines on an isolated network for lab and test purposes, we provide instructions on how to set up the GW01 virtual machine so it is configured as a virtual router.

If your virtual platform is already configured to provide Internet access to your VMs, or if you are on a dedicated lab network that allows you to run your own DHCP server, you can skip creating the GW01 virtual machine.

> **Real World Note:** You also can use a Linux-based system for routing the network traffic. For detailed guidance on setting up a Linux-based virtual router for your lab environment, see this article: http://tinyurl.com/usingvirtualrouter.

Setting Up the Hydration Environment

Again, to enable you to quickly set up the servers and clients used for the step-by-step guides in this book, we provide you with a hydration kit (part of the book sample files) that builds all the servers and clients. The sample files are available for download at http://deploymentfundamentals.com.

How Does the Hydration Kit Work?

The hydration kit that you download is just a folder structure and some scripts. The hydration kit scripts help you create the MDT Lite Touch offline media, and the folder structure is there for you to add your own software and licenses when applicable. In addition to the scripts to set up the MDT offline media, you also use other PowerShell scripts to perform post-deployment OS configuration on the virtual machines after they are deployed. The overview steps are the following:

1. Download the needed software.

2. Install MDT 2013 Update 2 and Windows ADK 10.

3. Create an MDT deployment share.

4. Populate the folder structure with your media and any license information.

5. Generate the MDT media item.

6. Create a few virtual machines, boot them on the media item, and select which servers they should become, and then about one hour later you have the lab environment ready to go.

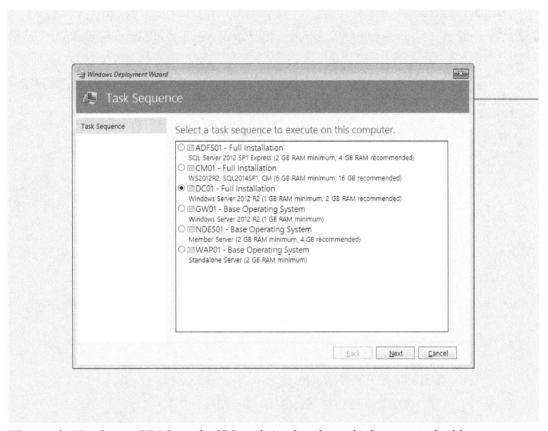

The result: You boot a VM from the ISO and simply select which server to build.

Preparing the Setup Folder

You should perform these steps on the Windows machine that you use to manage Hyper-V or VMware. If you are using Hyper-V or VMware Workstation, this machine also can be the host machine.

Download the Software

1. On the Windows machine that you use to manage Hyper-V or VMware, create the **C:\Setup** folder.

2. Download the book sample files from **http://deploymentfundamentals.com** and extract them to **C:\Setup**.

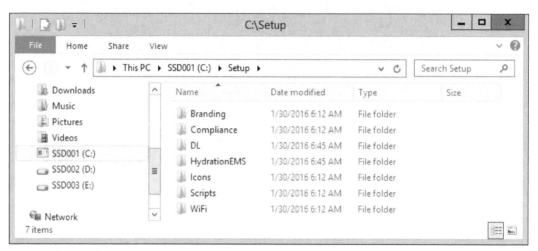

The book sample files extracted to C:\Setup.

3. Download the following software from Microsoft:

   o BGInfo (http://live.sysinternals.com)

   Download to **C:\Setup\DL\BGInfo**.

   o MDT 2013 Update 2 build 8330 (http://tinyurl.com/MDT2013U2)

   Download to **C:\Setup\DL\MDT 2013 Update 2**.

   o Windows ADK 10 build 10240 (http://tinyurl.com/ADK10Build10240)

   Download to **C:\Setup\DL\Windows ADK 10**.

Note: To download the complete standalone Windows ADK 10 setup, run adksetup.exe /layout "C:\Setup\DL\Windows ADK 10".

---

   o Windows Server 2012 R2 (trial or full version)

   Extract the ISO to **C:\Setup\DL\Windows Server 2012 R2**

   o SQL Server 2012 Express with SP1 x64 with Tools.

   Download to **C:\Setup\DL\SQL Server 2012 SP1 Express**.

   o SQL Server 2014 Standard with SP1 x64.

   Download to **C:\Setup\DL\SQL Server 2014 SP1 Standard**.

- ConfigMgr (the download is named System Center Configuration Manager Current Branch)

  Download to **C:\Setup\DL\ConfigMgr**.

- ConfigMgr Prerequisites (run the SMSSETUP\BIN\X64\Setupdl.exe application from the ConfigMgr installation files)

  Download to **C:\Setup\DL\ConfigMgrPreReqs**.

> **Note:** To download the ConfigMgr prerequisites, run the SMSSETUP\BIN\X64\Setupdl.exe application from the ConfigMgr installation files.

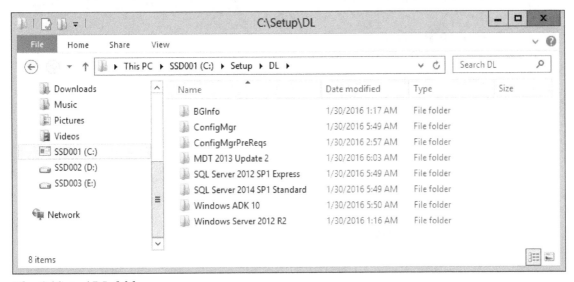

The C:\Setup\DL folder.

Preparing the Hydration Environment

The Windows machine that you use to manage Hyper-V or VMware needs to have PowerShell installed.

> **Note:** MDT requires local administrator rights/permissions. You need to have at least 60 GB of free disk space on C:\ for the hydration kit and about 500 GB of free space for the volume hosting your virtual machines. Also, make sure to run all commands from an elevated PowerShell prompt.

Create the Hydration Deployment Share

In this guide, you install some of the applications you downloaded to C:\Setup\DL:

1. On the Windows machine that you use to manage Hyper-V or VMware, install **MDT 2013 Update 2 (MicrosoftDeploymentToolkit2013_x64.msi)** with the default settings.

2. Install **Windows ADK 10 (adksetup.exe)** selecting only the following components:

   o **Deployment Tools**

   o **Windows Preinstallation Environment (Windows PE)**

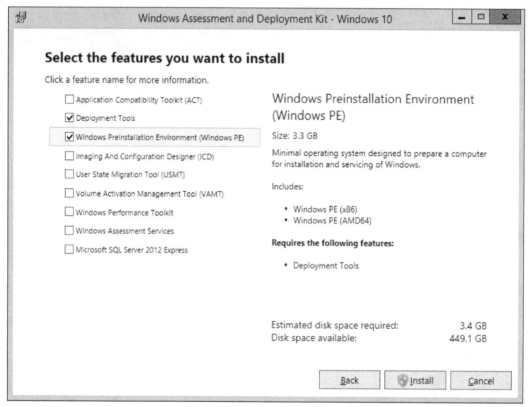

The Windows ADK 10 setup.

3. In an elevated **PowerShell prompt**, create the hydration deployment share by running the following command:

```
C:\Setup\Scripts\New-HydrationDeploymentShare.ps1
```

4. After creating the hydration deployment share, review the added content using the **Deployment Workbench** (installed as part of the MDT setup).

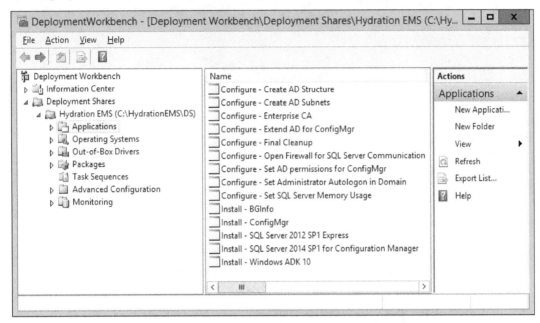

The Deployment Workbench with the ready-made applications listed.

Create the Hydration ISO (MDT Update Offline Media Item)

1. Using the Deployment **Workbench** (available on the **Start screen**), navigate to **Deployment Shares / Hydration EMS**.

2. Review the various nodes. The **Applications**, **Operating Systems**, and **Task Sequences** nodes should all have some content in them.

3. Navigate to **Advanced Configuration / Media**.

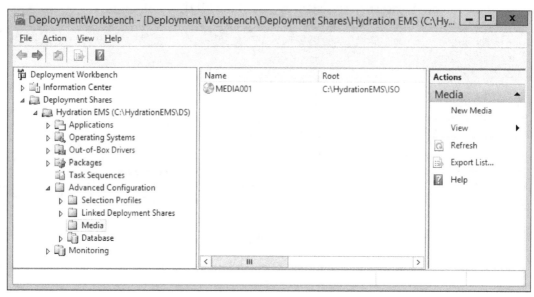

The Media node in the Hydration EMS deployment share.

4. In the right pane, right-click **MEDIA001** and select **Update Media Content**.

Note: The most common reason for failures in the hydration kit are related to antivirus software preventing the ISO from being generated correctly. If you see any errors in the Update Media Content process, disable (or uninstall) your antivirus software, and then try the update again. The media update takes a while to run, so it's a perfect time for a coffee break. ☺

After the media update, you have a big ISO (HydrationEMS.iso) in the C:\HydrationEMS\ISO folder. The ISO will be between 13 and 14 GB in size depending on which Windows media you have been using. (You have probably noticed that Microsoft offers Windows Server 2012 R2 ISO files with some updates already installed, and these ISO files are larger.)

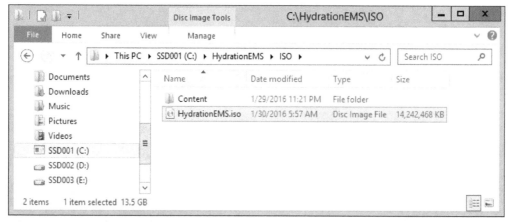

The Hydration ISO media item.

Deploying the New York Site VMs

In these steps, you deploy and configure the virtual machines for the New York site.

Deploy GW01

GW01 is an optional server used as a virtual router. Again, this allows for having the other virtual machines on an isolated network but still being able to access the Internet.

> **Note:** If your virtual platform is already configured to provide Internet access to your VMs (for example, you are using the NAT network feature in VMware Workstation, or you are on a dedicated lab network that allows you to run your own DHCP server), you can skip creating the GW01 virtual machine and go to the "Deploy DC01" section instead.

1. Using **Hyper-V Manager** or **VMware Sphere**, create a virtual machine with the following settings:

   a. Name: **GW01**

   b. Memory: **1 GB** (minimum, 2 GB recommended)

   c. Hard drive: **100 GB** (dynamic disk)

   d. Network: The virtual network you use for the virtual machines

   e. Image file (ISO): **C:\HydrationEMS\ISO\HydrationEMS.iso**

   f. vCPUs: **2** (minimum, 4 recommended)

2. Start the **GW01** virtual machine. After booting from **HydrationEMS.iso**, and after WinPE has loaded, select the **GW01** task sequence.

> **Note:** It might take some time before the task sequence list displays. WinPE tries very hard to get an IP address from the DHCP, but because we don't have one, we'll just wait.

3. Wait until the setup is complete and you see the **Hydration completed** message in the final summary. Verify that there is no ISO file mounted in the **GW01** virtual machine, and leave virtual machine running.

GW01 Post-Deployment OS Configurations

After the initial deployment of GW01 is completed, you need to do additional post-deployment OS configurations like adding a second virtual network adapter and installing Routing and Remote Access (RRAS).

Add a Second Virtual Network Adapter

Because the purpose of GW01 is to route Internet traffic, you need to add a second virtual network adapter and connect it to the external network on your host PC or server. In this guide, you learn how to do it in Hyper-V. When using VMware, you have to do the equivalent VMware operations.

1. Using **Hyper-V Manager**, create a virtual switch that is connected to the external network (your network card). In our sample, we named the virtual network switch **UplinkSwitch**.

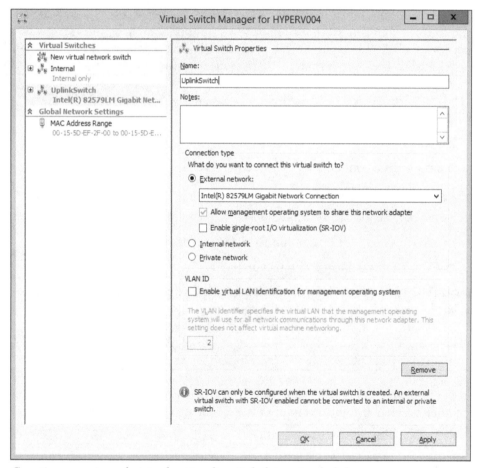

Creating an external virtual network switch for a simple lab setup.

2. Unless you are using Windows 10 as your Hyper-V host, shut down the **GW01** virtual machine before you continue. (Windows 10 allows you to add virtual network adapters while the virtual machine is running.)

3. Right-click the **GW01** virtual machine and select **Settings**.

4. In the **Hardware / Add Hardware** node, add a second virtual network adapter and connect it to the **UplinkSwitch** virtual network.

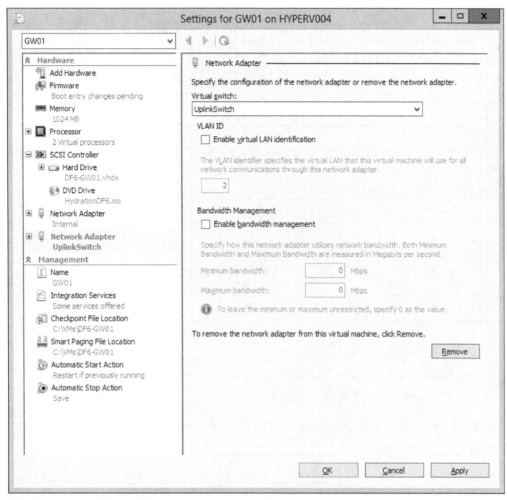

Adding a second virtual network adapter to GW01.

5. If you turned off the **GW01** virtual machine in this guide, now start it again.

Install Routing and Remote Access

In this guide, we assume you have copied the book sample files to C:\Setup on GW01.

> **Real World Note:** In addition to copying the files over the network, or via RDP (slow), one easy way to copy setup or sample files to a virtual machine is simply to mount the ISO file on the virtual machine. If you don't have an ISO file, but have Windows ADK 10 installed on a machine, you can open a Deployment and Imaging Tools Environment prompt and run the following command to create an ISO file: oscdimg.exe -u2 C:\Setup C:\ISO\SetupFiles.iso.

1. On GW01, log on as Administrator, and open an elevated PowerShell prompt.

2. Verify that the second virtual network adapter got an IP address from the external network by running the following command:

   ```
   Get-NetIPAddress | FT
   ```

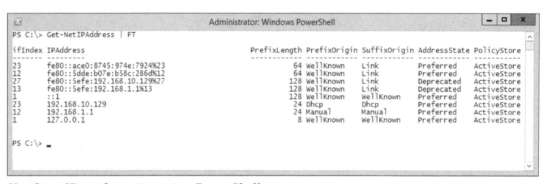

Verifying IP configuration using PowerShell.

3. Verify that **GW01** has Internet access by running the following command:

   ```
   Test-NetConnection
   ```

Verifying Internet access using PowerShell.

4. Install **RRAS** by running the following command:

   ```
   C:\Setup\Scripts\Install-VIARoles.ps1 -Role RRAS
   ```

Configure Routing and Remote Access

Now that Routing and Remote Access is installed, you need to configure it. During the configuration, the server will be a router with Network Address Translation functionality.

1. On GW01, open an elevated PowerShell prompt.

2. Configure **RRAS** by running the following command (the command is wrapped and should be one line):

```
C:\Setup\Scripts\Set-VIARRASNetworking.ps1
-InternalIP "192.168.1.1"
```

3. Restart **GW01** by running the following command:

```
Restart-Computer -Force
```

4. After the **GW01** virtual machine is restarted, log in again and start **Routing and Remote Access** to review the configuration.

> **Real World Note:** First, restarting GW01 is not required because of the Routing and Remote Access configuration, but it's nice to do a final reboot after completing the configuration and make sure everything starts properly. Also, please note that the Routing and Remote Access service is configured with a delayed start, so give it some time to start. A service configured for delayed start starts two minutes after the last "automatic" service has started.

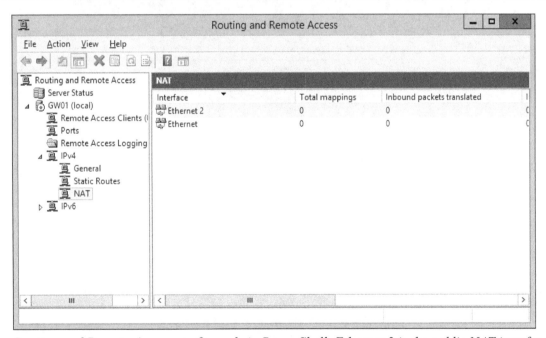

Routing and Remote Access configured via PowerShell. Ethernet 2 is the public NAT interface.

Deploy DC01

This is the primary domain controller used in the environment, and it also runs DNS and DHCP.

1. Using **Hyper-V Manager** or **VMware Sphere**, create a virtual machine with the following settings:

   a. Name: **DC01**

   b. Memory: **1 GB** (minimum, 2 GB recommended)

   c. Hard drive: **100 GB** (dynamic disk)

   d. Network: The virtual network you use for the virtual machines

   e. Image file (ISO): **C:\HydrationEMS\ISO\HydrationEMS.iso**

   f. vCPUs: **2**

2. Start the **DC01** virtual machine. After booting from **HydrationEMS.iso**, and after WinPE has loaded, select the **DC01** task sequence.

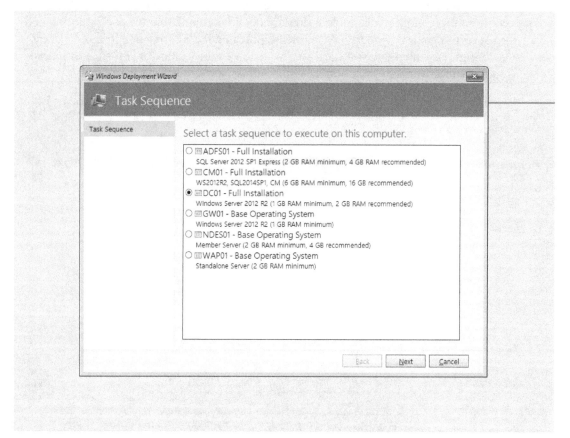

Selecting the DC01 task sequence.

3.   Wait until the setup is complete and you see the **Hydration completed** message in the final summary. Verify that there is no ISO file mounted on the **DC01** virtual machine, and leave the virtual machine running.

Real World Note: Using a dynamic disk is useful for a lab and test environment because the host PC uses only the actually consumed space on the virtual hard drive and not the size that you enter as a fixed disk would.

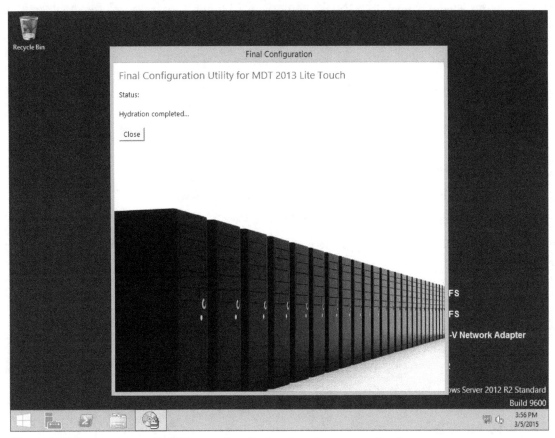

The initial deployment of DC01 completed, showing the custom final summary screen.

Deploy ADFS01

ADFS01 is the server used for Active Directory Federation Services.

1.   Using **Hyper-V Manager** or **VMware Sphere**, create a virtual machine with the following settings:

   a.   Name: **ADFS01**

   b.   Memory: **2 GB** (minimum, 4 GB recommended)

   c.   Hard drive: **300 GB** (dynamic disk)

       d.   Network: The virtual network you use for the virtual machines

       e.   Image file (ISO): **C:\HydrationEMS\ISO\HydrationEMS.iso**

       f.   vCPUs: **2** (minimum, 4 recommended)

2.   Make sure the **DC01** virtual machine is running, and then start the **ADFS01** virtual machine. After booting from **HydrationEMS.iso**, and after WinPE has loaded, select the **ADFS01** task sequence. Wait until the setup is complete and you see the **Hydration completed** message in the final summary. Verify that there is no ISO file mounted on the **ADFS01** virtual machine.

Deploy WAP01

WAP01 is the web application proxy server used for controlling access to internal resources based on conditions like network, device, group membership, and so forth.

1.   Using **Hyper-V Manager** or **VMware Sphere**, create a virtual machine with the following settings:

       a.   Name: WAP01

       b.   Memory: **2 GB** (minimum, 4 GB recommended)

       c.   Hard drive: **300 GB** (dynamic disk)

       d.   Network: The virtual network you use for the virtual machines

       e.   Image file (ISO): **C:\HydrationEMS\ISO\HydrationEMS.iso**

       f.   vCPUs: **2** (minimum, 4 recommended)

2.   Make sure the **DC01** virtual machine is running, and then start the **WAP01** virtual machine. After booting from **HydrationEMS.iso**, and after WinPE has loaded, select the **WAP01** task sequence. Wait until the setup is complete and you see the **Hydration completed** message in the final summary. Verify that there is no ISO file mounted on the **WAP01** virtual machine.

Deploy NDES01

NDES01 is the server used for Network Device Enrollment Service.

1.   Using **Hyper-V Manager** or **VMware Sphere**, create a virtual machine with the following settings:

       a.   Name: **NDES01**

       b.   Memory: **2 GB** (minimum, 4 GB recommended)

       c.   Hard drive: **300 GB** (dynamic disk)

       d.   Network: The virtual network you use for the virtual machines

       e.   Image file (ISO): **C:\HydrationEMS\ISO\HydrationEMS.iso**

       f.   vCPUs: **1** (minimum, 2 recommended)

2. Make sure the **DC01** virtual machine is running, and then start the **NDES01** virtual machine. After booting from **HydrationEMS.iso**, and after WinPE has loaded, select the **NDES01** task sequence. Wait until the setup is complete and you see the **Hydration completed** message in the final summary. Verify that there is no ISO file mounted on the **NDES01** virtual machine.

Deploy CM01

CM01 is the ConfigMgr Site Server.

1. Using **Hyper-V Manager** or **VMware Sphere**, create a virtual machine with the following settings:

    a. Name: **CM01**

    b. Memory: **6 GB** (minimum, 16 GB recommended)

    c. Hard drive: **300 GB** (dynamic disk)

    d. Network: The virtual network you use for the virtual machines

    e. Image file (ISO): **C:\HydrationEMS\ISO\HydrationEMS.iso**

    f. vCPUs: **2** (minimum, 4 recommended)

Make sure the **DC01** virtual machine is running, and then start the **CM01** virtual machine. After booting from **HydrationEMS.iso**, and after WinPE has loaded, select the **CM01** task sequence. Wait until the setup is complete and you see the **Hydration completed** message in the final summary. Verify that there is no ISO file mounted on the **CM01** virtual machine.

Appendix B

Setting Up a Basic Office 365 Environment

In Chapter 2, the Office 365 trial is set up. To support the basics in the proof-of-concept environment, you need to configure some services.

Assign Office 365 Licenses

You can assign Office 365 licenses via the Office 365 Portal or via a PowerShell script.

1. Go to **https://portal.office.com** and log on with the administrative credentials created earlier.

2. Click **Admin** and go to **Users / Active Users**; select a user and click **Edit** at the **Assigned license** section in the user details of the selected user.

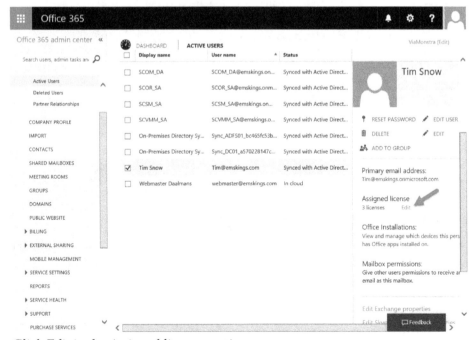

Click Edit in the Assigned license section.

3. Select the license and click **Save**.

Another way is to automate the assignment of the licenses via a PowerShell script based on an Active Directory security group:

```
# Assign license based on membership of a group for SharePoint

[array]$licensed = ""

$GroupObjectID = Get-MsolGroup -SearchString "SharePoint Online
Users"

$GroupObjectID = $GroupObjectID.ObjectId

$userlist = Get-MsolGroupMember -GroupObjectId $GroupObjectID

foreach ($user in $userlist) {

  $licensed = (Get-MsolUser -UserPrincipalName
$user.EmailAddress).Licenses[0].ServiceStatus | Select-Object
-ExpandProperty ServicePlan

  If ( ($licensed.servicename -like "SHARE*").count -eq 0) {

    # No license, license needs to be added

      Get-MsolGroupMember -GroupObjectId $GroupObjectID  | Set-
MsolUser -UsageLocation US

      Get-MsolGroupMember -GroupObjectId $GroupObjectID  | Set-
MsolUserLicense -AddLicenses emskings:ENTERPRISEPACK

    }

  }
```

Configuring Exchange Online

When starting with Office 365 and you want to use Exchange Online, you must apply some basic configuration to be able to send and receive email. This section describes some basic configuration.

Correct Email Addresses

Because the domain is federated and equal to the domain name that also is used for Exchange Online, you cannot set this domain as the default domain.

The only way to configure the default domain name for a user is by selecting the default email address in the Exchange Admin Portal or via PowerShell.

1. Log on to **http://portal.office365.com** and with the administrative credentials.

2. Select **Admin / Exchange**, and click **Recipients**. Double-click a mailbox and select **email addresses**.

3. Select the email address you want to make the default and click the **pencil**.

4. Click **Make this the reply address** and click **OK**.

Select Make this the reply address.

To use the User Principle Name as the default email address in Exchange Online, the following script needs to be run every time a mailbox is created in Exchange Online:

```
$UserCredential = Get-Credential

$Session = New-PSSession -ConfigurationName Microsoft.Exchange
-ConnectionUri https://outlook.office365.com/powershell-liveid/
-Credential $UserCredential -Authentication Basic
-AllowRedirection

Import-PSSession $Session

get-mailbox -resultsize unlimited | Where-Object
{$_.UserPrincipalName -ne $_.WindowsEmailAddress} | foreach {
set-mailbox $_.identity -windowsemailaddress $_.UserPrincipalName
}

Remove-PSSession $session
```

Appendix C

Test Scenarios – Completing the Microsoft EMS PoC

Running a successful EMS proof-of-concept (PoC) environment depends on the results of the tests and of course the initial goals of the PoC. One way to measure the results is to walk through use cases and document the results.

Admin Experience

Test scenarios and checklist about the admin experience, security, and compliance. All the scenario actions are done from the Microsoft Intune console.

Selective Wipe of Devices

If a user leaves the company and uses their own device to connect to ViaMonstra resources, the IT department can wipe the corporate data from the device without touching the personal data.

Use Case	Expected Result	Result	Status
Android: 1. Select the Android device that needs to be selectively wiped. 2. Right-click the device and select **Retire Wipe**. 3. Select **Selectively wipe the device** and click **Yes**.	The user receives the following message: "Your device is no longer managed by your IT admin. Access to company data, apps, and email might have been removed. To regain access, enroll your device."		
iOS: 1. Select the iOS device that needs to be selectively wiped. 2. Right-click the device and select **Retire Wipe**. 3. Select **Selectively wipe the device** and click **Yes**.	Only the corporate data managed by Intune is removed. Native apps, installed by Intune are removed, as are the data of apps that are managed via Mobile		

Use Case	Expected Result	Result	Status
	Application Management policies. Apps disappear, and the management profile is removed from the device. Per managed app, a message that the corporate data is removed is shown when starting the app for the first time. The device is removed automatically from the Microsoft Intune console.		
Windows Phone 8.x: 1. Select the Windows Phone 8.x device that needs to be selectively wiped. 2. Right-click the device and select **Retire Wipe**. 3. Select **Selectively wipe the device** and click **Yes**.	The user receives the following messages; "Password no longer required" and "Account deleted." All apps and policies required by the company are removed.		
Windows 10 Mobile: 1. Select the Windows 10 Mobile device that needs to be selectively wiped. 2. Right-click the device and select **Retire Wipe**. 3. Select **Selectively wipe the device** and click **Yes**.	User receives a notification with the "following message: "<Company> has removed your workspace account and deleted all of the information associated with…." All apps and policies required by the company are removed.		

Remote Lock of Devices

If a user loses the phone or control over it, an Intune admin can remotely lock the device.

Use Case	Expected Result	Result	Status
Android: 1. Select the Android device that needs to be locked. 2. Right-click the device and select **Remote Lock**.	The device is locked without any warning.		
iOS: 1. Select the iOS device that needs to be locked. 2. Right-click the device and select **Remote Lock**.	The device is locked without any warning.		
Windows Phone 8.x: 1. Select the Windows Phone 8.x device that needs to be locked. 2. Right-click the device and select **Remote Lock**.	Device is locked stating "Your company has locked your device. You can use your PIN to unlock it."		
Windows 10 Mobile: 1. Select the Windows 10 Mobile device that needs to be locked. 2. Right-click the device and select **Remote Lock**.	The device is locked without any warning.		

Passcode Reset of Devices

If a user forgets the passcode of the device, an Intune admin can change the passcode remotely.

Use Case	Expected Result	Result	Status
Android: 1. Select the Android device for which the passcode needs to be reset. 2. Right-click the device and select **Passcode Reset**. 3. Select the Android device and click **View Properties**. The new passcode is listed.	Device shows a notification "Update your passcode, your passcode has been reset, contact…." The Intune admin is able to communicate the new very strong password.		
iOS: 1. Select the iOS device for which the passcode needs to be reset. 2. Right-click the device and select **Passcode Reset**.	The passcode is removed from the device and no new passcode is applied. Some device types cannot issue a passcode reset.		
Windows Phone 8.x: 1. Select the Windows Phone 8.x for which the passcode needs to be reset. 2. Right-click the device and select **Passcode Reset**. 3. Select the Windows Phone 8.x device and click **View Properties**. The new passcode is listed.	Device is locked stating "Your company has reset your password. Contact your company's support person to learn the password." The Intune admin is able to communicate the new PIN.		
Windows 10 Mobile: 1. Select the Windows 10 Mobile device for which the passcode needs to be reset.	Device is locked stating "Your company has reset your PIN. Contact		

346

Use Case	Expected Result	Result	Status
2. Right-click the device and select **Passcode Reset**. 3. Select the Windows 10 Mobile device and click **View Properties**. The new passcode is listed.	your company's support person to learn the PIN." The Intune admin is able to communicate the new PIN.		

User Experience

Test scenarios and checklist about the user experience, Office apps, and enrollment.

Enrolling Devices as Discussed in Chapter 6
Devices need to be enrolled so Microsoft Intune can manage them.

Use Case	Expected Result	Result	Status
Android device	Device is enrolled.		
iOS device	Device is enrolled.		
Windows Phone 8.x device	Device is enrolled.		
Windows 10 Mobile	Device is enrolled.		
Rooted Android device	Device is blocked after enrollment.		
Jailbroken iOS device	Device is blocked after enrollment.		

Installing Apps Automatically from the Company Portal
While enrolling, apps are installed automatically.

Use Case	Expected Result	Result	Status
Android device	Apps are not installed automatically but are available in the notification bar / screen.		
iOS device	Apps are installed automatically.		

Installing Apps Manually from the Company Portal

Applications can be installed from the Company Portal.

Use Case	Expected Result	Result	Status
Android: 1. Open the Company Portal. 2. Authenticate if necessary. 3. Select **All Apps**. 4. Tap an application. 5. Tap **View in Google Play**. 6. Tap **Install**. 7. Tap **Accept**.	App is installed, but the user is redirected to the Google Play store.		
iOS: 1. Open the **Company Portal**. 2. Authenticate if necessary. 3. Select **Company Apps**. 4. Tap an application. 5. Tap **Get**. 6. Tap **Install**. 7. Tap **Install** when an installation prompt appears.	App is installed straight from the Apple App Store.		
Windows Phone: 1. Open the **Company Portal**. 2. Authenticate if necessary. 3. Select **Apps**. 4. Tap an application. 5. Tap **Store**. 6. Tap **Install**. 7. Tap **Allow**.	App is installed, but the user is redirected to the Windows Phone Store.		

Use Case	Expected Result	Result	Status
Windows 10 Mobile: 1. Open the Company Portal. 2. Authenticate if necessary. 3. Select **Apps**. 4. Tap an application. 5. Tap **Install**.	App is installed straight from the Windows App Store.		

New Passcode Enforced with Different Passcode Length

When implementing a new password policy, users are prompted for a new passcode or password after enrolling their devices.

Use Case	Expected Result	Result	Status
Android: 1. Tap the notification bar that states "Secure your device. You need to update your device passcode." 2. Confirm the old PIN and click **Next**. 3. Tap **PIN**, enter the new PIN, and tap **continue**. 4. Confirm PIN and Tap **OK**.	When a user does not change their passcode according to the compliance settings, email is blocked. After the passcode is changed, the compliance of the device must be rechecked and email is downloaded again.		
iOS: 1. Tap Continue in the Passcode Requirement message box. 2. Supply the old passcode and tap **continue**. 3. Enter the new passcode and tap **continue**. 4. Reenter the new passcode and tap **Save**.	The user receives a message that within 60 minutes the passcode needs to be changed. After 60 minutes the user is forced to change the passcode.		

Use Case	Expected Result	Result	Status
Windows Phone: 1. Straight after enrollment, the user gets a notification to Create a new password. 2. Tap **Set**. 3. Supply the old password and then the new password twice. 4. Tap **Done**.	The user is forced to change their passcode. The device remains compliant.		
Windows 10 Mobile: 1. Straight after enrollment, the user gets a notification to Create a new password. 2. Tap **Set**. 3. Supply the old password and then the new password twice. 4. Tap **Done**	The user is forced to change their passcode. The device remains compliant.		

Check Whether the Email Profile Is Configured

Mail profiles are deployed and configured automatically.

Use Case	Expected Result	Result	Status
Android: 1. Tap the native Email client, or the Validate account settings notification. 2. Supply the user password. 3. Tap **OK**.	Email is downloaded.		
iOS: 1. Select Settings / Mail, Contacts, Calendars and access the ViaMonstra email profile.	After verifying, email is downloaded.		

Use Case	Expected Result	Result	Status
2. Tap the account. 3. Add the password and Tap **Done**. **Real World Note:** Just after enrollment, a password popup also can be displayed to allow the user to access email.			
Windows Phone 8.x: 1. Go to the notification screen and tap the Your ViaMonstra Email account needs attention notification. 2. On the **email+accounts** screen, click **ViaMonstra Email**. 3. Supply the password. 4. Tap **Save**.	Email is downloaded.		
Windows 10 Mobile: 1. Go to the notification screen and tap the Your ViaMonstra Email account settings are out of date notification. 2. In the notification, tap **Fix Account**. 3. Supply the password and click **Sign In**. 4. Tap **OK** and **Continue**. 5. Supply the password again and tap **Save**. **Real World Note:** At the time of writing, Windows 10 Mobile was	Email is downloaded.		

Use Case	Expected Result	Result	Status
still in beta, so the process may be slightly different.			

Retire Device

When supporting Bring Your Own Devices, users should be able to remove management from their device. Users are able to retire devices themselves.

Use Case	Expected Result	Result	Status
Android: 1. Open the Company Portal. 2. Authenticate via AD (FS) if necessary. 3. Tap **My devices**. 4. Tap **(thick) Android device**. 5. Tap **Trashcan**. 6. Tap **OK** to remove management.	Management of device is removed, and the device is retired in Intune. Policies that were restrictive can be undone by setting a different, less restricted value.		
iOS: 1. Open the Company Portal 2. Optional: Authenticate via AD (FS) if necessary 3. In **My devices**, swipe to the **iOS** device. 4. Tap the **iOS** device. 5. Tap **Trashcan (Remove)**. 6. Tap **Remove** to remove management.	Management of device is removed, and the device is retired in Intune. Policies that were restrictive can be undone by setting a different, less restricted value.		
Windows Phone: 1. Open the Company Portal. 2. Optional: Authenticate via AD (FS) if necessary.	Management of the device is removed. Policies that were restrictive can be		

Use Case	Expected Result	Result	Status
3. Swipe to **My Devices**. 4. Tap the **Windows Phone** you are using. 5. Tap the **Trashcan**. 6. Tap **Remove**. 7. Tap **Close** when a message appears saying the password no longer required or that the account is deleted.	undone by setting a different, less restricted value.		
Windows 10 Mobile: 1. Select **Settings**. 2. Select **Accounts**. 3. Select **Work Access**. 4. Tap **ViaMonstra connected**. 5. Tap the **Trashcan**. 6. Tap **Remove**.	Management of device is removed. Policies that were restrictive can be undone by setting a different, less restricted value.		

MAM Policies: Copy / Paste

With Mobile Application Management policies, you are able to control the data flow in and from managed apps like Microsoft Word, Microsoft Excel, and more.

Use Case	Expected Result	Result	Status
Android: 1. Open **Microsoft Word** on an Android device. 2. Supply a PIN (optional). 3. Open a document, and select and copy text. 4. Switch apps and open a non-managed app. 5. Try to paste the text in the app. 6. Open **Microsoft Excel**.	Pasting the text in the non-managed app is not possible. Pasting the text in Microsoft Excel (which is managed) is allowed.		

Use Case	Expected Result	Result	Status
7. Paste the text.			
iOS: 1. Open **Microsoft Word** on an iOS device. 2. Supply a PIN (optional). 3. Open a document, and select and copy text. 4. Switch apps and open a non-managed app. 5. Try to paste the text in the app. 6. Open **Microsoft Excel**. 7. Paste the text.	Pasting the text in the non-managed app is not possible. Pasting the text in Microsoft Excel (which is managed) is allowed.		

Open a Managed Document and Save It to the Non-Managed Dropbox

Documents from managed apps cannot be saved to non-managed locations like Dropbox.

Use Case	Expected Result	Result	Status
Android: 1. Open **Microsoft Word** on an Android device. 2. Supply a PIN (optional). 3. Open a document. 4. Tap **Save** and try to save it to **Dropbox**.	The user receives a message that "Your IT policy doesn't allow saving of this file."		
iOS: 1. Open Microsoft Word on an iOS device. 2. Supply a PIN (optional). 3. Open a document. 4. Tap **Save** and try to save it to **Dropbox**.	The user receives a message that "Your IT policy doesn't allow saving of this file."		

Recover a Managed App PIN

All those different PINs can be confusing for users. Users are able to reset managed app PINs by using their corporate credentials.

Use Case	Expected Result	Result	Status
Android: 1. Start Word, for instance, and click Forgot your PIN? 2. Authenticate with corporate credentials. 3. Set a new PIN. 4. Repeat new PIN.	User is able to reset the PIN, which allows access to the managed app again.		
iOS: 1. Start Word, for instance, and click Forgot your PIN? 2. Tap **OK**. 3. Authenticate with corporate credentials. 4. Set a new PIN. 5. Confirm the new PIN.	User is able to reset the PIN, which allows access to the managed app again.		

Azure Rights Management Service

Azure RMS is used to protect the documents. The protection travels with the document, so this is the ultimate way to prevent data leakage.

Users Setting Up RMS

Users need to be able to use Azure RMS. This is done by enabling users to set up Azure RMS themselves.

Use Case	Expected Result	Result	Status
1. Go to http://ref.ms/rmsplugin. 2. Supply your email address and click **Next**. 3. Log on with corporate credentials.	The computer is configured for Azure RMS. The RMS application is installed. Sharing for protected files is		

Use Case	Expected Result	Result	Status
4. Download and install the **Azure Sharing App** for Windows. 5. In the **Setup Microsoft RMS** window, click **Next** to configure RMS for the computer. 6. Click **Restart** to restart the computer.	enabled for Microsoft Office.		

Creating a Document in Word and Sharing It Protected

After the RMS Sharing App is configured, a plugin for Microsoft Word also is installed.

Use Case	Expected Result	Result	Status
1. Open Microsoft Word and create a new document. 2. Click **Share Protected** on the Home ribbon. 3. Log on with corporate credentials. 4. Add an email address from the user to whom you want to email the document. 5. Select **ViaMonstra – View for everybody**. 6. Select **Email me when someone tries to open these documents**. 7. Select **Allow me to instantly revoke access to these documents**. 8. Click **Send**. 9. Click **Yes**.	An email message is sent via Outlook with a protected document created in Microsoft Word and initiated from Microsoft Word. The recipient within the company is able to view the document.		

Use Case	Expected Result	Result	Status
10. Add content to the email message opened in Outlook and click **Send** to send the protected files.			

Sending a Protected Attachment via Email in Outlook
Sharing via Outlook also can be done with people outside the company.

Use Case	Expected Result	Result	Status
1. Start Outlook and create an email message for an internal user. 2. Attach an **Office** document to the email. 3. Click **Share Protected** and authenticate if necessary. 4. Click **Viewer – View Only**. 5. Select **Email me when someone tries to open these documents**. 6. Select **Allow me to instantly revoke access to these documents**. 7. Click **Send Now**.	Documents that are shared with people from outside of the company need to be sent and protected from Outlook itself.		

Sending a Protected Email Message
Instead of sending a protected attachment, RMS is able to protect the email message.

Use Case	Expected Result	Result	Status
1. Start Outlook and create an email message for an internal user and write the secret content. 2. Click **File / Set Permissions**.	The receiver of the email is not able to forward the email to another person.		

Use Case	Expected Result	Result	Status
3. Select **Do Not Forward** and go back to the email. 4. Click **Send**.			

Using In-Place Protection
Documents also can be protected in place.

Use Case	Expected Result	Result	Status
1. Select an Office document and right-click the document. 2. Select **Protect with RMS / Protect In Place / ViaMonstra – Expires after 7 days** 3. Open the document and click **View Permissions**.	The document is protected in place and can be shared with colleagues.		

Opening a Document by a User without Permissions
Try to open the document with an account without permissions to the document.

Use Case	Expected Result	Result	Status
1. Open the PPDF or the protected Word document with an account that is not part of the ViaMonstra domain and not used in the sharing tool. 2. Click **Close** after access has been rejected.	Open the email inbox of the sender. You see an email message stating that access to the document has been blocked.		

Opening a Document by a User with Permissions
Try to open the document with an account that has permissions to the document.

Use Case	Expected Result	Result	Status
1. Open the Outlook WebApp.	Content of the attachment is shown.		

Use Case	Expected Result	Result	Status
2. Log on as the user who has access to the document. 3. Open the email message and click the attachment.			

Using the Tracking Tool to See Access to a Document

With Azure RMS, it is possible to track usage of documents you share.

Use Case	Expected Result	Result	Status
1. In Outlook, click Track Usage. 2. Click **Login** and log in with the credentials of the user sending and protecting the documents. 3. In **Your shared documents**, click the document for which you want to track usage. 4. Click **List**. 5. Click **Timeline**. 6. Click **Map**. 7. Click **Settings**.	On the Summary screen, you are able to view who has accessed the document, who was denied access, and the activity. On the List screen, a list displays with all users who accessed the document. On the Timeline screen, a diagram is plotted with all activity. On the Map screen, access from the several locations is plotted.		

Sending mail in OWA

OWA also supports sending RMS-protected email.

Use Case	Expected Result	Result	Status
1. Log in to https://outlook.office365.com. 2. Click **New**. 3. Click **...** (ellipsis) / **Set Permissions**. 4. Select **Do Not Forward**. 5. Send an email message to a colleague.	Azure RMS policies are available. Email is sent, but the colleague cannot forward the message. The Forward option is disabled.		

Appendix D

Setting Up Active Directory Federation Services

Like ViaMonstra, many companies do not allow synchronizing the hash of the passwords to Azure Active Directory. Only local authentication to the on-premises Active Directory is allowed. This appendix describes the setup of AD FS for the EMS PoC environment.

Note: Setting up AD FS as described in this appendix is allowed only in a lab environment for the EMS PoC.

Install and Configure AD FS

To install and configure AD FS in the PoC environment, follow these steps:

1. Log on to the domain controller DC01.

2. Start **PowerShell ISE** as administrator and open the **ADFS_Commands_on_DC01.ps1** script, shown here, from the book files.

```
#Setting Up new AD FS Service

$ADFSServerIP = '192.168.1.244'

#Add new KDS Root Key

Add-KdsRootKey -EffectiveTime (Get-Date).AddHours(-10)
-Verbose

#Create New AD FS Server group - only these AD FS servers
can query the Managed Service Account Password

New-ADGroup -Name 'AD FS Servers' -GroupScope Global
-Verbose

$Server = Get-ADComputer -Identity 'ADFS01' -Verbose

$ADGroup = Get-ADGroup -Identity 'AD FS Servers' -Verbose


#Add the ADFS01 to AD FS Servers AD Group

Add-ADGroupMember $ADGroup -Members $Server -Verbose

#New AD Managed Service account
```

```
New-ADServiceAccount -Name 'ADFSGMSA' -DNSHostName
'DC01.corp.viamonstra.com' -
PrincipalsAllowedToRetrieveManagedPassword 'AD FS Servers'
-Verbose

#Print out the new AD Managed Service Account

Get-ADServiceAccount -Identity 'ADFSGMSA' -Verbose

#Restart AD FS Server

Restart-Computer -ComputerName ADFS01 -Verbose -Wait -Force
-For PowerShell
```

3. Review the script and run it using the **F5** key.

4. Log on to **ADFS01** and install the **Microsoft Online Services Sign-In Assistant for IT Professionals** (http://ref.ms/msolsignin) and the **Azure Active Directory Module for Windows PowerShell (64-bit version)** (http://ref.ms/Azureposh).

5. Open **MMC.exe** via the **run** command box, select **File / Add/Remove Snap-in**, select **certificates**, and click **Add**.

6. Select **Computer account**, and click **Next**, **Finish**, and then **OK**.

7. Expand **Certificates**, right-click **Personal**, and select **All Tasks / Advanced Operations / Create Custom Request**.

8. Select **(No Template) Legacy key** and click **Next**.

9. Select **Proceed without enrollment policy** and click **Next**.

10. Click **Next** again and expand the details.

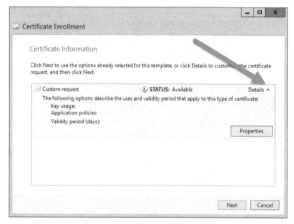

Click the Details arrow to expand the certificate request details.

11. Click **Properties** and add a friendly name, e.g., **AD FS Cert**.

12. Click the **Subject** tab and add the following information, making sure the certificate has all these fields:

    a.   Subject name

        ▪   Type: **Common name**

        ▪   Value: **sts.emskings.com**

    b.   Alternative name

        ▪   Type: **DNS**

        ▪   Value: **sts.emskings.com**

    c.   Alternative name

        ▪   Type: **DNS**

        ▪   Value: **enterpriseregistration.emskings.com**

    d.   Alternative name

        ▪   Type: **DNS**

        ▪   Value: **workfolders.emskings.com**

Adding subject alternative names for the AD FS certificate.

13. Click the **Private Key** tab.

14. Expand **Key options**, select **2048** as the key size, and then select **Make private key exportable**.

15. Click **OK**.

16. Click **Next** to save the request. Supply a file name and click **Finish**.

17. Submit the saved request to a certificate provider like **DigiCert** and acquire a certificate that supports two or more subject alternative names.

    After the certificate provider creates and supplies the certificate, the certificate request needs to be completed.

18. Expand **Certificates**, right-click **Certificate Enrollment Requests**, and select **All Tasks / Import**.

19. Click **Next** and browse for the certificate file. Click **Next** twice and then click **Finish** to import the certificate.

    After you complete the request, there should be a new certificate in the Personal certificate store.

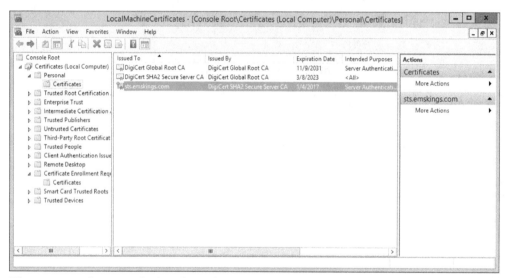

The new certificate in the local machine's Personal certificate store.

20. Right-click the **sts.emskings.com** certificate, and select **All Tasks / Export**.

21. On the **Welcome to the Certificate Export Wizard** page, click **Next**.

22. On the **Export Private-key** page, select **Yes**, export the primary key, and click **Next**.

23. On the **Export File Format** page, select **Include all certificated in the certification path if possible** and **Export all extended properties**. Click **Next**.

24. On the **Security** page, enable **Password**, type **P@ssw0rd** and click **Next**.

25. On the **File to export** page, save the certificate as **C:\Documents\AD FS_STS.pfx** and click **Finish** to complete the wizard.

26. Log in to the **ADFS01** server and start **PowerShell ISE** as administrator.

27. Open the **ADFS_Commands_on_ADFS01.ps1** script as shown here. The script is divided into three steps. Be sure to run the steps separately because the results of step 1 need to be used in step 2. Copy the Certificate Hash gathered in step 1 and replace 'sts.emskings.com Certificate HASH' in the following script:

```
#Step 0 - Install AD FS Role

Install-WindowsFeature -Name ADFS-Federation
-IncludeManagementTools -Verbose

#Step 1 - Print out certificates hashes

Get-ChildItem Cert:\LocalMachine\My

#Step 2 - Modify certificate Thumbprints and then run the
Install-ADFSFarm cmdlet

Install-ADFSFarm -CertificateThumbprint 'sts.emskings.com
Certificate HASH' -FederationServiceName sts.emskings.com
-FederationServiceDisplayName 'ViaMonstra AD FS'
-GroupServiceAccountIdentifier 'VIAMONSTRA\ADFSGMSA$'
-Verbose

#Restart the AD FS Server Service

Restart-Service -Name ADFSSRV -Force -Verbose
```

28. Log in to **WAP01** as administrator, remove the server from the **ViaMonstra** domain, and reboot the server. Log in to **WAP01** as administrator again.

29. Add the internal AD FS server to the hosts file as follows:

```
192.168.1.244 sts.emskings.com
```

30. Import the **ADFS_STS.pfx** certificate from **ADFS01** to the local machine Personal certificate store.

31. Start **PowerShell ISE** as administrator and open the **AD FS_Commands_on_WAP01.ps1** script shown here. The script is divided into three steps. Be sure to run the steps separately because the results of step 1 need to be used in step 2. Copy the Certificate Hash gathered in step 1 and replace 'AD FS Server certificate thumbprint' in the following script:

```
#Step 0 - Install Web Application Server Role

Install-WindowsFeature -Name Web-Application-Proxy
-IncludeManagementTools -Verbose

#Step 1 - Print out the AD FS Server Certificate Thumbprint

Get-ChildItem Cert:\LocalMachine\My

#Step 2 - Install Web Application Proxy
```

```
Install-WebApplicationProxy -
FederationServiceTrustCredential (Get-Credential)
-CertificateThumbprint 'AD FS Server certificate thumbprint'
-FederationServiceName 'sts.emskings.com' -Verbose
```

32. Publish **port 443** of the **WAP01** to the Internet, and you are all set to go.

Enable Federation with Azure AD

After AD FS is successfully configured, the ViaMonstra AD needs to be federated with Azure Active Directory.

1. Log in to ADFS01, start PowerShell ISE as administrator, and open and run the ADFS_Fed_on_ADFS01.ps1 script shown here:

```
#add Global Admin account plus password in variable

$cred=Get-Credential

Connect-MsolService -Credential $cred

Set-MsolADFSContext -Computer sts.emskings.com

#Convert the normal domain to a federated domain
Convert-MsolDomainToFederated -DomainName emskings.com

#Get the results
Get-MsolFederationProperty -DomainName emskings.com
```

2. Supply the Global Admin (**admin@emskings.com**) credentials so you can connect to the Microsoft Online Services.

3. Supply domain credentials to connect to the **ADFS01** server in the **ViaMonstra** domain and click **OK**.

Supplying domain credentials.

After a couple of minutes, the Active Directory domain is converted to an Active Directory domain that is federated with Azure AD.

```
PS C:\Users\administrator.VIAMONSTRA> Convert-MsolDomainToFederated –DomainName emskings.com
Successfully updated 'emskings.com' domain.
PS C:\Users\administrator.VIAMONSTRA>
```

Successfully updated the domain.

Configure Branding

As explained in Chapters 4 and 5, changing the branding of the AD FS pages helps establish trust between the user and Azure AD. You change the branding for AD FS via PowerShell:

1. Log in to ADFS01 and start PowerShell ISE as administrator so you can open and run the scripts in the following steps.

2. To set the company logo, execute the following:

```
Set-ADFSWebTheme -TargetName default -Logo @{path="C:\setup\
Branding\logo.png"}
```

3. To set the company illustration, execute the following:

```
Set-ADFSWebTheme -TargetName default -Illustration
@{path="C:\setup\Branding\illustration.png"}
```

4. To change the AD FS sign-in page description, execute the following:

```
Set-ADFSGlobalWebContent -SignInPageDescriptionText "<p>
Please sign-in to ViaMonstra and prepare to learn stuff.
</p>"
```

Appendix E

Installing SCEP Using Microsoft NDES

To be able to deploy certificates from your own Certificate Authority via Microsoft Intune or System Center Configuration Manager, you need a solution like Simple Certificate Enrollment Protocol (SCEP). The Microsoft solution for SCEP is the Network Device Enrollment Service (NDES). This appendix helps you configure NDES so that it can be used with Microsoft Intune.

Note: This is an optional configuration and is typically completed after setting up either the EMS standalone solution, or the EMS hybrid solution.

Prerequisites

For NDES, you need a separate server that complies with the following requirements:

- Windows Server 2012 R2

- The server cannot be combined with the local Certificate Authority.

- The NDES server needs to be reachable not only from inside but also from the Internet to work with Internet-connected mobile devices.

Create an NDES Service Account and SPN

You need a service account for NDES. This account is just a member of the Domain Users group. After creating the service account, you need to create a service principal name (SPN):

1. Log on to **DC01** and start **dsa.msc**. Create a new service account, for example **NDES_SA**, in the OU for service accounts.

2. Create an SPN for the service account used for NDES by starting an elevated **Command prompt** and run the following command:

   ```
   setspn -s http/NDES01.corp.viamonstra.com VIAMONSTRA\NDES_SA
   ```

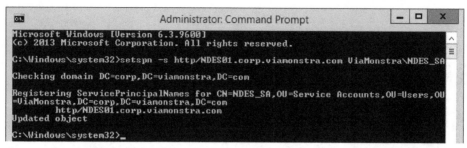

Setting the service principal name.

Create and Configure Certificate Templates for NDES

1. Log on to DC01 and start certsrv.msc. In the Certification Authority management tool, right-click the CA and select Properties.

Selecting Properties for the CA.

2. From the **CA Properties**, select the **Security** tab and make sure that the **NDES_SA** service account has permissions to

   o   Issue and Manage Certificates: **Selected**

   o   Request Certificates: **Selected**

3. Click **Apply** after setting the permissions for **NDES_SA**.

4. Still in the properties of the CA (corp-DC01-CA), click the **General** tab and click **View Certificate**.

5. Click **Details / Copy to file**.

6. Click **Next**, make sure **DER encoded binary x.509 (.CER)** is selected, and click **Next** again.

7. Type **C:\corp-DC01-CA.cer**, click **Next**, and then click **Finish**.

8. Click **OK** twice.

After you configure the permissions, you need to create three certificate templates. You use the certificate file corp-DC01-CA.cer of the root CA when creating the profiles in System Center Configuration Manager or Microsoft Intune.

Configure UserSignTest Certificate Template

1. Right-click **Certificate Templates** and click **Manage**.

2. In the **Certificate Templates** console, scroll down to the **User template**, right-click it, and select **Duplicate Template**. Configure the template as listed in the table:

Setting	Value
General > Template display name	UserSignTest
General > Template name	UserSignTest
Request Handling > Purpose	Signature
Subject Name > Supply in the request	Selected
Extensions > Key Usage	Clear the **Signature is proof of origin (nonrepudiation)** check box.
Security tab	Add NDES_SA with permissions: **Read and Enroll**

3. Click **Apply** after configuring the new certificate template.

4. In the **Certificate Templates console**, scroll down to the **User template**, right-click it, and select **Duplicate Template**. Configure the template as listed in the table:

Setting	Value
General > Template display name	UserGeneralPurposeTest
General > Template name	UserGeneralPurposeTest
Subject Name > Supply in the request	Selected
Security tab	Add NDES_SA with permissions: **Read and Enroll**

5. Click **Apply** after configuring the new certificate template.

6. In the **Certificate Templates console**, scroll down to the **Workstation Authentication template**, right-click it, and select **Duplicate Template**. Configure the template as listed in the table:

Setting	Value
General > Template display name	NDES Communication
General > Template name	NDES Communication
General > Validity period	5 years

Setting	Value
Subject Name > Subject name format	Common name
Extensions > Application Policies	Click **Add / Server Authentication**.

7. Close the **Certificate Template console** and right-click **Certificate Templates** in the **Certificate Authority console**. Select **New / Certificate Template to issue**.

8. Select the newly created templates and click **OK**.

Enabling the new certificate templates.

Configuring NDES Roles and Features

After configuring all certificate prerequisites, you need to configure the NDES Roles and Features on the NDES server. This section helps you configure the NDES server for use with Intune standalone or in a hybrid scenario:

1. Log on to **NDES01** and start **PowerShell ISE** as administrator.

2. Open and run the following scripts:

```
#Install NDES prerequisites

Install-WindowsFeature -Name "NET-Framework-45-ASPNET"

Install-WindowsFeature -Name "Web-WebServer"

Add-WindowsFeature -Name "Web-Asp-Net", "Web-Net-Ext", "Web-
WMI", "Web-Metabase", "NET-Framework-Core", "NET-HTTP-
Activation", "NET-Framework-45-Core", "NET-WCF-HTTP-
Activation45", "Web-ASP-Net45", "Web-Net-Ext45";

Install-WindowsFeature -name "ADCS-Device-Enrollment", "Web-
Mgmt-Console", "Web-Filtering";
```

Add the Service Account to the Local IIS_IUSRS Group

1. On **NDES01**, open **Computer Management**.

2. Expand **Local Users and Groups / Groups** and open **IIS_IUSRS**. Add the **NDES_SA** service account to **IIS_IUSRS**.

3. Click **OK** to finish.

Complete Configuration of the NDES Role

After installing the prerequisites and the NDES role, the configuration needs to be competed:

1. Log on to **NDES01** and go to the **Server Manager**.

2. Click the **yellow exclamation mark** in the upper right corner and then click **Configure Active Directory Certificates Services on the....**

Click Configure Active Directory on the...

3. Supply the domain admin credentials (**VIAMONSTRA\administrator**) and click **Next**.

4. On the **Role Services** page, select **Network Device Enrollment Service** and click **Next**.

5. Click **Select** and supply the service the credentials of the service account (**VIAMONSTRA\ndes_sa**).

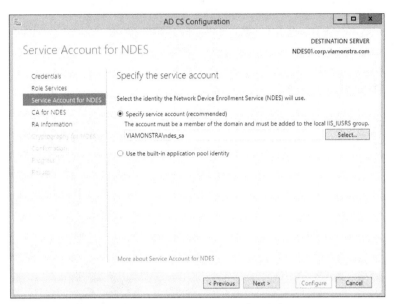

Supplying the NDES service account credentials.

6. Click **Next** and click **Select** to select the local CA (**DC01.corp.viamonstra.com\corp-DC01-CA**). Click **Next**.

7. On the **RA information** page, leave the default values and click **Next**.

8. Click **Next** on the **Cryptography for NDES** page.

9. On the **AD CS Configuration** page, click **Configure** to configure NDES.

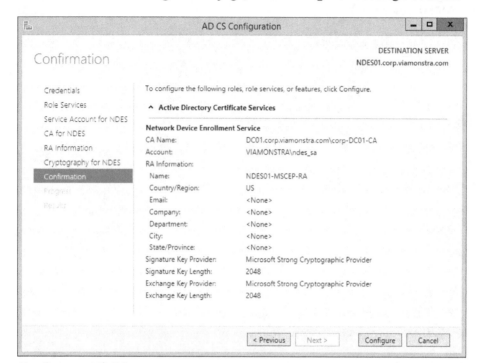

Configuring NDES.

10. Click **Close** after the configuration is finished.

Configure the Registry and IIS

To support longer URLs, You need to add two registry keys and change the configuration of the Internet Information Service (IIS):

1. On NDES01, start **RegEdit.exe** and add the following keys:

Location	Value	Type	Data
HKLM\SYSTEM\CurrentControl Set\Services\HTTP\Parameters	MaxFieldLength	DWORD	65534 (decimal)
HKLM\SYSTEM\CurrentControl Set\Services\HTTP\Parameters	MaxRequestBytes	DWORD	65534 (decimal)

2. On **NDES01**, open **Server Manager**.

3. Select **Tools / Internet Information Services (IIS) Manager**.

4. Browse to **Sites / Default Web Sites**, right-click **Request Filtering**, and choose **Open Feature**.

5. In **IIS Manager**, click **Edit Feature Settings** in the **Actions** pane and edit the values as follows:

   o   Maximum URL Length (Bytes): **65534**

   o   Maximum Query Length (Bytes): **65534**

6. Click **OK**.

Request and Configure Certificates

The NDES server needs a certificate from the local Certificate Authority installed to publish the NDES site in IIS in a secure way.

1. On **NDES01**, go to the **Start screen** and start **certlm.msc**.

2. Right-click **Personal** and select **All Tasks / Request New Certificate**.

3. On the **Certificate Enrollment** page, click **Next**.

4. Select **Active Directory Certificate Enrollment Policy** and click **Next**.

5. On the **Request Certificates** page, select **NDES Communication** and click **Enroll**.

6. Click **Finish**.

7. Next, the just requested certificate needs to be bound to the default web site in the IIS Manager. On the **NDES01** server, open **Server Manager** and select **Tools / Internet Information Services (IIS) Manager**.

8. Right-click the default web site, select **Site Bindings** and click **Add**. Then for **Type**, select **https**, supply the host name (**ndes01.corp.viamonstra.com**), and select the right **SSL certificate**.

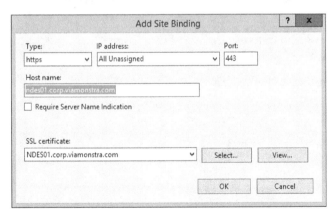

Configuring the IIS binding.

9. Click **OK** and close the remaining dialog boxes.

10. In an elevated **PowerShell Prompt**, use the following command to complete the setup:

```
Add-WindowsFeature NET-HTTP-Activation
```

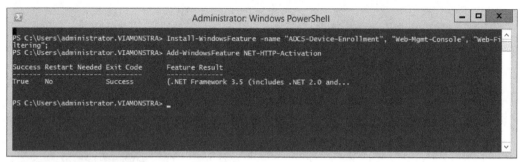

Adding HTTP activation.

Configuring EMS Standalone for NDES

Because Microsoft Intune is a cloud service, you need to configure a connector between the local NDES server and the Intune service. Also, be sure to make the NDES server available for devices connected to the Internet when using Microsoft Intune.

> **Note**: This guide is for EMS Standalone solution, if you are configuring the EMS Hybrid solution, skip to the next section.

1. Go to **https://manage.microsoft.com** and log on with the admin credentials (**admin@emskings.com**).

2. In the **Microsoft Intune console**, select **Admin / Mobile Device Management / Certificate Connector**.

3. The next step is to enable the subscription to use the Certificate Connector. Click **Configure on-premises Certificate Connector**.

4. Click **Enable Certificate Connector** and click **OK**.

Enabling the Certificate Connector.

5. Next, click **Download Certificate Connector**.

6. On **NDES01**, start the downloaded file **ndesconnectorsetup.exe** and click **Next**.

7. Click **I accept the terms in the License Agreement** and click **Next**.

8. Click **Next** and select **SCEP and PFX Profile Distribution**.

9. Click **Next**. Click **Select** and select the certificate of the NDES01 server. The certificate must have Client Authentication EKU and will be used for authenticating the Microsoft Intune NDES Connector.

Selecting the Client Certificate for Microsoft Intune Connector.

10. Click **Next** twice and then click **Install**.

11. Select **Launch Intune Connector** and click **Finish**.

12. In the **NDES Connector**, click **Sign in** and provide the Global Admin credentials of the Intune tenant.

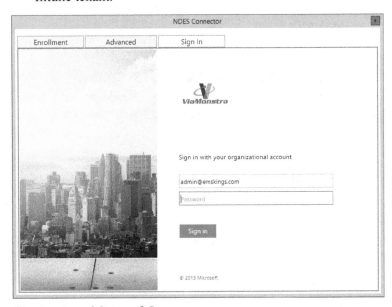

Signing in to Microsoft Intune.

13. Click **Sign in**.

14. Click **OK** in the message box that tells you **Successfully Enrolled**.

15. Click **Close** to close the **NDES Connector**.

16. Logging in to the Microsoft Intune Admin portal shows whether the connector is up-to-date. Click **Admin / Mobile Device Management / Certificate Connector**.

The Certificate Connector is up-to-date.

Configuring EMS Hybrid for NDES

When using EMS in a hybrid environment, you need to configure System Center Configuration Manager to use the NDES server to deploy certificates. This section describes the ConfigMgr configuration.

Prepare Certificates for ConfigMgr

1. On **CM01**, in the **Start screen**, type **certlm.msc** and press **Enter** to open the Certificates Local Machine MMC.

2. Right-click **Personal** and select **All Tasks / Request New Certificate** to request a new certificate for NDES Communication.

3. Click **Next** on the **Certificate Enrollment** page.

4. Click **Next** and select the **NDES Communication** certificate.

5. Click **Enroll**.

6. After enrolling the NDES certificate, it needs to be configured in IIS so that ConfigMgr can use it. On **CM01**, open **Server Manager** and click **Tools / Internet Information Services (IIS) Manager**.

7. Right-click the default web site and select **Site Bindings**. Click **Add**, for **Type**, select **https**, and then select the right **SSL certificate**.

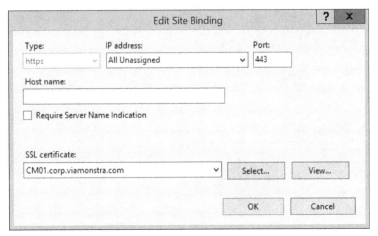

Assigning the SSL certificate.

8. Click **OK** and close the **Internet Information Services (IIS) Manager**.

Configure ConfigMgr for NDES

ConfigMgr uses the Certificate Registration Point role to communicate with the NDES server.

1. On **CM01**, start the **ConfigMgr console** and go to the **Administration** workspace.

2. Expand **Site Configuration / Servers / Site System Roles**.

3. Right-click **Primary Site Server** (CM01.corp.viamonstra.com) and select **Add Site System Role**.

4. Click **Next** twice.

5. Select **Certificate Registration Point Role** and click **Next**.

6. Click **Add** and supply the **URL of the Network Device Enrollment Service** (**http://ndes01.corp.viamonstra.com/certsrv/mscep/mscep.dll**).

7.   Click **Browse** and browse to the exported root certificate.

Configuring the certificate registration point.

8.   Click **Next** twice and then click **Close** to complete the **Add Site System Roles Wizard**.

You need to verify the installation of the certificate registration point before continuing with the configuration:

1.   On **CM01**, open **E:\Program Files\Microsoft Configuration Manager\Logs\CRPMSI.log**. The log should read:

Installation success or error status: 0

2.   On **CM01**, open **E:\Program Files\Microsoft Configuration Manager\Logs\crpsetup.log**. This log must read:

CRP.msi exited with return code: 0

If errors like **GetIISWebServiceStringProperty failed** are listed, make sure the correct SSL certificate is bound and no host name is specified in the Edit Site Bindings window of the binding in the Internet Information Services Manager.

3.   On **CM01**, open **E:\Program Files\Microsoft Configuration Manager\Logs\crpctrl.log**:

   o   It should show that CRP status is **0 (online)** like this line:

CRP's previous status was 0 (0 = Online, 1 = Failed, 4 = Undefined)
SMS_CERTIFICATE_REGISTRATION_POINT   4/25/2014 9:50:21 PM
6496 (0x1960)

o   However, right after installation of CRP, it might not show that yet. The self-health check runs every 10 minutes, so after 10 minutes, it should change from 4 to 0 (online). You can speed this up by restarting the SMS_CERTIFICATE_REGISTRATION_POINT thread if desired.

4.   On **CM01**, open **E:\Program Files\SMS_CCM\CRP\Logs\CRP.log**:

o   This log should not contain any errors.

o   If you see a security exception path error, grant the Network Service account read permissions to the HKLM\SOFTWARE\Microsoft\SMS\MPFDM\Inboxes registry key.

5.   Restart **CM01**.

Install the ConfigMgr NDES Plugin

After the certificate registration point installation is finished, it may take up to one or two hours to generate the certificate needed for the NDES plugin. The certificate ends up in the E:\Program Files\Microsoft Configuration Manager\inboxes\certmgr.box folder.

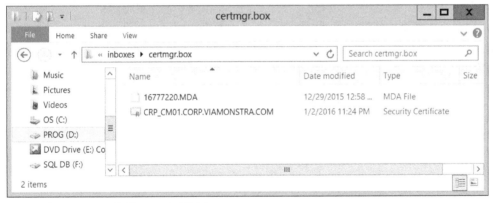

Copy the generated file to NDES01.

After generating the certificate, you are ready to continue the ConfigMgr NDES plugin installation:

1. Copy the generated certificate from **certmgr.box** to the **NDES01** server in the **C:\NDES** folder.

2. Next, you need to mount the Configuration Manager installation media and copy the content of **SMSSETUP/PolicyModule/x64** to the **C:\NDES** folder on **NDES01**.

3. Go to **C:\NDES** and start **PolicyModuleSetup.exe**.

4. Click **Next** and then click **I accept the license agreement**.

5. Click **Next** twice, and in the **Certificate Registration Point** step, enter the URL of the CRP: **https://CM01.<YourPubliclyRegisteredFQDN>/CMCertificateRegistration**.

6. Leave the **HTTPS Port Number** at **443**.

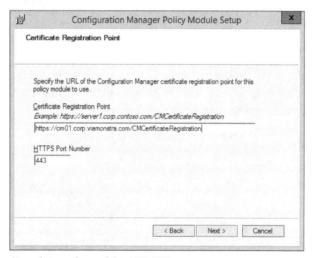

Supplying the public FQDN.

7. Click **Next**.

8. Click **Select** and then select the NDES certificate.

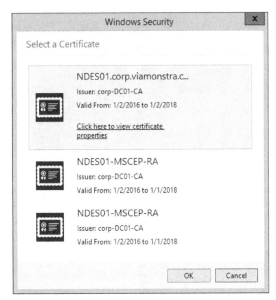

Selecting the NDES certificate.

9. Click **OK** and click **Next** twice.

10. Click **Browse**, select the certificate in **C:\NDES** that you copied previously from the **certmgr.box** folder on **CM01** in step 1, and click **OK**.

11. Click **Next**, **Install**, and then **Finish**.

12. Next, start **Regedit.exe**, browse to **HKLM\SOFTWARE\Microsoft\Cryptography\MSCEP**, and change the values of the following keys to the values listed:

    o   EncryptionTemplate: **UserEncryption**

    o   GeneralPurposeTemplate: **UserGeneralPurposeTest**

    o   SignatureTemplate: **UserSignTest**

13. Open an elevated command prompt and run **IISRESET**.

Create a Trusted Certificate Profile

Next, you need to create a trusted certificate profile with the certificate of the Root CA of ViaMonstra. The cert (corp-DC01-CA.cer) is exported earlier in this appendix.

1. On **CM01**, start the **ConfigMgr console** and go to **Assets and Compliance**.

2. Expand **Compliance Settings / Company Resource Access** and select **Certificate Profiles**.

3. Click **Create Certificate Profile** from the **Home** ribbon.

4. Give the profile a name (**ViaMonstra CA Certificate**) and select **Trusted CA Certificate**.

5. Click **Next**.

6. Click **Import**, browse to the exported root certificate, and click **Open**.

Importing the root CA certificate.

7. Click **Next**.

8. Select the supported platform and select **Windows 10**.

Selecting Windows 10.

9. Click **Next** twice and then click **Close**.

10. Select the certificate profile and click **Deploy** from the **Home** ribbon.

11. Click **Browse** to select the collection (**All Intune Users**) to which the certificate needs to be deployed and click **OK** twice.

Create SCEP Certificate Profile

ConfigMgr is able to deploy SCEP certificates to all kinds of operating systems. ViaMonstra only wants to deploy SCEP certificates to Windows 10 devices.

1. On **CM01**, start the **ConfigMgr console** and go to the **Assets and Compliance Workspace**.

2. Expand **Compliance Settings / Company Resource Access** and select **Certificate Profiles**.

3. Click **Create Certificate Profile** from the **Home Ribbon**.

4. Supply a **Name** (ViaMonstra SCEP User Certificate Windows) and select **Simple Certificate Enrollment Protocol (SCEP) settings**.

5. Click **Next** twice.

6. Select **Allow certificate enrollment on any device** and click **Next**.

7. Configure the **SCEP properties** like described in the following table:

Setting	Value
Certificate template name	UserGeneralPurposeTest
Certificate type	User
Subject alternative name	User principal name (UPN)
Certificate validity period	1 Year
Key usage	Key decipherment Digital Signature
Key size (bits)	2048
Hash algorithm	SHA-2
Root CA Certificate	ViaMonstra CA Certificate

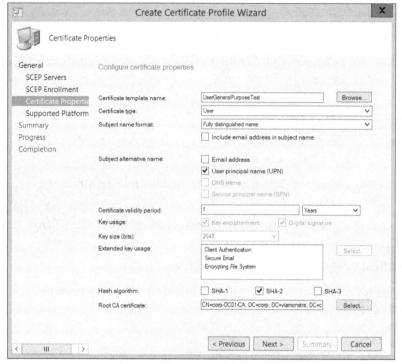

Creating the SCEP certificate profile.

8. Click **Next** and select all **Windows 10** operating systems.

9. Click **Next** twice and then click **Close**.

10. Select the **Certificate** and click **Deploy** from the **Home** ribbon.

11. Click **Browse** to select the collection (**All Intune Users**) to which the certificate needs to be deployed and click **OK** twice.

Check the Certificate on a Device, the CA, and in ConfigMgr

To check the deployment of the SCEP certificate, use a Windows 10 machine that is enrolled via MDM and not domain joined. This way you know that the device is not able to contact the CA directly.

1. On a MDM-managed Windows 10 machine, type **Manage User Certificates** in the **Search** box. Click **Manage User Certificates** in the search results and expand **Personal**.

2. Click **Certificates** to see the user certificates.

3. Double-click the user certificate with the name of the user (e.g. Tim Snow) and check whether it is issued by the domain CA, for instance **corp-CA-DC01**.

Issued certificate via SCEP/NDES.

4. In the **Certificate Authority** on **DC01**, go to **Issued certificates** and double-check whether the right certificate template is used.

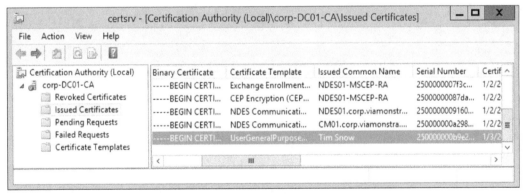

Issued certificate with the UserGeneralPurposeTest certificate template.

5. On **CM01**, start the **ConfigMgr console** and go to the **Monitoring** workspace.

6. Expand **Reporting / Reports**. In the **Reports** node, click **Company Resource Access**.

7. Select **Certificate issuance history** and click **Run**.

8. Supply the information (e.g. start date, end date) to be able to create the report. Click **View Report** to see the results.

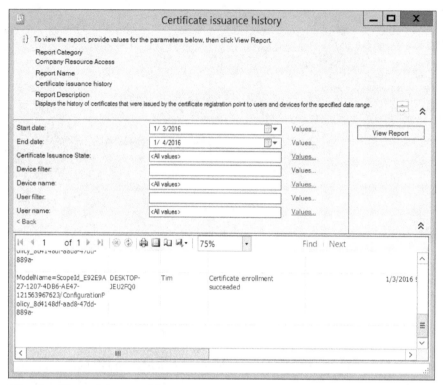

The Certificate issuance history report.

Index

Beyond the Book – Meet the Experts

If you liked their book, you will love to see and hear them in person.

Live Presentations

Kent Agerlund frequently speaks at conferences around the world, such as Midwest Management Summit (MMS), IT/Dev Connections, System Center Universe, and Microsoft Ignite.

Peter Daalmans also speaks at conferences like Midwest Management Summit (MMS), IT/Dev Connections, and BriForum.

You also can find Peter and Kent at infrastructure tours and local events like Microsoft Campus Days/TechDays, the Nordic Infrastructure Conference (NIC), and user group meetings around the globe.

For current tour dates and presentations, see

- http://blog.coretech.dk/kea (Kent)
- http://configmgrblog.com/speaking (Peter)

Live Instructor-led Classes

Kent conducts instructor-led classes in the United States, Asia Pacific, and Europe. For current dates and locations, see the following sites:

- www.coretech.global
- www.truesec.com
- www.labcenter.se
- www.labcenter.dk
- www.glasspaper.no

Beyond the Book – The Community

What would we be without the IT pro community? As writers of this book, we embrace the community and live it by sharing their knowledge via our blogs, by running user groups, and by speaking at user group events or conferences. As we gain from the community by learning from others, we also give back. That is the way to do it. We dedicate this last element to our fellow IT pros in the community who feely share their knowledge.

Fellow Enterprise Mobility MVPs

Worldwide, more than 60 Enterprise Mobility MVPs with a focus on Configuration Manager and the Enterprise Mobility Suite share information about experiences from the field. In this section, you can find some great resources. We highly recommend that you read their blogs and follow them.

James Bannan
James Bannan is an MVP based in Australia. He blogs and presents about all things Microsoft (and a few things not related to Microsoft). James used to be an Enterprise Client Management MVP, but he switched focus to Cloud and Datacenter Management.

- James' blog: http://www.jamesbannanit.com
- Follow James: @jamesbannan

Kenny Buntinx
Kenny is one of the reviewers of this book and has blogged about his experience with Configuration Manager and the Enterprise Mobility Suite for years now.

- Kenny's blog: http://www.scug.be/sccm
- Follow Kenny: @kennybuntinx

Mirko Colemberg
Mirko shares lots of information about Configuration Manager and the Enterprise Mobility Suite via his blog.

- Mirko's blog: http://blog.colemberg.ch
- Follow Mirko: @mirkocolemberg

Gerry Hampson

Gerry Hampson Device Management blog specializes in Microsoft technologies: System Center Configuration Manager, Intune, and Enterprise Mobility Suite.

- Gerry's blog: http://gerryhampsoncm.blogspot.com

- Follow Gerry: @GerryHampson

Cliff Hobbs

Founded in 2003 by Microsoft MVP Cliff Hobbs, FAQShop.com provides the answers to frequently asked questions (FAQs) on Microsoft System Center Configuration Manager and its related technologies.

The site is unique in its approach of combining a traditional website organized by category with corresponding Microsoft OneNote Notebooks.

- FAQShop: http://FAQShop.com

- Follow Cliff: @CliffHobbs

Kaido Järvemets

If you say Configuration Manager and PowerShell in one sentence, you say Kaido. He lives and breathes PowerShell when it comes to automating processes around Configuration Manage and the Enterprise Mobility Suite.

- Kaido's blog: http://cm12sdk.net/

- Follow Kaido: @kaidja

Garth Jones

Garth specializes in reporting and inventory collection, so his blog provides many useful tips for ConfigMgr admins.

- Garth's blog: http://www.enhansoft.com/blog/author/garth

- Follow Garth: @GarthMJ

Ronny de Jong

Ronny blogs mainly about the Enterprise Mobility Suite and Azure Remote App.

- Ronny's blog: http://ronnydejong.com

- Follow Ronny: @ronnydejong

Tim De Keukelaere

Tim is one of the reviewers of this book. He loves to learn and share knowledge about Enterprise Client Management and Mobility topics and products. He is based in Belgium and a board member of the Belgian System Center User Group. He is also active in the global System Center Community as a speaker at various events and a frequent blogger.

- Tim's blog: http://www.scug.be/tim
- Follow Tim: @Tim_DK

Brian Mason

Brian runs the Minnesota System Center User Group (MNSCUG) as well as the Midwest Management Summit (MMS). Brian also reviewed this book and blogs on MNSCUG.

- Brian's blog: http://www.mnscug.org/blogs/brian-mason
- Facebook: https://www.facebook.com/brianmasonmn
- Follow Brian: @abetterpc

Torsten Meringer

Torsten writes his blogs in German and has blogged about Configuration Manager since 2007.

- Torsten's blog: http://www.mssccmfaq.de
- Follow Torsten: @tmeringer

Chris Nackers

Mac dude who lives Mac devices and managing them with EMS. He blogs about Intune and Configuration Manager.

- Chris' blog: http://www.chrisnackers.com
- Follow Chris: @chrisnack

Nash Pherson

Nash is active in the Minnesota System Center User Group (MNSCUG).

- Nash's blog: http://myitforum.com/myitforumwp/author/npherson
- Follow Nash: @kidmystic

Greg Ramsey

Greg likes automating everything with PowerShell and blogs about Configuration Manager and Intune-related subjects.

- Greg's blog: http://gregramsey.net
- Follow Greg: @ramseyg

Nico Sienaert

Nico runs the Belgium SCUG and blogs about Configuration Manager and EMS.

- Nico's blog: http://scug.be/nico/
- Follow Nico: @nsienaert

Steve Thompson

The focus of Steve's blog is System Center and SQL Server, particularly as they relate to Configuration Manager. It is a great resource if you want to install, configure, and tune SQL Server the right way for Configuration Manager.

- Steve's blog: http://stevethompsonmvp.wordpress.com
- Follow Steve: @Steve_TSQL

Peter van der Woude

A blog about more than just ConfigMgr. This blog is about everything related to ConfigMgr and Microsoft Intune.

- Peter's blog: http://www.petervanderwoude.nl
- Follow Peter: @pvanderwoude

Other Great Resources

Besides all the personal blogs, there also are very valuable online community platforms and, of course, the very valuable local user groups around the world!

Valuable Online Community Platforms

Online Platforms	Website
MyITForum	http://www.myitforum.com
Windowsnoob.com	http://www.windowsnoob.com

User Groups around the World

User Group	Website
Configuration Manager User Group Switzerland	http://configmgr.ch
System Center User Group Belgium	http://www.scug.be
System Center User Group Denmark	http://www.scug.dk
System Center User Group Netherlands	http://www.scug.nl
System Center User Group Norway	http://www.scug.no
Windows Management User Group UK	http://www.wmug.co.uk
Windows Management User Group Netherlands	http://www.wmug.nl
Minnesota System Center User Group	http://www.mnscug.org
New England Area Systems Management User Group	http://ref.ms/neasmsug/

Community Tools

Microsoft EMS Resources

Marius A. Skovli created a free community Windows tool that brings all the Microsoft Enterprise Mobility Suite resources together. This community tool offers a "single pane-of-glass" into the Microsoft Enterprise Mobility Suite where you have a single hub for all the necessary information to get you started with EMS and hybrid-cloud services.

Download the tool here: https://www.microsoft.com/en-us/store/apps/microsoft-ems-resources/9nblggh6j3fq

Wi-Fi Profile Generator

Johnathon Biersack created two free Wi-Fi XML generators for all of us who need a quick-and-easy way to create Wi-Fi profiles for Android and iOS.

Access the tool here: http://johnathonb.com/category/blog/

CPSIA information can be obtained
at www.ICGtesting.com
Printed in the USA
LVHW060340151019
634227LV00008B/1463/P